Déjà Rêvé
& Love at Second Sight

"An extraordinary exploration of how dreams shape destiny, *Déjà Rêvé and Love at Second Sight* reveals the mysterious phenomenon of meeting in dreams before meeting in life. Rich in historical accounts, cross-cultural lore, and contemporary testimonies, this book illuminates the uncanny power of dreams to guide love, friendship, and fate. Daniel Bourke has gathered compelling evidence that dreams are not mere illusions but doorways into future encounters. His meticulous research and captivating stories demonstrate how déjà rêvé has profoundly shaped lives throughout history—and continues to do so today. A fascinating and inspiring read that blends folklore, parapsychology, and modern dream studies, this book shines light on one of the most mysterious dimensions of human experience: precognitive dreams. *Déjà Rêvé and Love at Second Sight* is both deeply researched and highly readable—a groundbreaking work on the hidden influence of our dream life."

DAVID JAY BROWN, AUTHOR OF *DREAMING WIDE AWAKE* AND *THE ILLUSTRATED FIELD GUIDE TO DMT ENTITIES*

"Dreaming about future life turning points is an important but sadly under-researched part of human life. Its most magical manifestation is dreaming of future encounters with people who are destined to change our lives. Daniel Bourke has made a valuable—and fascinating—contribution to the study of precognitive dreaming across time and cultures."

ERIC WARGO, AUTHOR OF
PRECOGNITIVE DREAMWORK AND THE LONG SELF
AND *TIME LOOPS*

"If you have ever doubted that dreams and visions instruct us, read Daniel Bourke's book *Déjà Rêvé and Love at Second Sight*. The profusion of examples he offers will convince you that, inexplicably, the future—as recorded in dreams and visions—comes toward us. I personally can attest to having met both my teacher and my husband through clear visions and dreams that guided me to them. It is a common phenomenon that is not talked about a lot. Bourke's new book fills the gap."

CATHERINE SHAINBERG, PH.D., AUTHOR OF
KABBALAH AND THE POWER OF DREAMING
AND *THE KABBALAH OF LIGHT*

"In his lively book, Daniel Bourke shares fascinating accounts of those who dream about life events before they occur. Exploring other times and cultures, as well as our own, Bourke reveals how such dreams can shape our destiny—wars won, treasures found, mysteries solved, soul mates at last embraced. Not so important is the 'how' or 'why' of this, but that the encouraging dream comes, inviting us to steer our path more knowingly into the future."

DAWN BAUMANN BRUNKE, AUTHOR OF
SHADOW ANIMALS, *ANIMAL VOICES*,
AND *SHAPESHIFTING WITH OUR ANIMAL COMPANIONS*

Déjà Rêvé
& Love at Second Sight

The Experience of Meeting in Dreams Before Meeting in Life

A Sacred Planet Book

Daniel Bourke

Destiny Books
Rochester, Vermont

Destiny Books
One Park Street
Rochester, Vermont 05767
www.DestinyBooks.com

Destiny Books is a division of Inner Traditions International

Sacred Planet Books are curated by Richard Grossinger, Inner Traditions editorial board member and cofounder and former publisher of North Atlantic Books. The Sacred Planet collection, published under the umbrella of the Inner Traditions family of imprints, includes works on the themes of consciousness, cosmology, alternative medicine, dreams, climate, permaculture, alchemy, shamanic studies, oracles, astrology, crystals, hyperobjects, locutions, and subtle bodies.

Cataloging-in-Publication Data for this title is available from the Library of Congress

ISBN 979-8-88850-271-6 (print)
ISBN 979-8-88850-272-3 (ebook)

Printed and bound in the United States by Lake Book Manufacturing, LLC

10 9 8 7 6 5 4 3 2 1

Text design and layout by Priscilla Harris Baker
This book was typeset in Garamond, with Big Caslon, Classico, Gill Sans, and Legacy Sans used as display typefaces

To send correspondence to the author of this book, mail a first-class letter to the author c/o Inner Traditions, One Park Street, Rochester, VT 05767, and we will forward the communication, or contact the author directly at **daniel_bourke_89@hotmail.com.**

Contents

Two courses are open to us at the outset. Either we can find out what meaning has come to be attached to the word "uncanny" in the course of its history; or we can collect all those properties of persons, things, sense-impressions, experiences and situations which arouse in us the feeling of uncanniness, and then infer the unknown nature of the uncanny from what all these examples have in common. I will say at once that both courses lead to the same result: the uncanny is that class of the frightening which leads back to what is known of old and long familiar.

SIGMUND FREUD, *THE UNCANNY*

FOREWORD

In Your Dreams

Gary Lachman

Have you ever dreamt of someone and then met them in "real life"? I have, although not in the romantic or dramatic settings that are the main focus of this engaging book. On more than one occasion, a situation that was merely awkward and could have easily escalated into something more unpleasant was neutralized because I remembered that the bothersome character troubling me was the same one I had encountered in the previous night's dream. In the dream the situation got out of hand and turned nasty. But because I remembered it in real life, I was able to exert some self-control and deflect the conflict. Would that I had more such early nighttime warnings and could pass through more tight squeezes so frictionlessly.

The phenomenon of *déjà rêvé*, "already dreamed," as the French have it, can be seen as a subset of the experience of precognition. It is a precognitive experience had while dreaming. Precognitive means knowing something before you know it—before, in fact, you could possibly have known it, because that which you are knowing hasn't happened yet, and so, is not available for you to know. The array of strange phenomena making up the repertoire of parapsychology contains some very odd things—telepathy, for example, "reading someone's mind," or telekinesis, moving an object by pure thought. But precognition has to be the strangest of them all, an observation made by Frederic Myers in his classic *Human Personality and Its Survival of Bodily Death* when, speaking of precognition, he called it "a category of phenomena which at present I can make no attempt to explain."

Other forms of paranormal phenomena could eventually be accounted for by some so far undiscovered property of the mind (whether they will or not is a separate issue). But by no twist or turn of mental acrobatics can precognition be so accommodated, no matter the quantum hijinks enlisted to do so. Logic alone tells us that if something does not yet exist, we can't possibly "know" it. But as Daniel Bourke makes clear in this thorough, readable, and well-documented account, this is what seems to have happened over the centuries and around the globe.

My own interest in and experience of the strange character of dreams began some years ago, when I was a musician. It began with a series of shared dreams and telepathic experiences my girlfriend and I had at the time. While I was on tour and she was back in New York, we discovered that we were having the same sorts of dreams, sharing them, as it were. We also discovered that we were experiencing some sort of telepathic contact. Whenever one of us thought of telephoning the other, we discovered that the other had had the same idea at the same time. This was well before the advent of cell phones, when one had to be at a certain place at a certain time either to make or to receive a call. After that tour, I thought about our experiences, and the result of my ponderings was a song, "(I'm Always Touched By Your) Presence, Dear," which became a top ten hit. As the author makes clear, the notion of meeting one's "destiny"—or "kismet," which I refer to in the song—in a dream, has launched more than one romance. And as I know from the people who have told me, not a few have had my song as their soundtrack.

Not long after the experiences that led to the song, I began to record my first experiences of precognitive dreams—admittedly a more abstract term than the poetically suggestive French. I read a remarkable book, *An Experiment with Time*, published in 1927, by the aeronautics engineer J. W. Dunne. By chance, Dunne had discovered that he dreamt the future—or, to be precise, that bits and pieces of his own personal future, were turning up in his dreams. Readers familiar with the literature on precognition will remember Dunne's account of his dream of reading a newspaper story about the terrific eruption on Mount Pelée on the island of Martinique, before it had taken place. Other items of Dunne's personal future seemed to be jumping the queue and reaching him ahead of time in his dreams.

Dunne suggested that this apparent temporal anomaly was not peculiar to him, but was something available to everyone, in our dreams. If we wanted to confirm this, all we had to do was record our dreams and pay attention to what happens in our daily life. I took Dunne at his word and began writing down my dreams. No sooner had I started recording them than I was given my first "Dunne type dream," as they are called in the literature. At least it was the first I remembered. Not long after that, I had another and then another. It did not take long for me to recognize that Dunne was right. I dream the future—and so do you, dear reader, even if you have not yet noticed it.

I continued to keep a dream journal and have done so from that time. By now I have recorded dozens—scores—of precognitive dreams. In 2019, I gave a talk in London about hypnagogia, the liminal state between sleeping and waking in which we can observe dreams take shape while still conscious. Hypnagogia is associated with various paranormal phenomena, but one it is peculiarly prone to is precognition; indeed, Dunne had experimented with it to confirm his precognitive visions. At the end of my talk I tagged on a few accounts of precognitive dreams, my own and others, and suggested that the audience do as I did, and record their dreams to see if any of their own future turns up in them. The next day I received a message on Twitter from someone who had attended the talk, telling me that, yes, she had taken my advice and had a precognitive dream. I took that as a sign and proposed a book on my experiences to my UK publisher. The result was *Dreaming Ahead of Time: Experiences with Precognitive Dreams, Synchronicity and Coincidence* (Floris Books, 2022), which I wrote over the first Covid-19 lockdown.

One of the odd things I discovered writing the book is that most precognitive dreams are about fairly pedestrian events, boring, everyday things. The ones we tend to hear about are those that fall under what I call the "two D's," Disasters and the Derby, dreams of catastrophes and those of winning at the races. Most aren't about these extremes, or about the sort of life-changing experiences that are the focus of this book. This is one of the reasons why Frederic Myers was so stumped by them, by their "definiteness," "purposelessness," and "isolated unintelligibility." Other researchers have commented similarly. One, the psychologist Stan Gooch, remarked that the only thing that made these dreams interesting, is that they were precognitive. Were it not for that, no one but one's therapist would be interested in them.

One interesting area the author of this book enters is the difference between *déjà vu*, "already seen," and déjà rêvé. The author remarks cogently on the confusion about the two, which often equates one with the other. I don't know about anyone else, but for me they are clearly distinct and cannot be mistaken for each other. When I experience déjà vu I am unsure if what I am experiencing at that moment has happened before. There is an unsettling feeling of uncertainty, a sense that I am going through something I have gone through already, but it is not definite and I cannot "place" the other experience of it. With precognitive dreams it is completely different. When I feel what I call the "precognitive tingle," I know, without doubt, that I have dreamt what is now happening. One reason I know is because of my dream journal. The other is that the felt experience, the "phenomenology" of it, is unmistakable. Most times it raises a laugh. Although I have had the experience scores of times by now, I am still surprised by it and somewhat in awe. I have no interest in or desire to explain it. I am happy that it happens and I am reminded of just how odd reality can be.

The reader of this stimulating book may find that the numerous accounts of dreaming ahead of time it provides may well have just the same effect.

GARY LACHMAN is an author and lecturer on consciousness, counterculture, and the Western esoteric tradition. His works include *Touched by the Presence, Dark Star Rising, Beyond the Robot,* and *The Secret Teachers of the Western World.* A founding member of the rock band Blondie, he was inducted into the Rock and Roll Hall of Fame in 2006. He lives in London.

PREFACE

Dreams Come True

Is it possible to dream or otherwise mysteriously envision a future spouse, acquaintance, helper, healer, or even a shaman or saint before meeting them in life? To literally see the face, hear the voice, or sense the presence of another whom you are yet to meet and are nevertheless destined to do so? If our only witnesses were the voluminous records of legend, lyric, and lore on all corners of the globe, the answer would be a resounding yes. These experiences are found widely among both the most renowned literary works and the most obscure folkloric memorates. Less commonly noted, however, and what is much of the subject of this work—as are the many historical and cross-cultural accounts—is that the very same extraordinary experiences are still being recorded and still profoundly affect individual lives. These mysterious experiences of ordinary people, along with those esteemed romantic and chivalrous adventures and tales that we will be exploring here, speak powerfully on the matter, and perhaps in doing so, speak to us of something more—some mysterious human faculty that often manifests when we least expect it.

Among the world's deep and wide reservoir of evergreen, legendary, and folkloric catalogs and chronicles, one of the most common of all tales spanning the genres of literature is that in which the individual, perhaps an earnest prince, dreams of another, often a princess. He might then set out across dark forests and vast plains to find the object of his heart's desire. Whatever its particular incidence, both in individual cases and in relation to other kinds of visionary narratives, there can be no doubt as to the compelling ubiquity of these stories and the extent to which they are often attached to both important and ordinary people, places, and things. These tales span the globe. *Telepathy? Déjà Vu? Déjà Rêvé? Precognition? Simple errors of memerory and perception?* While various explanations have been offered, many of which we will explore in this book, and none of which are mutually exclusive, the verdict is very much out. It is in that open and rarely traversed field of inquiry that we will find ourselves.

Something else of great importance that emerges in the reading of these tales is that while some will dismiss these experiences as the workings of the mind or the machinations of chance coincidence etc., whatever their origin, they have (as we will see) sometimes *greatly* affected both the individual and the group, and therefore left their mark upon the historical record. Despite how little known they may be, these strange, mysterious, and seemingly veridical or truth-telling visionary experiences have been pivotal in setting many people upon entirely different life paths and determining their futures in various important and fascinating ways. Love, career paths, healing, and aid: it is not just those romances, dream visions, and other ancient tales where one's dream might literally move the individual and set them to action in the world. Just as Macsen Wledig, in his famous and most ancient dream recorded in the *Mabinogion*, had moved entire armies at the whim of such an experience—and for the sake of love—still our contemporaries do the same. Still they are moved by the same magic. As will become clear while the stories unfold, the old and the new are inextricably linked in this way.

One could find numerous examples in the scholarly literature of writers puzzling over the origins of these widely found dreams and visions in which people meet before meeting in life. "No one knows just how or why this type arose at Alexandria," writes Allen Godbey, for example, before continuing:

> Xenophon and Chares cited such tales from Persian sources. The theme is familiar in Arabian tales. Did the Persians in Alexandria furnish the model for the Greeks? Or is this a Jewish protest against the vulgar comedy, maintaining that a "lily among thorns" may remain a lily nevertheless? The notion of predestination of the maiden points perhaps a little more to Semitic than Persian ideas.[1]

Of course, such borrowing and diffusion occur. That these very same dreams and visions are still actively reported among ordinary people, and in surprising numbers, however, is very rarely mentioned. While scholars are often reluctant to link the old and the new, in this case, the old tales often tell true. It is those very tales and what seem to be their more recent counterparts that the reader will be presented with here, and while the individual truth of each and their relationship to each other will be for each to decide, their romantic, social, and very much personal reality and impact are undeniable, profound, and plain for all to see. For this reason, as much as any other, they deserve more significant attention.

While there will be some cross-pollination where necessary or illustrative throughout the book, the accounts will be sorted by type rather than geographically or temporally in order to more easily appreciate the similarities between what are sometimes greatly disparate sources, many of which will be brought to bear; we begin, however, how we also intend to continue, with some more recent accounts that speak to the very much ongoing and affecting nature of these déjà rêvé experiences in the individual's life. More so than my previous works, and with the dearth of research in mind, the idea is to make clear the extent to which men and women still dream these dreams and are still moved by this same mysterious magic. The phenomenon of "already dreamed"!

INTRODUCTION

Déjà Rêvé and Precognition

The Phenomenon of "Already Dreamed"

> The crucial issue about the paranormal is not the mechanism through which it operates—which might perfectly well be in itself entirely material—but its irreducibly uncanny, *unheimlich* quality, the threat it poses to ego boundaries, which therapists often find at least as hard to bear as do their clients.
>
> NICK TOTTON

It would be impossible to simply turn our attention to the kinds of fascinating dreams, visions, fateful encounters, and adventures (worldly and otherworldy!) with which these pages will be filled without mention of the rarely explored category of phenomena under which they most often and easily fall, that being *déjà rêvé*. Déjà rêvé translates directly from the French to "already dreamed"[1] and the term is often applied to cover a number of related experiences. Fundamentally, and how the term will be made most accurate use of here, déjà rêvé is the conviction that after encountering a moment in life, be it a person, place, or thing, one has dreamed of it before, though meetings with people ahead of time will be the focus. As defined, it is often related to the absolute certainty that the moment or something specifically presaging the moment has definitely been dreamed of before. It is in this sense that déjà rêvé differentiates itself most starkly from the more popularly known *déjà vu* phenomenon (which speaks to novel experiences that feel only *generally* and not *specifically* familiar). Neuroscientist and philosopher Vernon Neppe, in what seems to have been the first book dedicated to the déjà vu experience, touched on this, noting the importance of delineating between the various types of "déjà experience" for the simple reason that déjà vu, meaning "already seen," was not a term accurate enough to account for the numerous kinds of these déjà experiences. Neppe came up with *déjà entendu* (already heard) and *déjà recontre* (already met), a term that would, in fact, neatly or partly cover the majority of the accounts in this present work. With that said, and as was pointed out by Harvey Irwin in his review of Neppe's monograph, the variety of permutations often warrants the adoption of the broader and more general term *déjà experiences.*[2] Here, and in the same helpful spirit, we similarly adopt the broader term *déjà rêvé* to describe the majority of the accounts, many of which include aspects of some of those latter mentioned

Déjà vu has been most helpfully and acceptedly defined as "any subjectively inappropriate impression of familiarity of a present experience with an undefined past."[3] In the experiences with which we will be dealing, however, there *is* a defined past; there *is* a dream or visionary experience pointed to from the outset in almost every case. This truth is certainly the prevailing rule in the literary and legendary accounts, as we will see, although not only there. In many more recent accounts, too, the individuals even knew or assumed during or just after the dream that it portended future events. The sense that the experience was uniquely meaningful among other dreams often turns up during or right after the dreams themselves, setting them apart from others before even their fulfillment. In many cases, they have acted on those dreams. They have been impelled to significant movement or great change. It is for this reason among others, in fact, that déjà rêvé has sometimes been considered precognitive. If one is convinced they have dreamed of or otherwise envisioned a person, place, or thing before the encounter, it is entirely understandable that the individual might consider this some form of legitimate future sight when those very events play out before their eyes, even to the extent that they themselves seem to preempt them in real time. A typical example, recorded in the *Philadelphia Telegram* and reported in 1888, was the case of a Pennsylvania lady who dreamed that she was met by a "peculiar looking man" while she was visiting various points of interest in London. He would always ask her, "Are you ready?" The dream recurred, and she remarked to a friend before its truth was discovered that she could never forget the face of that man. Some time later, having returned to the States and while staying in a lodge, she entered an elevator after breakfast to return to her room. The man in charge of it suddenly turned to her and asked, "Are you ready?" Being very much struck by these words, she looked at the man and "instantly recognized the hero of her singular dream."[4]

It should be noted early that there are many examples of déjà experiences in which the dream was recorded or told *before* the event unfolded, a number of which will be presented. Psychotherapist Arthur Funkhouser considered that such instances "support the notion that at least some occurrences of déjà vu result from precognitive dreams."[5] Funkhouser himself gives an example in which he, having been playing a game of hide and seek at the age of fourteen, was suddenly, and in his own words, "seeing all this for the second time, and I had the impression that I had been through this experience once before while asleep. I felt I knew what was to come—I could 'remember' what was to be." Of interest here, Funkhouser noted that he knew what was going to occur next according to his memory of a dream, and according to him, this came to pass when he saw a quarry laying down his bike in the front yard.

Funkhouser noted this was "just as I knew it would be."[6] Strange indeed. These ideas were entertained over a century before, with W. Sander suggesting in 1874 that experiences of *paramnesia* (a term that references a group of pathological and non-pathological memory anomalies) could instill the conviction that the future could be foretold.[7]

It would, of course, be challenging to prove that such impressions are not quickly formulated in the seconds during or after the event and remembered as if they had happened before. Likewise, some form of "telepathy" might as easily be invoked in many cases (if the new reader will allow for its existence, at least insofar as this has been genuinely posited). Le Lorrain, in fact, long ago argued that paramnesias that presented with ostensible premonitions should be classified as telepathic phenomena.[8] Again, while these do not specifically reference déjà rêvé and are more to do with déjà vu, it is the case that historically, the attitudes toward one affected by those toward the other, and their conflation, runs surprisingly deep. Thankfully, outright discerning whether such things are either actually the case or possible is not the primary goal here.* It is enough for us to know that, regarding the accounts to be found throughout these pages, everything is on the table. These are strange, enduring, and often profound occurrences with a long and impressive pedigree regarding (which we do not in the historical and cross-cultural sense have) some grand trove of synthesized literature to appeal to or some great annals attended and upkept by historians of religion and other scholars. It should nevertheless be made clear that if déjà rêvé is defined as primarily the *conviction*—if perhaps sometimes the *feeling* (later being confirmed) that something occurring in the moment has been dreamed of before—then it is a major, and to this point, fairly hidden historical and social phenomenon. Although limited, the research, including the work presented here, supports this notion.

---

*The interested reader should consider the following 90 study meta-analysis regarding scientific work on precognition. Bem, Daryl, et al., "Feeling the future: A meta-analysis of 90 experiments on the anomalous anticipation of random future events."

While very little work has been done at all pertaining to the incidence of déjà rêvé among the general population, the indications are that these are not overly rare events. Certainly, they are not rare enough to warrant the distinct lack of work that has been done regarding, at the very least, their clinical significance. Eranimos and Funkhouser found in one survey of 500 participants done in India that most reported having the experience, with 32 percent claiming this was something that happened often.[9] Funkhouser and Schredl's 2010 study of students in Gemany found that only 4.8 percent said that they had never had a déjà vu experience.[10] These tentative suggestions that the experience is surprisingly common might speak to the impressively large number of accounts that one may with relative ease find scattered in online forums all across the web and across the gamut of nonfiction and popular fictional works. It was for this very reason that psychologist David Ryback wrote the following:

> The larger the number of people who report such dreams, the less confidently the dreams can be explained by chance alone. Also, the more the details of the dreams coincide with the details of the actual events, the less plausibly such concurrence can be explained as random.[11]

With this said, there is no great collected literature where disparate accounts of déjà rêvé may easily be found, but rather they are notably scattered, something that will be addressed for the first time in this volume. Indeed, up until 2018 Curot et al. suggest their own work as being the very first scientific study to focus solely on déjà rêvé at all.[12] While the accounts are out there to be found, they are often not specifically labeled or categorized in this way—there is much work to be done.

DÉJÀ VU AND PARAPSYCHOLOGY

Explanations for anomalous errors in memory and perception have historically been centered on disorders of memory, such as dementia.

However, from the outset the experiential strangeness of the broader déjà experience has seamlessly allowed for the introduction of parapsychological or other "non-ordinary" explanations (as we had touched on with precognition and telepathy). Indeed, while it is not the entirety of the explanation, the extent to which this baggage attached itself to déjà experiences has plainly played a role in how understudied they have been. A significant portion of the published literature on déjà vu and related experiences deviates from the mainstream and is to be found in parapsychological and related literature. Many dozens of accounts could be pointed to between the likes of astronomer Camille Flammarion and classicist Frederic Myers in their respective parapsychological works alone. Researchers such as Gary Lachman and Eric Wargo have similarly contributed with their work. Rather than offer the parapsychologists and other scholars their flowers, however, there seems to have been a historical antagony between a parapsychological and "naturalist" or even psychological approach. This is ongoing, and while unhelpful at their extremes, these dichotomies are not entirely without merit.

Historically, non-ordinary states of consciousness have been directly associated with psychopathology. This kind of supernatural baggage seems to have been a key influence regarding how little has been published on these experiences up until the last few decades. Alan S. Brown noted that in the three decades prior to 2004, there had been a "nearly uniform silence" on the topic, offering dozens of examples of general memory and cognition books that uphold this strange omerta.[13] There is still reticence throughout the mainstream in these fields to take the work of parapsychologists and others seriously. Numerous historians of religion still consider it to be a pseudoscience, a rather outdated characterization. Brown made the somewhat strangely definitive statement in this regard that, "It should be strongly emphasized that such explanations are not useful for the goal of gaining an understanding of déjà vu."[14] This seems to be a conclusion a little ahead of itself in an area so neglected outside of popular literature (and even there, it is not greatly ubiquitous). From the beginning, however, even the mainstream conclusions, definitions, and parameters themselves were loaded with key assumptions.

Most importantly for us, and for those experienced throughout these pages, we can look again to the word *paramnesia*, coined in 1887 by Emil Kraepelin. This is ultimately a reference to false memory, deriving from the Greek *para* (from the side), beside, near, against, beyond, and *-mnesis* (meaning memory).[15] With rare exception, these are considered hallucinatory or illusory memories by definition.* Of course, it is nothing more than a circular assumption in and of itself that every instance of memory relating to paramnesia is therefore false or related to psychopathology of some kind. These category assumptions can be traced back further still to the influential theologian and philosopher Augustine of Hippo, who referred to the phenomenon of déjà vu as *falsae memoriae*.[16] This, however, is where the parapsychological rub comes in.

There seems, then, to have been something of an at times unwarranted gaze of disdain cast upon the work of psychical researchers and spiritualists and perhaps somewhat lazy finger-pointing of this kind regarding their role in muddling these areas.† The likes of Brown, for example, hold that such ventures have been an "impediment to empirical research," as the involvement in the field of such actors causes "serious" scientists to keep their distance.[17] This seems to be an unsatisfying summary and perhaps speaks to an unfamiliarity with the often entirely and often carefully applied methods of the parapsychologists and those otherwise dealing with related phenomena. The truth seems more related to the discomfort of the scientist himself with a subject due to its association with another of lesser repute. And while psychical

*The reader should see Sno, "Déjà vu and Jamai vu," 339–42, for some varying interpretations and definitions of paramnesia.

†Much more could be said of this; however, these surprisingly complex historical dynamics spoken of are wonderfully spoken to in Luckhurst's *The Invention of Telepathy* and Monk's *Trauma and the Supernatural in Psychotherapy*.

researchers were by no means immune from such things themselves, in this case the impediment is simply a shoe on the other foot.*

THE FATE OF THE DÉJÀ EXPERIENCE

Perhaps the issue of most contention regarding the approach of the naturalists and others to déjà experiences and the cause of the aspersions cast in that direction toward the more parapsychologically inclined—and even the lack of research in the area—are the philosophical and other biases involved. The assumption in that literature has been that such experiences are psychopathologically tinted, and particularly early on, they were mostly filed away as disorders of memory or disturbances of perception, and the key, if not thrown away, was certainly not placed within reach. Furthermore, these are the very areas of research that, unfortunately, scientists often tend to sidestep. A lack of research is then erroneously conflated with a phenomenon lacking credence. But, despite their conspicuous absence from the scientific literature, these relatively forgotten, legitimate, and often powerful human experiences still require interdisciplinary apprehension and explanation today.

Regarding déjà rêvé in particular, there can be no doubt that the historical fate of déjà vu, being clinically forgotten and primarily relegated to popular media, has extended to the other déjà experiences. Furthermore, the ongoing conflation of it with déjà vu has certainly played a part. In the case of déjà rêvé, as we have alluded to, this may not be entirely without justification, at least on its face. A number of the early déjà case reports were plainly related to those mentally compromised, such as a man who upon admission to the hospital, "immediately recognized everything he saw, including the rooms, the park outside, the staff,

---

*This "hostility" between men and women of science and spiritualists and even between spiritualists themselves dates back to the Victorian era and can be seen in Crookes, William, "Spiritualism Viewed by the Light of Modern Science," where he lambastes spiritualists for their often less than scientific approaches and calls for adhering to the methods of what were then the emerging institutions of science.

their words and gestures and his own responses." This man, as given in a paper by Arnaud in 1896, developed cerebral malaria in childhood and suffered from anterograde and retrograde amnesia. He underwent many déjà vu experiences in his life, and despite it being known even early on that such things occur in both the well and the unwell—and that therefore generalizations based upon a sample of compromised persons would be unhelpful—it seems the pathological aspect curried the most favor in later generalization.[18] Arnaud, using this case and others, suggested déjà vu to be an error in perception rather than memory as such. Even in these cases, however, it may not be easy to discern between actual and imagined déjà experiences. The kinds of simplifications that often turn up in this regard are unhelpful. There is nothing to say that a legitimate déjà experience might not be one of those among the number of others related to psychopathology. Conclusions in these areas must be carefully considered, and the data parsed with great care.

There is still much confusion regarding the terminology surrounding the varying déjà and particularly déjà rêvé experiences. Consider an article from *Bustle* entitled *Déjà Rêvé Is Déjà Vu, But For Dreams,* an inaccurate comparison.[19] Likewise, the popular website *Wikihow* incorrectly explains déjà rêvé as déjà vu but in your dreams.[20] CNN ran an article in which they described déjà rêvé as "dream déjà vu."[21] Some have gone so far as to suggest that "in all cases of déjá rêvè, the subject believes they have somehow prophesized an event that happens."[22] However, this is also without basis. This confusion is very much historically entrenched. For example, the English romantic poet Percy Bysshe Shelley is often cited as being the first on record to suspect a connection between déjà vu and dreaming. The related experience often cited, however, falls under the category of déjà rêvé,* something that generally

*Being yet more specific, this experience would fall under the category of *déjà visité*, specifying that one considers themselves to have dreamed of a place or the details of a place at some time before. This term, however, has not gained either popular or clinical traction, and often doesn't relate to an actual phenemon or experience of this kind. This will be addressed in a future work.

goes unmentioned. The experience, which Shelley powerfully called the "most remarkable event" of this kind in his life, occurred while he was at Oxford. While walking with a friend, Shelley turned a corner and recognized every little detail of the scene as if this moment had occurred in exactly this way before, right down to the layout of the brickwork on the ground. "The effect which it produced on me," Shelley wrote, "was not such as could have been expected. I suddenly remembered to have seen that exact scene in some dream of long ago."[23]

Clearly, the terminology continues to be unsettled. Others consider déjà rêvé "re-experiencing a dream you've had previously—but fully awake."[24] In many of our own examples, however, it is not a straight reenactment at all; it is a directly, thematically, tangentially, or otherwise related one. For instance, in some of the accounts, the imagery can be rather elaborate and full of symbolism, while the meeting with the person who was seen within that romance and strangeness of the dream world is met without any of these more flamboyant aspects at all.

With all of this said, even further complications may arise. Déjà rêvé itself could, in fact, be the initial cause of multiple déjà experiences, the original dream having simply been forgotten and prompting a less defined déjà vu experience. Strictly then, even these previous and seemingly incorrect at face value (and by current standards) definitions may ultimately prove correct, if it will ever be possible to know. Augustine may have been correct after all! If this wasn't enough, in some cases it may even be that these visionary experiences which occur at night—typically at the time during which we dream—are not even dreams at all, at least not of the typical kind. As Funkhouser very astutely and importantly noted in one of his own related déjà vu experiences, his experience related to something that occurred while he was "asleep" as opposed to dreaming.[25] This is an important distinction often overlooked. As he explains, "I have deliberately not used the phrase 'in dream' as, the 'preview' is not at all like a normal dream. It feels entirely different, almost foreign. The problem is that I have no better word to describe this while-asleep forward-in-time glimpse." So commonly in accepted definitions, déjà experiences are initially defined as "glitches" or "errors" of memory. The reality, however, is that we don't know enough to state this broadly of every instance, particularly as it pertains to déjà rêvé.

In the old tales, too, everything is not always so easy to categorize. Consider the romance or the dream vision in which the dream is known at the time of its occurrence to be portentous. It is already believed to have meaning for the future; is it still a definitional déjà rêvé when it comes to pass? Furthermore, one can imagine a déjà vu experience retrospectively becoming a déjà rêvé if the dream is remembered much later as the vague sequence of the initial sensation, etc. Such accounts feature through these pages, but let's keep it simple. Here, for our ease, we generalize all the experiences within as déjà rêvé with the caveat that some more granular analysis and future additions to the terminology might sift accounts further from each other and into varying subcategories of what are all nevertheless déja experiences. These, themselves, of course, may later be placed under even broader categories such as telepathy or precognition.

FIRST STEPS TAKEN

While much more could be said here of the historical origins and course of the déjà experiences and the paramnesias, these have been covered with great skill before and are not as relevant to us. The interested reader should consider Alan Brown's *The Déjà vu Experience (Essays in Cognitive Psychology)* or the excellent *Memory Disorders in Psychiatric Practice* edited by Berrios and Hodges. For our purposes, it is more than enough to say and to establish before beginning properly that déjà rêvé—and specifically in the context of the stories presented here—is still of a fundamentally mysterious and understudied nature. While the research and thinking around the phenomenon make for fascinating reading, they are far from conclusive or singular in those conclusions, and a significantly more robust body of knowledge will be required in order for the likes of the scientist, the historian of religion, the parapsychologist, or the psychologist to draw final conclusions. Here, we are concerned with these questions to some degree; however, they are not the focus. The focus here is the subjective (although seemingly veridical in many cases) and wonderful world of the individual, their dreams, their visions, their lives, their loves, and the meaning with which they both imbue the experiences and the meaning taken from those experiences out into the world. We are concerned with how these strange happenings have impacted and continue to impact the individual and the wider world in a manner so far underappreciated. More often than not, for him or her there is no doubt as to the importance of these experiences, which have helped them find lovers, acquaintances, healers, shamans, doctors, guides, and so much more alike. And that should be important to us.

1

Déjà Rêvé, Belief, and the Power of Dreams

Meeting in Dreams Before Meeting in Life

We must remember that the rationalistic attitude of the West is not the only possible one and is not all-embracing, but is in many ways a prejudice and a bias that ought perhaps to be corrected.

C. G. Jung

The idea and widely lived experience that the location and/or identity of another person may be mysteriously revealed in a vision or dream and later confirmed turns up in a surprisingly large variety of legend, lore, and literature of all kinds. Particularly from a cross-cultural and historical perspective, little work has been done in synthesizing these strange occurrences. These are experiences, after all, which are as much if not more reported in numbers by our own contemporaries as they have turned up in the renowned dream visions, romances, and folklore of old. Just as the troubadours and knights of the old lays and lyrics might dream of their maidens to be, ordinary people are still dreaming the same dreams. Just as the shared dream of two distant knights might bring them together in the waking world, still our contemporaries claim the same mysteriously shared spaces. The past and the future are firmly connected at least in this way and speak to us of a genuine and mysterious continuum of variously neglected human experience. In this first chapter, therefore, it would be well to establish—with a significant number of more comparative examples—just how widely recorded and believed these déjà rêvé related experiences have been and continue to be. Furthermore, these opening accounts will primarily speak to the kinds of surprising and powerful real-world effects these experiences have in the life of the individual. They will establish a ground floor upon which those of the following chapters will elaborate, and expand.

DESTINY, DECISIONS, AND DREAMS

Karilee Shames, a specialist in psychiatric nursing, writes that when she and her husband, Rich, were living in Hawaii she had a "powerful dream." She met a woman with distinctive dark eyes and a graying bun who told her in no uncertain terms, "Go to Phoenix." "I had awakened Rich shaking, so powerful was this dream," Shames wrote. "Within me a seed began to grow. Maybe it was time to leave the island." As Shames further explains, the power of the dream is made clear in that "The next thing we knew we had our belongings shipped from Hawaii to Phoenix."* Her husband, Rich, was hired as a general practitioner attending home births and was to work with Dr. Gladys Taylor McGarey, the so-called "mother of holistic medicine."[1] Shames points out that McGarey "turned out to be the woman from my dream, with the gray hair and the bun." Of interesting relation, the Hawaiian *Legend of Kepakailiula* speaks to just how old the idea that a dream could be the impetus for such movement on those islands is. In this tale, Kepakailiula is instructed by a spirit in a dream to move over forty miles south to Paliuli and live there with his wife. While she doesn't initially take this very seriously, she and her husband later have the very same dream at the same time and therefore decide to take up their lives and move together to Paliuli.[2]

Cheryl Heppner, former President of the Association of Late-Deafened Adults (ALDA), wrote briefly of a similar dream in her fascinating work *Seeds of Disquiet: One Deaf Woman's Experience.* Having returned home from a trip to Richmond, she found two strangers being entertained by her husband, Fred, in their living room. One of them told Heppner that she lived in New York, had a dream about her, and on the authority of that dream flew to Heppner's home in Norfolk. Arriving at the airport, she picked up a newspaper and happened to find Heppner's picture inside, and as the author explains it, "she recognized me as the person from her dream. She decided it was her mission to find me." Heppner continued, "I was flabbergasted. The woman seemed to know a lot about me. I didn't know whether she had picked up details from talking to Fred or from the newspaper article, but it was still spooky."[3]

Heppner was right; these absolutely are important dreams, often set apart from others at the very outset. Once more speaking to this capacity of the dream to quite literally move the individual, John Broomfield gave the case of an Argentinian woman he had met at the Esalen Institute, a nonprofit retreat center in Big Sur, California. She sat down beside Broomfield, and in reply to his question as to what had brought her all this way, she said it was because of a certain dream. "I couldn't have made it up," she told him. "At that stage I didn't know any of the circumstances revealed to me in the dream. It was only four weeks ago that I found out that the people and objects I saw in the dream do in fact exist."[4]

As noted, some of these dreams are much more than a simple visualization of the vision's object, but are often full of more elaborate and more typically symbolic dream imagery. During a strange dream or vision in which he felt his bed was in the middle of a vast, dark ocean, author Joseph Jenkins "recognized a human form within the fog, appearing very distant." The largest of what seemed to be five figures "had a human face, a man's face, dark-skinned and bearded." Whatever the experience was, it stayed with Jenkins strongly afterward. For various reasons, the dream ultimately convinced him that he should travel to Peru, as he had been previously considering. Some time after, his daughter Sarah arrived with her friend Michael. "I immediately recognized him as the one I saw in my dream," Jenkins wrote, "and I couldn't help but stare at him when we were introduced."[5]

American "astrologer to the stars," Sydney Omarr, gave the similar case of a Florida woman, Hazel West, who moved to Omarr's own hometown of Cassadaga directly "as the result of a dream she had in 1963." While living off the mainland on Merritt Island with her first husband, West dreamed of an elderly man in a wheelchair who was requesting her help writing a book. Some months after the dream, which West had noted before its fulfillment as seeming important, a friend of hers brought her to Cassadaga to have a reading with medium Anne Gehman. They formed a bond and West would return multiple times over the next year. Some time later, Gehman invited West to a spiritualist community in Wisconsin—an offer she reluctantly took up—of which Omarr writes, "She met the elderly white-haired gentleman in the wheelchair who had appeared in her dream." He turned out to be one of the best-known mediums in Cassadaga. "He was thirty-five years older than me," West wrote, "a very private person, and I was too intimidated to tell him about my dream. But we became good friends." She later moved to Cassadaga on the advice of these experiences.[6]

Similarly, author Francis Fontana credits his own dream as being one of two events that led to his collaboration with his future wife Sara on a book about marriage, the book from which this following account is taken. While the visual identification is not made as such, the extent to which these dreams might move the individual to creative endeavors in this seemingly lesser form warrants their inclusion. Fontana dreamed he was to direct the next meeting of a men's retreat and that there was someone he was meant to meet. He later agreed to do this, meeting many men and women and sharing their stories. "There was one man whom I connected with in a special way," Fontana wrote, "and I believe was the man from my dream. He was persistent in encouraging me to write the book."[7]

It is not just that they pin their hopes to a dream or aimlessly wish upon a star; in the minds of the experiencers, the experiences are veridical or truth telling. Whatever the actual nature of the dynamics at play, their visions and dreams coincide with reality. They are "confirmed" in the waking world, and this is often powerfully received. It should perhaps be no surprise then how prominently they feature through time and space. After being shipwrecked off the coast of the western Sahara and captured by slave traders in 1815, Captain James Riley of the United States merchant ship *Commerce* documented just such an episode.[8] During the episode, he saw himself being rescued by a stranger from Morocco, who reassured him that he would see his family again. Riley, although he admitted he never believed dreams, was fully convinced of their truth in this case and told his captors they had a friend in Morocco who would pay their ransom. As Shema Rismay powerfully noted, "He trusted his life to a dream."[9] Later, Riley wrote almost with a tinge of embarrassment that "I must add that when I afterwards saw Mr. Wilshire, I knew him to be the same man I had seen in my sleep. He had a particular mark on his chin—wore a light colored frock coat, had on a white hat, and rode the same horse."[10]

Kristin, an informant of author Louisa Oakley Green, told poignantly of a dream that "shaped her destiny." She found herself in a gymnasium, being greeted by thousands of people she seemed to know. A frail elderly woman grabbed her from out of the crowd and told her she would be going to North Carolina and that she was needed there. Seven years later, Kristin took a different path after trying LaHo-Chi for the first time, a healing technique that she wanted to use to help with a personal crisis. These events culminated in Kristin studying LaHo-Chi at a North Carolina institute run by Dan and Rio. "When Rio made her first appearance to the students," Kristin recalled, "there was a big hush as she descended the stairway into the classroom. I kept thinking the woman looked very familiar to me, but we had never met before." Later, on her return trip, she "had this sudden realization." Kristen continued, "She was the woman from my dream seven years earlier!"[11]

One of our own unique informants, the first of a number who have so graciously offered their experiences through the internet and most of which are recent, was especially impressed and entirely convinced as to their reality, meaning, and significance:

> Last June I took my three-year-old son to visit my parents in my hometown. We made plans one evening before bed to go check out a park the next day. That night I had a very vivid and realistic dream that I met a woman and her son there and the kids played and we talked. She had a pretty distinct look and voice, short red hair, and certain mannerisms. Her son was about my son's age and had blonde hair. I thought about it the next morning, how real it seemed and how it felt like I knew her. The next morning when we went to the park, there they were. I almost felt like I was expecting them, which is insane. The kid ran up to mine and introduced himself and they played and I talked to her for a little while. I thought about that for weeks, it was just so weird. I had never seen them before, don't know them, don't even live in that city.

Our "Jane Doe" noted that she had seen the family multiple times after and discovered that they had moved into her neighborhood, but not at the time of the first experience.

> *This is a town of 250k+ people, and we only visit maybe 2–3 times a year, and yet 3 different times we have been out doing the same things*

at the same moments with our sons . . . and our first meeting was in a dream!! I have never given much credence to this kind of thing but I know my experience was real and not some kind of déjà vu / dual processing brain error.[12]

Such conviction turns up commonly in these accounts. Our contemporaries often express the same conviction that turns up so commonly in the legends, the lyric, and lore. Holding our focus upon more recent times for now, at ten years old, author Senaria Bridges very briefly referenced a related dream. While heading to visit the parents of her stepfather, Bridges noted—without a detailed description of the dream itself—that "In my mind, I needed to see Franco's mother. There was something about her that I needed to see, and I needed to hear her voice." This conviction seems to have arisen in a dream. "After I put my bags up, I rushed to that porch to see who this grandmother was. And it was just like I had seen her in my dream, sitting on the porch. She had on the same dress, and she wore glasses, and she had that same apron on. I told her that I had seen her in a dream before I had gotten there, and she smiled and said [in relation to the dream] that was something good."[13]

According to Swami Sivananda Radha, a German *yogini* (a kind of female yoga practitioner or spiritual teacher) who founded Yasodhara Ashram in British Columbia, a psychiatrist she met told her, "You know, I had an extraordinary and clear dream of your ashram after you were here the last time. Is there a guest lodge, a small office and bookstore, and an old house where you eat meals?" Radha confirmed. The psychiatrist went on to describe details of the grounds before asking, "And is there a young man there with particularly large blue eyes?" (along with other details as to the man's appearance). "Yes," Radha told him. "Why don't you come and see for yourself?" Taking up the invitation, this psychiatrist pointed out the landmarks and eventually saw a young man come along. "That's him, the one I saw in my dream," he said. Of importance here, the dream impacted the psychiatrist greatly, and he even became fearful of its implications. "I have to change my perception of my life. I have to change my idea of what my senses can do."[14]

These are no idle or transient effects. It becomes clear that these déjà rêvé experiences are more than the kinds of simple and dispensable anomalies or psychological oddities they have often been considered. As will continue to come into focus, they have the very real capacity to alter fundamental beliefs and engender real and strikingly similar action from person to person. And this, as we'll see, is no new idea.

STRANGE RECORDS AND SEER TYPES

Sigmund Freud claimed to have met Austro-Hungarian Jewish journalist and political activist Theodor Herzl in a dream before actually meeting him in life.[15] The number of these visions and dreams, which may be found almost hidden away in biographies, journals, memoirs, and letters—sometimes those of people of renown, at other times those much lesser known—is particularly striking. The extent to which the references are often in passing and rarely elaborated upon may speak to their perceived flimsy or flaky status. While a number are presented here, many more will also be found scattered across other chapters to which their content is better suited.

In the memoir of Mintauts Blosfelds, a Latvian who fought for the Germans, he very briefly recorded a strange experience he had while on the Eastern Front in 1944. While asleep in a German bunker, Mintauts had what he called a "curious" dream in which a German entered the bunker, took his rucksack from its place on the wall, and exited while saying they had to leave. "I was therefore more than a little surprised," Mintauts later wrote, "when we were given the order to withdraw for real. My dream had come true and the person giving the order was the same German I had seen in my dream."[16]

Olaudah Equiano was a writer and leading abolitionist born in

Nigeria and shipped as a child slave to the Caribbean. His memoir, first published in 1789, *The Interesting Narrative of the Life of Olaudah Equiano, or Gustavus Vassa, the African*, is one of the earliest published writings by an African to be widely read in English and was later published in numerous European countries. While still a slave and heading to Philadelphia, Equiano heard of Mrs. Davis, a wise woman who lived there and whom people said could reveal secrets and foretell events. "I didn't put much faith in this story," Equiano wrote, "but then, the very same night, I dreamed of her! When I got there, she came to the door—wearing the very same dress I had seen in my dream!"[17]

Harriet Tubman, when she came into the acquaintance of the abolitionist John Brown, claimed that she had "seen him in a dream before they met."[18] "I was in a wilderness sort of place," as she told it, "all rocks and bushes, when a big snake raised his head from behind a rock, and while I looked at it, it changed into the head of an old man with a long white beard on his chin, and he looked at me wishful like, just as if he was going to speak to me." It was said that Tubman "laid great stress" on this dream and that she, in fact, was the recipient of a number of other seemingly prophetic episodes.[19]

While repeated general déjà experiences are relatively common, it is nevertheless the case that many people speak of *these* kinds as distinct from ordinary dreams or as the only experience of this kind in their lives. However, like Tubman, there is often a sense that a number of the percipients have rather been subject to such or related things throughout the course of their lives. The individual to whom various seemingly extrasensory occurrences are attributed is a common folkloric figure, often thought to be endowed with a particular capacity or receptivity. These individuals still exist and would likely be candidates for such categorization had they found themselves in a different cultural milieu. Theresa Cheung, for instance, had an informant who spoke of her own dreams of this kind following a pattern and suggesting she has had a number of them.[20] "These dreams," as she explained it, "seemed to follow a sequence of seeing the person in my dream followed by the dream actually happening in life . . . it's uncanny!" Much before Cheung's account, German poet and author Johann Peter Eckermann (1792–1854) was said to have had second sight,* something that, while often spoken of in relation to Scotland, Richard Friedenthal noted as being fairly common among those of the German State of Lower Saxony. Before meeting German polymath and influential German writer Johann Wolfgang Goethe, he "saw Goethe in a dream before he set out on his pilgrimage to walk to Weimar."[21] It is somewhat unclear as to whether or not this was their first meeting; however, the anecdote is patently relevant in that such a possibility is inherent within.

Relayed in an 1880 issue of *The Spiritualist* magazine was an account initially given to the *New York Sun* regarding a Kansas woman who was said to have had just such an "exceptional mental endowment." She was said to have had the capacity, with their Scottish descent being cited as relevant, to come to know of the misfortunes of distant family members, the dreams by which these intimations came being "subsequently confirmed in every instance by letters and telegrams." In one of those dreams, this woman was preparing for a visit from her brother, Dan. He would be coming from Pennsylvania to New York. A few nights before they were to meet for the first time, she dreamed of a white-haired man with a basket with a hole in it that was set on his knees opposite her on a train. It was full of fish. The dream was of a journey from Terre Haute, Indiana, to Altoona, Pennsylvania, where they were to meet. Later in the dream, she saw an expressman pass her as they left the train wheeling a great box on a truck, within which there was a coffin holding her brother. The man's unique clothing also caught her

*As long ago as 1652 in Scotland, the nobleman Lord Talbot wrote in a letter to a friend that those with second sight "will ordinarily see their absent friends, though at a great distance, sometimes no less than from America to Scotland, sitting, standing, or walking, in some certain place, and then they conclude with assurance that they will see them so and there." The implication that they might also "see" strangers in this way seems a reasonable inference. See Tibbits, *Folklore and Legends*, 176.

eye. The informant woke crying and entirely convinced her brother was dead, although some ridicule from those at the breakfast table apparently had an initially beneficial effect on her mood. The day she came to Terre Haute station to depart and meet her brother, as she states it, "In an opposite seat sat a white-haired man. I recognized him at once as the man I had seen in my dream. He had a fish basket on his knees. The faces of the passengers were familiar to me. At the dinner station I met the lady I had seen in my dream, and we had dinner together." Soon, too, she saw the expressman from her dream pass her with a box addressed to her father that said, "Dan is dead." He had indeed died.[22]

Influential British Neopagan and author Lois Bourne, relating a number of seemingly prophetic dreams from the historical past to her own present, also gave an example from among her own experiences.

> I once had a dream that I was in a large store and a woman quite close to me put something in her bag without paying for it. I saw her face quite clearly. A few days later whilst shopping in a store, I had a feeling of déja vu: I recognized the woman standing next to me as the person in my dream. She looked around quickly to see if anyone was watching, did not notice me, and stuffed something in her shopping bag. I did absolutely nothing.

While no further comment was made on this experience, the author did offer one other related to the publishing of her first book. One night, she dreamed of a "neat, petite and very pretty" woman who took her to her flat. When Bourne met the senior editor who would be working with her on the book, as she writes, "she was exactly as I had seen her in my dream."[23] Author Alexandra Chauran keeps dream journals and likewise suggests that such dreams are a relatively common occurrence for her. "For example," she writes, "I've seen a new person in my dream and then later met that person in real life."[24]

Author Miriam Minkoff, as recorded in her own journal, dreamed she was working on a project with a nice looking man with eyes that would apparently "sparkle like sunlight on river stones." A billboard comes into view flashing the words "don't be too grabby" with such a din that they both flee the scene. The next Monday, after a team-building session at work involving playing instruments, the man who was drumming mentioned that he couldn't go out with the group after work as he had just moved from California with his children. "That's when it hits me," Minkoff wrote. "He's the guy from my dream."[25] Others, too, such as author James Gollnick, have systematically recorded their dreams toward the same purposes. "Gradually," he writes, "I began to recall and record my dreams in greater detail. Over time, I was surprised to find that I could confirm a number of future references in my dreams, such as seeing a person in my dream—whom I had never met—a day or two before I first met them."[26]

Pioneering American psychical researcher and professor of philosophy and psychology, James Hyslop recorded and reported the case of a woman from a family in Toronto, where he was invited to conduct some research in 1904. She claimed to have been the subject of multiple premonitory experiences, including one in which she "had a dream of meeting a certain person on the cars on the way to this place where she arrived yesterday. She met this person as dreamed and there had been no prearrangement for the meeting and it was only a casual circumstance that they came together on the train."[27] Something else of great interest here was recorded in the 1788 diary of the Welsh author and salon holder of the prominent Salusbury family, Hester Lynch Thrale. Thrale was convinced, based on the dream experiences of certain others in her social circles, that dreams, as Homer put it, "do descend from Jove."* She thought they could offer legitimate "warnings from above"

*In the ancient Greek epic poem the *Iliad,* attributed to Homer, dreams are often portrayed as having the capacity to tell the truth. These are "mystic dreams" and were said in that work to "descend from Jove," a reference to Jupiter, the sky god and chief god of both ancient Rome and Italy. See Pope, *Pope's Translation of Homer's Iliad,* 19, for this account.

related to the individual's fortunes. The wife of a Colonel Gordon, a man intimate with Thrale's family, told her just such a dream, which she duly recorded. This woman insistently invited Thrale to walk with her in the Rhu Dee, a local meadow, an offer that was eventually taken up. While they walked together, this colonel's wife told her of a strange dream she had about this very walk, though Thrale was not of the mind at that point to put stock in such things and so attempted to steer the conversation elsewhere. Not long after, becoming more and more absorbed in thought, the colonel's wife suddenly shrieked and fainted. Becoming increasingly perturbed, Thrale saw a man on horseback wearing a black coat galloping toward town, apparently on some important errand. She called him over, and soon after, the colonel's wife awoke, fixed her eyes upon this man, and suddenly asked him about her brother, Colonel Ormsby, who was away. The man told her that he was dead. She then turned to Thrale and according to the diary said, "I saw the Man coming along & could not stand it; he is the very Person I saw in my Dream & it was to meet him that I tempted you hither, for I dream'd you were walking with me—I knew the Horse too from the Impression my Dream had made, for as to Horse or Man they neither of 'em ever saw me." This woman, then, had acted upon the dream itself in her actions. Thrale ended with the simple sentiment, "Is this not a very singular Story?"[28]

RETICENCE, EMBARRASSMENT, AND INCREDULITY

Author Rupert Isaacson, in his work on the Kalahari Bushmen, *The Healing Land*, wrote of an interesting incident that occurred while traveling to Tsodilo in southern Africa to see the famous UNESCO-protected rock paintings. The night before arriving, he dreamed that he was already there and that an old Bushman leader and he were speaking together beneath a tree in the moonlight. He asked the man if his people still used bone to make arrowheads (as he had previously been informed), to which the reply came that they were no longer allowed to hunt and that his people had been moved on from the hills. The following day, Isaacson found it to be true that the Bushmen had been moved away in this manner. Regarding that same day, when Isaacson finally met with the Bushman, he noted that he "could have picked him out in a crowd. The same man from my dream—the very one." Upon asking him the same questions he asked in the dream, Isaacson received answers that echoed those of the dream "almost verbatim."[29]

It is truly notable how often these accounts are simply mentioned in passing or given short shrift. So it was regarding an incident related to the wreck of the English-built *Dunbar* ship in 1857 on its way to Sydney. Mrs. Graham, the wife of the nearby lighthouse signal master, dreamed darkly that night as the storm was at its height. "Go down, Jim, and rescue the poor fellow in the sea," were her words as she suddenly woke. When the sailor James Johnson was found clinging to the cliffs thirty-six hours later, "she recognised him instantly as the man she had seen in her dream, struggling wildly in the surf."[30]

The true extent to which such seemingly extrasensory visions and dreams have helped shape and influence the color and course of history may always be hidden. Those who experience them, as is so commonly the case with most non-ordinary experiences in the West, are often extremely reluctant to relate them for fear of being disbelieved or ridiculed. How many pieces of literature, art, music, etc., have been inspired by such experiences, of which we may never know for this reason? Isaacson, the author of the previously quoted work on the Kalahari Bushmen, is a clear testament to these speculations in that the account itself was hidden away at the book's end and beyond the text of its main content. "There was already so much magic in it," he wrote, telling us that he "cut the story." "I was worried," Isaacson told, "that anything that seemed too 'New-Agey' might undermine the urgent reality of the Bushmen's struggle for survival and identity."[31] This ongoing refrain is an old one, and the same was true in the following account from 1803. Reprinted in the bimonthly *Zion's Landmark* journal was the case of Sarah Hamilton of South Carolina, who, in an episode worthy of the old romances, dreamed rather elaborately of a strange and beautiful place full of games, gaiety, and various fashionable things. She drank from goblets of gold and silver and saw a field full of shining people dressed in white robes with white palm in their hands singing more wonderfully than she had ever heard before. She saw an Episcopalian priest on multiple occasions, once drinking to his health and at another time looking dark and disagreeable. After some further elaborate adventures, the dream ended; however, it recurred some months later. While visiting her aunt and uncle, Hamilton struggled to find meaning in the experience. At one point, upon arriving at a certain destination, she noted that, "I no sooner came to the place that I saw the minister and knew immediately, although I had never seen him before, that it was the same man I saw in my dream." Hamilton, almost with embarrassment, noted the following of the experience: "Although some people may make light of all dreams, yet I would beg pardon for inserting this, for it was peculiarly interesting to me, however foolish it may look to others."[32]

In 1884, a Fellow of the College of Physicians—who refrained to give his name for fear of professional embarrassment—told of waking up one night and telling his wife, "I see the proprietor standing under the lamppost this side of the bridge with another man." The informant seemed to have dreamed of the location of one of his patients, although his wife was incredulous. Despite this, he went to the location and found that, "Sure enough, there he was under the lamppost, talking to a friend." This was seemingly something of a waking vision, and according to the informant, "he had never encountered the proprietor on the spot where he saw him, and it was not a likely thing that he should be standing talking in the street at so late an hour."[33]

Arthur Tudno Williams, in his memoir of his life with his father, Marcellus A. Williams—a deputy United States surveyor in Florida—recalls a dream he had in 1872 while staying in a surveyors' camp while his father was some miles off. In the dream, he and the resident cook heard shouting and saw Mark, a Seminole Indian man who worked for them arrive and tell Tudno that his father had sent him to tell the cook to prepare two days' worth of provisions and meet him and his crew at a specific corner post three miles or so from camp. "And the next afternoon," as he explains it, "we started out to meet them at the corner post." Tudno noted that "I had never been through this country before, but I had seen it so vividly in my dream that I would have had no difficulty in going to the designated spot." Just before awakening with a jolt, Tudno saw a mysterious, dark-skinned man attack and kill his father. "Mark, the Seminole Indian who'd given us the message, came into the camp and told the identical story I had dreamed. The provisions were cooked, and we started for the corner post." Everything was as Williams dreamed, and he soon saw his father in the distance.

Here again, we see the same reticence in accepting the experience. "I was ashamed to tell my father of my dream, for fear that he would ridicule me," Tudno wrote. After falling asleep the following morning having been awake all night, he writes, "I jumped to my feet, and came within an ace of shooting the very colored man I had dreamed of sticking the axe in my father's head! He had gotten up to replenish the fire and was in the act of throwing a stick of wood on it, which of course was the jolt which awakened me. I did not sleep any more that night."[34]

Increasingly and importantly apparent is that these accounts are commonly found outside of the realms of any patently psychical or occult literature or context. They are come upon incidentally and from various unrelated sources. One of those was recorded in *The Green Bag*, a popular legal magazine out of Boston published between 1889 and 1914 that offered news of legal events, essays, and biographies and often took a somewhat less serious tone. In one issue, Englishman Baxter

Borret states that his friend doctor Ralph Jackson moved to Australia, and their correspondence gradually grew less frequent. Many years later, Jackson was to return and around that time Borret dreamed vividly of his friend lying in his berth on a ship, pale, worn, and thin, as if he had a very serious fever. Standing by the berth was a man Borret saw as being a surgeon, holding Jackson's wrist in one hand and a watch in the other. "Borret, Borret," the figure of Jackson exclaimed, "I am dying Borret; Grayson of Rochdale has some deeds of property in Mason street; the proofs you want are with the deeds," he said before falling back dead. Even upon awakening to the afternoon sunlight streaming through the windows, Borret "felt certain" this was a "vision of what was happening afar off." He then set about writing the dream into his pocketbook along with the time. Around a fortnight later, Borret boarded the boat at Liverpool. "The first face I saw on board," he writes, "was the one I had seen in my dream, the ship's surgeon. I accosted him without hesitation." He continued, "You are the ship's surgeon; you have had my friend Ralph Jackson on your sick list; you need not tell me anything, he died on Sunday afternoon, the 22nd of September." These events all turned out accurately and to have occurred at the time of the dream. Borret, echoing the sentiments we have seen here, told Grayson when they met regarding the deeds that "If I had commenced my correspondence with you by telling you that it had been revealed to me in a dream that this evidence was to be found in your office, you would have put me down for a lunatic; yet here is the evidence, and I can give you my most solemn assurance that neither by letter nor vivo ore did Ralph Jackson tell me that I should find it here; it was revealed to me in a dream."[35]

MURDER, ROBBERY, AND DEATH

On the tail of this previous account, it is worthwhile to note that a significant number of these experiences pertain to murder and death and that they could have taken up their own study. It is especially the case that memories tied to emotionally charged events might be particularly well remembered. Where these déjà rêvé turn up in relation to something so involved as death, as when they turn up in relation to love, it could be speculated that these experiences were particularly well poised to effect or engender beliefs on their basis. Finally, then, a sampling is offered, and as we go on, a number of others related to death, dying, and even the dead will continue to turn up throughout.

One of the earliest memories of Dutchman Marinus B. Dykshoorn is of a vision that he claims to remember more clearly than any other event in his childhood. Standing at the window of his parents home in Honselersdijk in winter, the snow heavily falling, he saw a man enter a barn. This man then took a length of rope and hung himself. Even then, he knew this wasn't "real" as such; there was, after all, no actual barn where he was looking. His father told him he was "imagining things," and he was punished as this was not the first time something strange of this kind had occurred. Two weeks later, a man hanged himself in his barn from a beam, as Dykshoorn relays it, "exactly as I had described it to my father, and it was the same man I had seen in my 'dream.'"[36]

While Scottish author, physician, and philanthropist Dr. John Abercrombie (1780–1844) was careful to admit the number of falsehoods and cranks in this area, he nonetheless came across a number of dreams that he felt "compelled to receive" as "facts which we can in no degree account for." One of those related to the 1812 assassination of Spencer Perceval, the former British prime minister. A dream came to John Williams eight days before the event, in which he saw a small man enter the house of commons dressed in a blue coat and white waistcoat. Soon after, another man entered dressed in a brown coat with yellow basket buttons, drawing a pistol and killing Perceval. Williams took special note of the man's countenance before awaking and speaking of the dream to his wife. Just over a week later, Williams received news of the murder and a short time later "found in a news shop several colored prints depicting the scene, and recognized in it the countenance and dress of the parties, the blood on Mr. Perceval's waistcoat, and the peculiar yellow basket buttons on Bellingham's [the murderer's] coat, precisely as he had seen them in his dream."[37] English author Augustus Hare (1834–1903) in *The Story of My Life* told of something related that was given by a man from Chartwell, Kent, in England. This man, Mr. Colquhoun, was awoken by his wife, who dreamed that her aunt was going to be murdered and that she saw the person who was to carry out the crime. That morning, she went to Edinburgh and turned up at her aunt's home. The door was opened by a strange servant. "It was the man she had seen in her dream." The deed, as it happens, was supposedly attempted, though it was not carried out.[38]

Recorded in the *National Police Gazette*, a "legendary" American magazine founded in 1845 under the heading *A Wonderful Dream*, was another strange account wrapped up in a murder. The author notes of the case that it was an occurrence "so remarkable in its character that it would exceed the receptive capacity of the most credulous person were it not so well authenticated and so firmly established by the best of evidence." Rachel, an early Scottish-Welsh-Irish settler from Washington County, hadn't returned home after intending to travel three miles to visit the man to whom she was engaged. Indeed, it was found she had not even arrived. That same night, a woman living in the same country woke her husband in great distress, declaring she had just seen a murder done, going on to describe the place and the people involved. Many witnesses would testify that she had told them the dream that morning before anything came of it. Despite having never left her hometown, she later guided an interested reverend to the area, noting at one point, "This is the place that I dreamed of!" The body is soon found, and the woman's husband is arrested on suspicion. "The dreamer recognized him in a crowd of other men, and startled her companions still more by pointing out another young fellow [. . .] as his partner in the dream." The dream was brought to court, although it was not considered strong enough evidence for a conviction. *Her* conviction, however, and that of those she had told, was in their minds entirely with basis.[39]

Similarly, around the middle of the nineteenth century, miner Lloyd Magruder is murdered and robbed near the Clearwater River in Idaho. The perpetrators chose the spot as there was nothing within one hundred miles of it and nothing, as they thought, to connect them to the murder. That night, however, Hill Beachy, owner of the Luna Motel in Lewiston, "dreamed that the man of whom he had become a close friend was killed and robbed." He saw everything in "vivid detail," including the faces of the slayers. The following morning, a stagecoach arrived at Lewiston, and from among the travelers buying tickets at his hotel for the journey, "Beachy recognized the man in his dream." He could do nothing then; however, on the authority of his dream, the body was soon found, and the men were arrested in San Francisco and according to Glass, "found guilty, and hanged on March 4, 1865—because of a dream."[40]

Ruth Ammer, on a hot August afternoon in 1962, woke up from a sleep with the strangely distinct and powerful sense that she was now a widow. She had dreamed that her husband was assaulted in his shop. Ruth went to the shop when he was late home from work and found her husband dead. She gave the police a description of the man she had seen in her dream that, despite their initial skepticism, turned out to match the description of the murderer, who was later found guilty and sentenced to life in prison.[41] Stories of exactly this kind, often found scattered throughout the pages of various newspapers and periodicals, are, in fact, nothing new. They may as much be found in ancient China, where in 740, after a woman's grave was robbed and her corpse defiled by a number of men, she appeared to her son in a dream and gave their description. This later led to their apprehension and arrest, as well as the restoration of the stolen goods.[42]

Again and again it is the dream seen to move the dreamer to action. Recorded in the *Journal of the Friends' Historical Society*, a Quaker publication founded in 1903, was the dream of one Abiah Darby. In this dream, Darby sees a cook stirring something up by a fire. The cook suddenly leaves, and a strange man stealthily approaches the saucepan and drops something in. The cook then returns, pours the pan's contents into a basin, and brings it up to her ill master just before the dream ends. The dream came two more times, and it "so impressed Darby that she felt she must get up at once." She knew a young woman was sick in the local jail on suspicion of poisoning her master and made the connection. After the woman was found innocent, Darby, who said her face was exactly that of the cook in her dream, hired her. About twelve months later, the cook fell ill. Eventually, the nephew of her deceased master confessed to poisoning her. When Darby paid this man a visit, "the face of this gentleman corresponded with the face she had seen in her dream."[43]

We now return to the pages of *The Spiritualist*, a journal published between 1869 and 1882, where numerous related experiences may be found. One of those, reprinted from another publication, *Banner of Light*, has Mrs. Allen of Calaveras, California, as the subject of a burglary. The intruder entered her house, taking her watch and pocketbook before following the trail by the local river. That night she dreamed of the thief, followed the trail in the morning, and "discovered the man she had seen in her dream."[44] Another much older related dream comes down to us according to a history of Crowland Abbey in Lincolnshire, England, dealing with its destruction and restoration. The Benedictine abbot of Crowland from 1087, Ingulphus, dreamed while he was a monk at Fontanelle, Italy, that several bishops and saints appeared before him, leading an unknown person somewhere in a gold chain. While overseeing the restoration of the abbey, one of the objectives was to move the body of Waltheof, the last of the Anglo-Saxon earls, as it was exposed to the weather. When the tomb was opened, "Ingulphus looking in the face, immediately recollected the person he had seen in his dream at Fontanelle."[45] Similary, during the seventeenth-century patriarchate of

Nikon—and after the founding of a çertain monastery—Nikon records a dream in which he sees a wounded man lying on the ground whom he later realized was dead, his hands being arranged in a gesture of blessing. The very next day, Nikon opens the coffin of Iakov of Borovich, and "he recognized the man in his dream as Iakov and saw that his hands were making the same gesture of blessing." Speaking directly to the didactic utility of these account types, something that will be spoken to more as we continue, American historican Paul Bushkovitch considers the story from the perspective of speaking to the truth of Iakov's earlier recorded miracles.[46]

From all corners, dreams and other visionary experiences in which individuals are met, only then to be met later in life, are there to be found. They have been recorded in large numbers in diaries, biographies, the back notes of more serious studies, the newspapers, and the journals alike. Already it becomes clear that certain fundamental beliefs have been instilled or altered via these experiences and that action has been taken on their direct authority. This will continue to be explored. Whatever debates might occur between perhaps the parapsychologist, the opposed materialist, and others, these facts alone warrant much closer scrutiny of the déjà rêvé and other related phenomena clinically, historically, contemporaneously, comparatively, and otherwise.

2
The Old, the New, and Beliefs That Move
Déjà Rêvé as a Cross-Cultural Experience

> *The fate of our times is characterized by rationalization and intellectualization and, above all, by the disenchantment of the world.*
>
> Max Weber

The idea, as we have seen so well expressed, that these are visions and dreams that make tangible impression and impacts on the waking world is not something exclusive to our contemporaneous and other relatively recent accounts. This is an old and widely represented notion and experience that takes numerous forms. If there were no other reason for others to attend to these experiences more closely, this would be reason enough. In its most basic sense, déjà rêvé is a surprisingly common occurrence in legendary, folkloric, and other literature. While numerous older and cross-cultural accounts will continue to turn up as the chapters progress, here, in something of a primer, a particular focus will be put on those accounts along with some comparative examples of what seem to be their much more recent counterparts.

THE OLD MARVELS AND THE NEW MARVELS

Among the events of war, both today and in the distant past, there are many accounts of the kinds we are interested in to be found. From the most ancient records, extrasensory and supernatural phenomena abound in the records of conflict. Jirjis al-Makīn (1223–1273), a Coptic Christian historian who wrote in Arabic, recorded that an Abbasid Caliph named Motassem had knowledge "from a dream" of a Greek invasion, led by Byzantine emperor Theophilus in 837. In this dream, he saw a noble Arabic woman seized by them and crying out for Motassem to help her. The invasion, which history indicates was an opportunistic one rather than part of an overarching strategy, was confirmed in the morning, and Motassem set out for the emperor's lands. Either the power of the dream itself, or the power the individual who put ink to paper sees in such dreams, is then brought to bear upon the narrative. It goes that the "strong conceit he entertained that the woman he saw in his dream was a prisoner in that city, induced him to undertake the siege of this place, preferably to any other." Later, the caliph finds the same woman in prison after picking her out of all those brought based upon his image of her from the dream. His strange conviction had told true. The dream, just as we have seen in the more recent accounts, is specifically cited as the impetus for action.[1]

While such "divinely inspired" actions are found in numbers in and around the events and course of war, other decisions are far less dramatic. Gersonides (1288–1344), the fourteenth-century French Jewish philosopher who often took a critical approach even to many of the miracles in the Bible, nevertheless offered numerous anecdotes that would have fit nicely among the writings of the parapsychologists. In one of those, he gave a dream from a man who saw someone sitting in the street with the intention of hurting the dreamer. "I had never seen this man previously," the dreamer said, "but an impression of his likeness stayed in my imagination. The next day," he continued, "I saw the man whom I had seen in my dream. I knew it was the man whom I had seen in my dream because of his likeness, his dress, and the other details I had seen in the dream." Based on the dream's conclusion, the man changed direction and avoided the stranger entirely.[2]

In an account from many hundreds of years later, the dream similarly revealed to the dreamer a potential future quarrel. Reported in an 1889 issue of the *Nevada State Journal* newspaper was the dream of one J. E. J. Buckley of Maryland. "I dreamed one night last summer," he told it, "that I met a man of small stature, dark complexion, black haired, and heavy black mustache, fashionably dressed, on the corner of the Center and Baltimore streets in this city." A scuffle soon broke out in the dream, and the dreamer shot the man. The next morning, while turning the corner on that street, as Buckley explained it, "I met the dream man." He jumped back and begged Buckley not to shoot him. "We had both dreamed the same thing," Buckley discovered and concluded.[3] In a example relayed in an 1883 issue of *The Spiritual Record*, the visionary was not so lucky as these previous two.[4] Living in Bornesketaig on the blustery Isle of Skye off Scotland, Daniel Dow was frequently troubled by the "sight of a man threatening to give him a blow." This individual whom he didn't recognize turned up about a year later when Dow went south to Kyle-Raes. No sooner had he arrived, he saw the man who had so often appeared to him, and unlike these previous dreamers who took helpful action, they happened to come to blows after all.

Some of the oldest Christian apocryphal works implement numerous dreams of this kind in a manner that would foreshadow many of the dreams of, for just one example, the various Mormon denominations. One of those incidents is recorded in the Acts of Andrew, composed before the turn of the third century. After the Ascension, a rich noble youth makes company with Andrew and asks him to travel to Thessalonica in Greece. This boy preached in a theater there as Andrew watched on in silence. The people would cry out, "Save the son of

Carpianus who is ill, and we will believe." When Carpianus returned home to his ill son, Adimantus, Adimuntus told him he saw a "man in a vision" healing him. He got up, dressed, and ran to the theater before falling at Andrew's feet, clearly the man of his dreams.

Just as we see so commonly among the medicine men and and shamans, the supplicant here dreamed of the healer. This was neither the first nor the last instance of déjà rêvé related to Andrew's life. This phenomenon, it seems reasonable to suggest, was both long and well known, and either experienced often enough or implemented widely. Furthermore, the phenomenon is remembered strongly in the folklore and continues to be well remembered. Continuing the story, while Andrew was in Corinth, one named Sostratus, father of Philopator, was "warned in a vision to visit Andrew." Upon the authority of this vision, in which he had clearly visualized the man, he traveled from his home to Achaea and finally to Corinth. He met Andrew while he was walking with another and "recognized him by his vision and fell at his feet." The vision is later clarified as having been sent by God, something that will be explored in chapter 7.[5]

According to the records, and speaking once more to the great age of accounts of this kind, Alexander the Great in 333 BCE came to Tyre at the borders of Palestine during the course of his adventures. A procession of priests had come from distant corners to greet him. It is recorded that Alexander, upon seeing one of them in particular (the High Priest), bowed before him in reverence. He explained himself later by saying that he had "seen the figure of the priest before in a dream while he was in Macedonia."[6]

Already we can clearly see that the records, legends, and tales record not only the same kinds of events but remember the very same effects upon the individual as do our more recent and contemporary accounts, a truth that will continue to unfold. These accounts are connected through time in this way. As we have seen also, they might even retain the kind of narrative or "epic" feel of their romantic and certain historical counterparts. Author Wanda Easter Burch relates just such an example in her 2003 book, *She Who Dreams: A Journey Into Healing Through Dreamwork.* At age nine, she dreamed of a boy with brown hair who was drowning in shallow water near a boat, after which she reaches in and helps him up. Burch later discovers for herself that this person is historian and author Robert Moss. He himself had noted in the books foreword that "as our friendship developed, we were able to validate and confirm each other's experiences." Burch then writes, "When I pulled a drowning boy from the shallow water, I recognized him over thirty years later." Speaking to the kinds of beliefs these experiences might engender, Burch continues on to say, "How could I have dreamed this person when I was nine years old if dreams did not hold some reality far beyond my ability to grasp and—even more telling—how could I have come to meet him thirty years later and both of us recognize the story of my dream being the story of his waking reality at the same time as my dream?"[7] These are the powerful questions that may arise in the face of such uncanny experiences.

While little work has been done on the shared dream, it is a fascinating and legitimate historical, cross-cultural, and literary entity.* The confirmation offered by one to another after a shared dream is a powerful one and often leads to real-world effects, something that sometimes comes out in these very tales. There is just such a story from the time of Gazi Husrev Bey (1480–1541), who was an Ottoman Bosnian governor in the sixteenth century. It is said that a shared dream, an apparently shared déjà rêvé, was the very reason that the legendary character of

*The reader may find dozens of shared dreams in the final chapter of the present author's *Telepathic Tales.* While these connections have been dealt with in some detail there, the same conviction, so anciently recognized, still comes to these dreamers. In 1995, Cindy McGill and her husband, Tim, for example, both dreamed the same dream about flying. McGill noted that this dream "put us on a path of seeing dreams as a valid and tangible way to receive information that would help us in life. We started putting more weight on dreams as a source of communication." See McGill, *What Your Dreams Are Telling You,* 25, for this account.

Derzelez Alija and the Serbian Prince Marko Mrnjavčević became blood brothers. After their respective dreams of one another, clearly impressed they had "gone out into the world in search of one another."[8]

As with so many recognized extrasensory and other non-ordinary phenomena, these déjà rêvé dream and vision types turn up in impressive numbers throughout the lives of the saints, mystics, and others of renown. This will be a recurring theme. Legend tells us that Francis de Sales (1567–1622), a celebrated French saint, found himself the recipient of something alike. It is said of both him and the French Catholic noble St. Jane Frances de Chantal, who had set off to meet him in Dijon for this very reason, that they "had been presented, each to the other, in dreams, before they met."[9] Longer in the past, Dominic de Guzmán (1170–1221), founder of the Order of Preachers and a good friend of Saint Francis of Assisi, is said to have "beheld [Francis] in a dream before meeting." Both Dominic and Francis were said to have had dreams the night before they actually met.[10] There is a related and more symbolic dream recorded of Pope Innocent III in which for several nights he saw a bearded man in a brown robe holding up the tottering structure of the basilica of St. John Lateran. At some point later, the pope "recognized the man in his dream as a supplicant who wanted him to approve his idea for a new and different kind of order." The man turned out to be St. Francis, and the order, of course, was the Franciscans.[11] One might easily write off such narratives as literary devices of various kinds were it not for how commonly the same things are still recorded in earnest. Though the two, of course, are not mutually exclusive.

Author and philosopher Michael Gurian heard a story with the ring of folklore from eastern Turkey in 1995 in which a woman named Serpil was living unhappily with her husband. One day, while out walking, and having crossed a river her husband would always warn her not to cross, she fell asleep and dreamed of an old woman working over a fire inside a cave. This stranger was seemingly brewing some sort of herbal concoction. The woman was directed to walk until she found a forked road. Upon awakening, traveling as directed and asking for further directions on the outskirts of a village, she came to a cave, out of which "the wise old woman from the dream came." She had been expecting the dreamer.[12] While it is not made clear if the object of the dream was visualized, the same dynamics and beliefs are very much spoken to in the following ancient Persian account. In the *Shahnameh*, a large epic poem from between 977 and 1010 CE, an angel is the messenger of a person's location. When a certain child, a future King Kay Khusrow, is born in Turan, his identity is kept a secret. Meanwhile, the Iranian hero Gudarz "sees in a dream a cloud full of water ascending from Iran, and an angel informs him of the existence of a new king called Kay Khusrow." Gudarz, acting on the experience, sends his son to find Khusrow and bring him back to Iran.[13] Again from the *Shahnameh*, and from a tale that echoes many found in folk literature, we have Saum, a monarch who left his child on a mountain to die. Saum, later regretting his act, "was told in a dream his son still lived" and where he was located. He was being cared for by a strange creature called a Simurgh, and Saum "accordingly sought the nest, and carried his son away with great thanksgiving."[14] While a stranger is not being discovered in accounts such as these, they speak directly to the possibility that they might as easily be.

Echoing some earlier accounts in which murderers or robbers are identified during the course of such experiences, a popular story from Saudi Arabia has two men planning to steal the body of the prophet Muhammad. They dug a tunnel, reached the grave, and began their work. Apparently, a distant king "saw the two men in a dream digging a tunnel in order to reach and remove the body of the Prophet." He traveled to Medina and directed the leader to invite every inhabitant. This was "because he saw them in the dream, thus he could recognize them." The last two in a mosque were brought before the king, "and he recognized them as the men from his dream once he saw them."[15]

Clearly, the belief that unknown individuals involved in crimes may be dreamed of and later found is one that permeates the legend and the lore. It is always of particular interest in the folktales when the belief is implied to have been so taken for granted that it is used to the advantage of the protagonist in some manner. In the Romanian folktale "Red King and Green King," for example, we read of Petru, a young, poor boy who takes a nap after a hard day of plowing and dreams a strange dream, the contents of which he won't divulge. The king imprisoned Petru for nine years for not telling his dream to anyone, but the king's daughter secretly brought him food. Petru learned that the king was looking for a specific man who could shoot an iron arrow that weighed ninety-nine pounds and send it to the bottom of his wineglass. Petru asked the king's daughter to tell the king that she had a dream that identified Petru as the man they were looking for and that he must be freed. The trick worked, and freed he was. This reinforces the idea that certain individuals can be identified through dreams.[16]

Coming again to a much older account, Gregory, nephew of Czech Hussite theologian Jan Rokycana (c. 1396–1471), underwent torture for his proto-Protestant religious beliefs in the fifteenth century. He was stretched out on the rack, during which he fainted and seemed dead until he was later revived with smelling salts. "I have had a dream," he weakly whispered. "I saw a beautiful tree in a meadow. The tree was covered with fruit and beautiful birds were carrying the fruit away. In front of the tree I saw Jesus standing, and in the meadow, watching over the tree, were three men whose faces I seem to know. I shall never forget them." Some time later, in 1467, three men were chosen to be ministers of the brethren at a synod (council of a Christian denomination). Gregory, who was president of the synod at the time, lifted his hands in prayer when the three men were chosen and said, "These are the men whose faces I saw in the dream I had as I lay upon the rack."[17]

SOUTH ASIA, EAST ASIA, AND THE FAR EAST

According to Indian legends, around the time that Gautama Buddha had started preaching his new doctrine, two merchants in the eastern Indian state of Orissa dreamed they would meet the Buddha the following day.[18] The strange shared experience prompted them to buy honey-cakes soon after, which they later offered to Buddha "as soon as they recognized him from their dreams."*

The idea itself that one may be discovered in a dream and later found comes into play in the somewhat darkly humorous southeastern Indian oral folktale "It's Done with Mirrors," which is in the Telugu language. A certain harlot once dreamed of a particular Brahman who came to visit her for her services. When she awoke, she called her servant and recommended this man to them so that they might find him, which they did, and they later made payment for the service rendered in the dream.[19] However humorous, these ideas were widely believed across India, and it is not surprising that they would be remembered or implemented through folklore. According to a legend from Orissa, a northeastern Indian state, the goddess Durga manifested on earth as two beautiful girls in the house of Vasu Praharaja, a Tantric scholar living in the Ganjam district. After their sudden disappearance, their foster father made a wide-reaching search for them, but they couldn't be found. Later, "he saw them in a dream and came to know that they have installed themselves as deities on the top of a nearby hill (the present Tara-Tarini hill)."[20]

While in this previous case, the girl was known *of* (if not known) before the dream that located her, such dreams are importantly similar

*The preparation of food after dreams and visions is a common and clearly old one and speaks to how seriously they are often taken in the moment. The reader will find a number of relevant examples from a wide variety of sources in chapter 1 of the present author's *Telepathic Tales.*

and related to those in which the object of the vision is unknown and speak to the same ultimate capacities. Importantly, too, in many of those cases, there is still new veridical information discovered. In this case, it was the recognition of both the village and the house from the dream. The Chinese folktale "The Pearl that Shone by Night" has Ah Er, dreaming that a maiden waits for him by the riverbank and finds her exactly there. This is part of a longer tale in which the Dragon King of the Eastern Sea is protesting that his daughter should not marry this man as had been arranged, as he was not of the sea; he was a man of land. The dream had been sent by the king's courtier specifically in order to alert him to the princess's location.[21]

In the Far East, these accounts, both past and present, sometimes turn up in relation to reincarnation beliefs and often give rise not only to action, but to tangible things, such as poetry and art. Among the public records of Xiushui County of Jiangxi toward the east of China is a report concerning a woman reborn as a scholar named Huang Shangu. On his twenty-fifth birthday, he dreamed of a silver-haired old woman making offerings outside her house. A bowl of wonderful-smelling noodles sat on her altar, and Huang Shangu grabbed them to eat, still tasting the noodles when he awoke in that borderland state. While initially passing off the experience, when the dream repeated, Huang Shangu became concerned and specifically decided to try and find the place he had dreamed of. After walking some distance, "he came upon a house in front of which was the same old woman from his dream." The same bowl of noodles sat piping and invitingly on her altar. After a conversation, Huang Shangu realized he was her daughter in a past life, and in order to mark the occasion, he wrote the following short piece:

> *Like a monk with hair, like a layman free of*
> *worldly dust, Having a dream within a dream,*
> *I see existence beyond existence.*[22]

Somewhere around 1000 BCE, a Chinese emperor "met a man in a dream and [therefore] caused a search to be made for him everywhere, finding him at last employed on some embankment works."[23] The Chinese have historically taken dreams very seriously and commonly allowed room for their potentially veridical or truth-telling nature. It should not be surprising, then, to find a number of accounts wherein the dream spurs the individual to action. According to Chen Shiyuan's 1562 work compiling over 700 dreams related to the thoughts and experiences of the educated class, a man named Zhao Jianzi dreamed he had been taken to heaven and saw another man standing beside the supreme god Di (the highest deity in the theology of the classical texts). Later, while out and about, Zhao met a person blocking the road, "who was the person he had seen in his dream standing beside Di."[24]

That such déjà rêvé or related visionary experiences may occur in relation to death-related and other visits to otherworldly realms is something that turns up, even in the modern accounts. Furthermore, these stories speak to whether or not all of these are actually dreams in the typical sense at all, despite often being remembered in this language. Leaving this aside, Shiyuan had compiled a number of these déjà rêvé–type dreams, including one of a man named Han Yu who dreamed that someone had given him a book containing seal-script (a style of writing) graphs written in cinnabar ink. He was forced to swallow the book while someone beside him clapped and laughed, which caused Han Yu to wake up as if he were choking. Later, he met Meng Jiao, who was, as it turned out, "none other than the man laughing beside him in the dream."[25]

As with the case of St. John Lateran, a number of these and related experiences present themselves symbolically; however, they are generally not quite of the kind required for the present study. With that said, an illustrative example of those that do follows. Chang Tzu Ya, a minister of the royal court during the Shang Dynasty, recognizing his emperor's court had been reduced to a "pack of fawning sycophants," decided to leave the court to become a hermit fisherman. He became known as the man who could fish with a straight hook due to his unwavering honesty. The emperor he had left, Jou, released King Wen from his custody, and the king had a dream that a large bear with wings jumped on him, after which he awoke. His minister told him this bear was an image of someone he would be able to trust as a general to fight his enemies. Embarking right away on a hunting trip, King Wen encountered the hermit and "knew at once that this was the man who had appeared in his dream!"[26]

A medieval Japanese story has a king dreaming more directly of a man whose eyebrows were unusually far apart and was planning to kill him. The king later sends a proclamation to every quarter of his kingdom, saying that "somewhere in the land there is a man whose eyebrows are nine inches apart. Whoever arrests him and succeeds in bringing me his head, I will reward with a thousand pieces of gold." The man is later found hiding in the mountains, and his head, with his eyebrows indeed nine inches apart as they had been in the dream, is brought to the king.[27]

Some of these experiences involve much longer time frames before the fateful fulfillment of the vision or dream. Irish journalist Brian Inglis spoke to this when he noted that "the case for predestination is at its strongest in two types of precognitive dreams," including "those in which the action of the dream is fulfilled a long time in the future."[28] These longer periods of time between the dream and the dreamed event come out not just among the careful records of the parapsychologists, but in the folklore too. "Long ago," according to the Japanese folktale "The Mandarin Ducks," the Lord of the Castle at Tsu crossed a bridge, drew his arrow, and shot one of two mandarin ducks in the water. A beautiful girl appears in his dreams and accuses Toda of shooting her husband. One year later, he shot four or five ducks at the same spot, picked one up, and "noticed that the head of the duck he had shot the year before was there." He concluded this was the girl who appeared in his dream the year before. Feeling sorrow, he built a temple in their honor.[29] While containing fantastical elements, it is interesting to see these same real-world effects echoing between the various sources wherein these experiences are found.

Author David Lewis had numerous accounts of déjà experiences from Mongolia. Two-thirds of his Mongolian informants, in fact, reported déjà vu experiences; however, most of those were rather vague. Others, though, were tied directly to dreams. In one of those, a twenty-four-year-old man told him that such dreams were common in his life, citing one case as follows: "For example, once in Ulaan Baator I was walking in the street past a little shop and suddenly saw a small man. Then I suddenly felt that I'd seen this person before, in a dream. I didn't remember when I'd had the dream but I was sure I'd had it."[30]

Coming to another more grounded anecdote from the Far East in 2016, we can read of Dave, a missionary working in Hong Kong and interviewed by D. B. Haire. He told of having the same detailed dream about three times a year for the previous six. In the dream, everything is black and white and he is searching for something, though always in vain. Toward the recurring dream's end, a young Asian girl would come into his view, and even though elements of the background and scenario would change, her appearance remained the same, and she was always in color for each of those six years. She wore a distinctive red pea coat with black buttons and had vibrant brown eyes. She would always grab the dreamer's hand and guide him to what he was looking for, and he would wake up soon after. Dave, at one point during his time as a missionary in Hong Kong, was invited to the local harbor to see the fireworks for the Chinese New Year. He was color-blind and reluctant to go, but ended up finally deciding to attend. At some point, hearing people to his left and right speaking of the fireworks and their colors—none of which he could detect—he felt a tug on his coat. "Instantly, I jarred my neck downwards and almost passed out. While shock and disbelief smashed against my brain waves, I locked eyes onto the bright red coat staring back up at me. It was the little Asian girl from my dreams! For years I had seen her face, and there was not a doubt in my mind that this was her! How could this be? Everything around us was like a black and white movie, but her coat was the most vibrant red I had seen in three weeks."[31]

More accounts from these regions will continue to turn up; however, a final account for this section has British Protestant Christian missionary and university evangelist David Howard Adeney—in Hunan, China, and East Asia—giving the case of a man in China who dreamed of a stranger selling books in a distant market. After the dream, and clearly acting upon its authority as had the emperors of the legends before him, the man traveled to that market "and saw the very man who had appeared in his dream."[32]

FURTHER AFIELD

These visions, these mysterious déjà rêvé and related experiences such as déjà visité, are at the heart of certain important native traditions and tales on the North American continent. Among one of those groups, the *pauau* (a gathering of people to sing or dance, often featuring elaborate costumes) had its very origins in such an experience. The oldest of these traditions comes from among the Pawnees of the Central Plains. Their *iruskha*, a related ritual dance meaning "they are inside the fire," came about after a man dreamed he had come upon certain unknown people dipping their hands in boiling water and playing with fire. They told the dreamer they had a new dance to teach him before holding him painfully over hot coals and teaching him a new song and dance. He was told to take it to his people. Just the next day, while traveling to a hill to fast, our Pawnee dreamer met a man who asked him to follow. "They came to a place," as the legend goes, "where the same humans who had appeared in the vision were sitting around a fire, singing and laughing."[33]

As is the case among so many Native Americans, The Pawnee considered many of the dreams implemented in their legends to have been literally and historically true experiences. Another comes in relation to the origins of their "Pipe-Stick Ceremony." Among the Skidi, one of the four bands of Pawnee, there was a seer known for his wonderful dreams. In one of those, he found himself confronting a large, many-colored water monster coming up a river he didn't recognize. For days after, he considered whether or not he should search for the place he had dreamed of, finally made up his mind, and set off. At last, coming to the same stream from his dream after traveling for days, the very monster he had encountered there reared up multiple times before holding a conversation with the dreamer. Although there is more to this story, of importance for us here is that not only was the being from the dream later met in life, but that being was actually a human in disguise.[34]

Technically, a typical déjà rêvé type experience of the kind with which we are interested here sits squarely at the center of this traditional tale, even if particular attention would not have been drawn to it. This idea comes out more clearly in a longer tale that involved the imparting of many skills, secret knowledge, and other information to Handsome Boy, a young Pawnee Indian, over the course of multiple dreams. The tale is directly tied to the origins of a certain whistle and dance that is used in battle alongside some other gifts. Handsome Boy makes repeated acquaintance with a mysterious person whom he doesn't recognize. This individual takes on the role of his guide and offers him much secret and veridical information in dreams regarding the location of people, places, and things. Having eventually been guided underground to an underworld village, Handsome Boy was told that he was not dead, that it was not his time, and that he must return and tell his people of this place. Just as he was leaving through a tunnel—putting the cap on imagery highly suggestive of an actual near-death experience—a being initially blocks his path. As the tale goes, "He saw the little being there as he had seen him before, but when he closed his eyes and opened them again there stood the man concerning whom he had been dreaming." He wore the very same robes, leggings, and feathers.[35]

Non-ordinary and extrasensory experiences are often unceremoniously woven into Indigenous tales. Long ago, among the Kwakiutl Indians of the Pacific Northwest Coast, there was a young girl named Ack-koo who was lonely, as the other children avoided her due to her cleft lip. After traveling to see the wise Kloksum for advice and returning home, she dreamed that night of a pretty woman rooted to the floor in the corner of a cabin. The woman's name was Zoh-la, and she sang a mysterious song. Some time later, while traveling home through the woods again, she tumbled and fell at the hairy feet of Dzonaqua—a giant from another tribe—who duly took Ack-koo and flung her into the basket she carried on her back where Ack-koo saw two other children. Ack-koo made a trail of hemlock branches as the giant carried them through the woods so they could find their way home later. When they reached Dzonaqua's cabin abode, Ack-koo saw, rooted to the floor up to her waist, "the pretty woman in her dream." Singing the magical song she had learned in the dream, Ack-koo sent Dzonaqua to sleep, and they later escaped her clutches together and returned to the village safely.[36]

As with the Pawnee accounts, among other groups, too, it is by no means that only humans or humans *as such* met in dreams before meeting in life. Any number of veridical visions among Indigenous people involving accurate dreaming of the location of game could be laid out here. A woman named Deceased, from among the Ojibwe Indians of the Subarctic and Northeastern Woodlands, for example, once dreamed just such a dream. Anthropologist Ruth Landes (1908–1991) tells us that once, while Deceased's husband was away hunting, she dreamed "of a nice-looking girl dressed in red."[37] This mysterious girl told the dreamer that she should find her early the following morning so that the bad luck of her husband's unsuccessful hunts would relent. Walking a half mile with great purpose following her dream, Deceased managed to kill a female bear on the path she had been guided along, although she could not carry it home alone and soon got help. As she later found, it was the bear itself, represented by the woman wearing red, that she had seen and been urged to seek out in a dream.*

Much further afield, from the southernmost island of the Marquesas Islands in French Polynesia, Fatu-Hiva, the chief, Mota-Hupu, seems to leave his body. He travels to a cave, where certain other islanders have fled due to a village fire. The "ghost of the chief" perceived these people sleeping in the *convolvulus* growing there (a plant in the bindweed family). Pulling aside their covers, he saw their faces before his ghost returned home and he woke up. This chief tells his wife, "I have just seen in a dream a man with his wife and child sleeping down below there clothed in convolvulus vine." When dawn came, Mota-Hupu went to the place he had seen, saw the same people he had visited during the night, and therefore "knew that his dream was true."[38]

In parts of South America, "The Underwater Woman" is an example of a common kind of myth in which the daughters of the chief of water spirits are said to take human form so that they may entice unwary fishermen. In a variant from among the Shuar of Ecuador (that recalls a previous Chinese folktale) that was recorded in 1978, there is a twist of particular interest here. When a man hunting by the riverbank hears a strange whistling sound, he suspects it could be the workings of the spirit world. For this reason, he himself returns home in order to induce a tobacco trance, what is referred to as a "dream," in order to discover more. The daughter of a water spirit appears to him and tells

*Similar things also occur outside of these cultures where they would be more commonly expected. A number of horse owners, for example, share close and spiritual bonds with their equestrian acquaintances. Pauline Patterson from Michigan, having just had what seems to have been something of a spontaneous mystical experience while combing her horse in the barn, soon took Kayla, that horse's mother, for a ride. She noted of Kayla that "we have connected spiritually in the deepest of ways. I had seen her in a dream before we first met, making her literally my dream horse." See Anderson and Anderson, *Horses with a Mission*, 152–55 for this interesting account.

him to go back to the river. Following the dream, he meets her where she had indicated she would be.[39]

Far distant among the Dodoth tribesmen of northern Uganda lived a man called Lomotin, an *emuron*, something of a prophet and renowned far and wide for his advice and doctoring skills. American author Elizabeth Marshall Thomas wrote in 1965 that "Many years ago [. . .]Lomotin dreamed that an old man witch was making the child ill [the child of a man he knew]." Lomotin awoke and crawled quietly so as not to awaken the family he was staying with, and after setting off, "he saw the old man witch, a stranger, sitting in the moonlight by the wall." The emuron, as it happens, was considered to have the power to dream of the identity of a witch.[40] From the farthest end of Africa—in a footnote of his historical work dealing with the freedom of the press in South Africa—formerly influential South African–based journalist Louis Henri Meurant writes how in the early nineteenth century, a "remarkable circumstance" had occurred to a young writer. This man dreamed one night of a gentleman walking into his printing office and handing him a copy of a leading article. "He took particular notice of the gentleman's features, and not long afterward came across a man in the streets who he at once recognized as the person he had seen in his dream." According to Meurant, "He had never seen Mr. Jardine before until he met him in the street, after his dream."[41]

Manifestly, there are no corners of the globe where these déjà rêvé and related experiences have not been reported and recorded in their various forms. British botanist, anthropologist, and author Francis Huxley (1923–2016), while traveling and working in Haiti, was on his way to see a supposedly rather powerful *mambo* healer. When Huxley arrived and sat with her for some time, she was ready for him. "You came to me in a dream last night," was her explanation. These are surprisingly common experiences among travelers in traditional communities. While Huxley doesn't make much of it, he notes that in this case, "I was able to flatter her in my turn, however, because two nights before

I had dreamt of a woman uncommonly like her, in just such a place as this, and she was hardly surprised when I told her so."[42]

Ancient China, North America, Africa, and Polynesia—while this has not been a comprehensive analysis, it is helpful to take a more general approach this early on and give an indication of just how widely in time and space these and importantly related experiences are to be found across the genres of literature. The cross-cultural nature of these strange occurrences will continue to be explored until the final page; however, it is enough for us to say here that these experiences, the experiences of dreaming of a person before later meeting them, are an ancient and widespread reality. These are encounters that legitimately engender beliefs, instill conviction and action, and result in creative and artistic endeavors alike. The changes that might be made in an individual's life path are particularly apparent in the examples in which they are led in dreams to their mentors or masters. This will be the subject of the following chapter.

3

Healers and Saints, Sufis and Sheiks

Eastern Religions and Other Visions of Esteemed Teachers

Two special factors have strongly influenced Western civilization: the first of these is the idea—also shared by Nietzsche—that we are alone in a hostile universe; the other is the notion that in the last resort life is meaningless. The shaman, on the other hand, speaks of the vitality of all that exists and of a global relatedness to all beings and phenomena at every level. To him the universe is pervaded by a creative essence which not only transcends normal existence but lends to it an inner cohesion.

HOLGER KALWEIT

As we have seen to some extent, visions and dreams involving the locating of persons afar are very commonly found around the lives of men and women of renown and esteem. They are found, perhaps, most readily there, at least in the old records. Whether in the lives of the saints, among the shamans and medicine men, or among the Sufi masters and other mystics, or even as they relate to healers and doctors in our own times, these strange dreams abound. As we'll see, they speak again both to the profundity of the effects they might impart upon the individual or the wider community. Both historically and in our own times, they often guide the individual or supplicant to the healer, or indeed, the healer to the supplicant. These are stories that can be found in particular abundance, for example, among some of the most important figures in Sufi and other Eastern traditions, past and present. Representatively, and regarding Indian professor and polymath Inayat Khan—a pioneer of the transmission of Sufism to the West—he is said to have been led to his master in a vision before meeting him. Furthermore, Khan's own first Western *mureed* (novice committed to the spiritual path under a guide), Rabia Martin, "saw him [Khan] in a vision before she met him in San Francisco."[1] This is the basic template of the experience in this context, and these visions continue to occur and unfold in similar forms.

THE SUFI AND THE SAINT

The Sufis give particular heed to the dream or vision and have traditions that speak directly to the kinds with which we are interested here. While traditionally, their most blessed dream is to dream of the prophet himself, their second most blessed are those in which the individual meets their *sheikh* (title of honor meaning elder often relating to a tribal chief or scholar). Just as we have seen with the Native American accounts, their guides are often met first in a dream, then later in life. It is said that in his youth, Baha' al-Din Naqshband (1318–1389), founder of the Naqshbandi (a Sunni order), dreamed that he was entrusted to a certain Turkish sheikh (*Yasavi*). He "preserved the image of the sheikh's face in his mind" before telling his grandfather of the dream. "Oh, my son! You will receive training from Turkish Sheikhs," he said. Some days later, while in the Bukhara market in Uzbekistan, "he saw the person who had appeared in his dream." His name was Khalil, and they later met again. The dream itself was cited as increasing Naqshband's affection for Khalil, and he began to attend his religious gatherings from that moment on. Similarly, his grandfather's acceptance of the dream as opposed to much of the reticence and relative personal secrecy we have seen among the modern accounts is a contrast worthy of note.[2]

Working in his rare bookstore in Istanbul in 1981, Muzaffer Ozak—formerly Sheikh Muzaffer—dreamed he was in the middle of the coastal town Bosphorus in a damaged sailing boat during a wild storm.[3] A stranger handed him a note explaining how he could avoid disaster. Having come back to his shop the following morning, according to Muzaffer, "I saw the very person who had given me the paper in my dream, passing in front of my shop." Muzaffer went on to dream of the man a couple more times before working up the courage to speak with him. The man turned out to be Seyyid Sheikh Ahmed Tahir ul-Marashi, sheikh of the Halveti-Shabani. Muzaffer became his dervish* and studied under him for seven years before going on to become a renowned author and *imam* in his own country and throughout the West.

Despite the patently helpful literary and didactic tools these kinds of tales often represent, they are fundamentally indistinguishable from the accounts collected more recently—both those attached to a more religious and even specifically Islamic context, and those that are not at all. American poet Coleman Barks spoke of a certain teacher, a Sufi mystic he would visit in Philadelphia named Bawa Muhaiyaddeen. "I first encountered him on May 2, 1977, in a dream, before we met," Barks claimed. Like some of our experiencers from the first chapter, he had recorded the experience in his dream notebook before its fulfill-

*The dervish is a member of a Sufi Muslim religious order who has taken certain vows and became known for their ecstatic rituals and dances. The imam is a Muslim leader who leads prayers in a mosque.

ment, and it involved seeing Muhaiyaddeen in a ball of light above him, saying, "I love you." The landscape where Barks grew up came into the picture too and it "felt saturated with love."[4] There are, in fact, numerous Western accounts across the literature in which Sufi informants claim to have dreamed of their sheikhs before meeting them in life. In one example told to Geaves in 1998, Haji Khurshid, while living in Birmingham, England, had a recurring dream of a certain man for nine months straight. After moving to London and going to Shacklewell Lane to join the prayers there, a man gave him a book to read. Kurshid was stunned. "This is the same person who came in my dream; same person, same face, same everything," he told his wife.[5]

In 1986, author Wayne Bloomquist was staying with his wife at the Furnace Creek in Death Valley. That night, he recorded a dream in his diary in which he seemed to be outside the Sri Aurobindo Ashram in Pondicherry, India. He was told by someone he didn't recognize that if he wanted to get in he should stand at a certain spot. A light then came down over his body, head to feet, before turning grayish and leaving, after which he entered. Bloomquist saw many people mingling together, people who seemed different from those we see on earth, "luminous and joyful." Soon a man appeared who seemed to know him and told him he lived on the Avenues in San Francisco, although Bloomquist recorded that he himself had no idea who this man was. A few years later, Bloomquist met Reverend Joseph Martinez, who worked at a spiritual healing center between 8th and 9th Avenue in San Francisco. "I believe this was the man I saw in the dream," the author wrote later. "I did not ask him about this, as I did not make the connection until after he passed away in 1995."[6]

A Muslim woman living in India told author and teacher Desiderio Pinto that while ill eight years previous, she dreamed of a very old man telling her not to worry and that all would turn out well. The woman woke up feeling an inexplicable sense of "deep peace and contentment." The problems cleared up, and three years later—when her husband was transferred to Delhi—she heard of a famous *dargah* (a kind of shrine or tomb) and decided to visit it. "When I arrived here," she told the author, "I recognized it as the surroundings of the old man in my dream. And I realized that the old man who had appeared to me was none other than Hazrat Nizamuddin Auliya [a very prominent Sufi saint]. Ever since I have come to visit him once every week and sometimes twice."[7]

As is also the case among the Irish saints and others—the Sufi and Indian mystics and saints in particular—more than one account often turns up in and around certain personalities. In this vein, a number of examples swirl around the life of philosopher and orator Uppaluri Gopala Krishnamurti. Once in 1957, while staying in the state of Karnataka's Chikkamagaluru district (famous for its coffee), he announced to his wife that they must leave. Suddenly, a stranger came into the traveler's lodge where they were staying and said he had heard that a yogi was staying there. "How does the Yogi look?" Krishnamurti asked the man. "Just like you," came the reply, along with a respectful salute. The man, it turned out, was Subbarao, the manager of a coffee estate. His servant had dreamed that a yogi in white pajamas and a *jubba* (long outer garmet often worn by public officials and professionals) taught him many philosophical truths in a language he couldn't understand. He told Subbarao that these truths went against what they both believed, and his sincerity convinced Subbarao. That morning, the servant saw Krishnamurti near the lodge and "identified him as the Yogi who had appeared in his dream" before fetching his master, Subbarao. Krishnamurti and his wife took up the offer that followed that they could stay with Subbarao, and they continued to return there whenever they returned to India.[8]

Narayan Nambiar, a man from Kozhikode (sometimes anglicized as Calicut) in Kerala on India's Malabar Coast, was a devotee of Krishna from a young age. In 1960, after one of his meditations, he dreamed of being in a courtyard full of colorful plants of various kinds. There were two figures in the courtyard: one, a holy man dressed in a bright orange gown with a mop of curly hair; the other, a holy woman dressed in white who made a particular sign with her right hand and beckoned Nambiar to follow them. "Though I knew it was only a dream," Nambiar writes, "I was firmly convinced that there must be some significance behind it." Nambiar later tells us in conclusion, "It was not until two years later, when he was first becoming known in our area, that I discovered that the man was Sri Sathya Sai Baba of Puttaparthi. Another twenty years passed before I realized that the holy woman whom I saw in the dream was Mata Amritanandamayi. In January 1985, I saw Her for the first time at the home of a devotee in Calicut."[9]

Doctor Hakam Singh, founder of the Sikh Welfare Foundation of North America, gave the case of an officer from a military garrison in India who left to visit his family back home—although he didn't return at the end of his allotted leave. All attempts to find him failed. It was suggested by a Sikh soldier to visit Baba Karam Singh Ji, who was a *parcharak* (preacher) and Sikh spiritual leader, as he apparently possessed "occult powers." When she visited the man, he took pity on her and closed his eyes, remaining silent for a while. "Do not worry dear lady," he told her, "your husband will be back in a couple of weeks." Just a few days later, she received a letter from her husband explaining that he had been unconscious for days and why he couldn't be found, that he was not carrying identification papers, and that he had a dream in which a saintly person had placed a hand on his head and said, "You are not going to die." The man then explained that after the dream, "I came out of my coma, which amazed even the doctors. Now I am recovering satisfactorily and will be discharged from the hospital in a few days." He soon returned to the garrison and heard the story of his wife's visit to Baba Karam Singh Ji, and he subsequently visited the man himself. When he arrived and Baba Karam Singh Ji emerged from the cave he had been meditating in, this English officer was apparently "completely flabbergasted." As the author explains, "Then he told his wife that the holy person who had appeared in his dream was no one else but Baba

Karam Singh Ji." They both visited him frequently from then on.[10]

Another example was published in a 1948 issue of *Prabuddha Bharata*, an English-language monthly journal of the Ramakrishna Order running since 1896. A man from Sind in southwest Pakistan had been initiated and received a *mantram* (holy name) in a dream. In this dream, he apparently received some meditation instructions, and before visiting the master Mahapurushji—a Hindu spiritual teacher far off in India—he wrote to him to see if he could help him understand the dream more fully. After meditating with Mahapurushji, the initiate said, "I have today found peace in the heart, thanks to your grace. My mind grew very restless after receiving the mantram in the dream. I failed to find peace by any means. I became exactly like one mad. Today after having received from you the same mantram which I got in the dream, I am firmly convinced that what I saw in the dream is true and that it is you who favoured me with your grace in the dream." Mahapurushji confirmed and corroborated his intuition on this matter.[11]

TIBET, NEPAL, NEW ZEALAND, AND BEYOND

Jetsun Milarepa is one of the most famous yogis and spiritual poets in Tibet. It is said of his master, Marpa Lotsawa, that he had known Milarepa would be one of his greatest disciples even before they had first made each other's company. As Chögyam Trungpa writes, "He had realized this in a dream before they ever met."[12] Spiritual leader Haipou Jadonang of the Rongmei Naga, a Tibeto-Burmese Indigenous ethnic group of northeast India, commonly relied on dreams in order to help his village in Manipur. More interestingly, it is recounted that he "dreamt of a *fakir* (a person who survives on alms) who he later met."[13]

Nearby in Nepal, and before arriving in Kathmandu for his studies in 1993, Sardar-Afkhami, a young Iranian American man raised in France, dreamed of a pristine landscape dominated by a pyramidal mountain. A Tibetan man on a white horse galloped toward him and silently pointed at a mountain. After arriving for his studies, his friend Baker suggested he travel up-country to see if Chatral Rinpoche, the now deceased Tibetan master, would attempt to interpret his dream. "When I came into his room," Sardar recalled, "we both instantly recognized each other. It was he who had been in my dream. He roared with laughter and invited me to sit at his feet." Rinpoche was then determined to be Sardar's teacher.[14]

A vision of Namkhai Norbu Rinpoche, a Tibetan Buddhist master of Dzogchen and professor of Tibetan and Mongolian language and literature at Naples East University, makes its meaning more patently clear. Soon after being sent to China as a Tibetan youth, Namkhai dreamed of a place unknown to him, a place with white cement houses in what he assumed was Chinese style. Inside one of the houses was an old man who bent to touch his forehead in the manner of a Tibetan master and began to recite a mantra. Unlike some of the other visionaries we have met, even within the dream itself Namkhai was sure this might be his future master. Returning to Tibet a year later, he heard of a man whom his father's friend had just met, and when the man's dwelling was described, Namkhai was immediately reminded of his dream. "I felt sure," he writes, "that the man he was describing was the same man I had seen in it." Five days later, after a journey on horseback with his father, as Namkhai describes, "when we got there, the old man I met really seemed to be the one I had seen in my dream. I really had the sense that I had been in that village before, with its Tibetan houses made in Chinese style concrete and the mantra over the old man's door." If the importance of these visions in an individual's life might dawn even in the dream, as in Namkhai's case, the later confirmation usually brings it home. "I had no doubt," he writes, "that he was to be my master, and I remained there to receive teaching from him."[15]

It is increasingly and unavoidably clear that despite the obvious utility of these types of visions toward various and particular ends, they are also an ongoing phenomenon entirely unrelated to how they may or may not be used or implemented in this way and certainly do not relate only to Eastern masters and mystics. They seem rather to relate to figures of authority or esteem of a wide variety of types. One could point to an admirer or "devotee" of German philosopher Arthur Schopenhauer, for example, who claimed that he had "seen Schopenhauer in a dream before making his acquaintance."[16] In more recent accounts of this kind, they certainly follow a similar pattern; however, sometimes it is not necessarily made clear to the dreamer or the object of the dream that this dynamic is involved. The events simply unfold and fall into this pattern. Over the course of ten years of traveling between China, Japan, the Philippines, and Hong Kong, native New Zealander Audrey Sharp had a recurring dream of an old and wise Chinese man. Sharp had a strange sense that she must actually go to meet this man. On her final day, having visited many sites in China, Sharp was taking photographs when she heard a voice from behind call to her. "It was the man from my dream," she said. They ended up having a rather fruitful rendezvous. Sharp writes that this experience changed her life dramatically. The man offered her much advice that changed her entire philosophy toward life that had been ingrained in her from a young age. She would now apparently take the world's injustices less to heart and live more peacefully.[17]

Psychologist and social worker Myron Eshowsky came close to death in his childhood and claims to have had numerous strange visionary experiences since. That someone who comes near death is later imbued with such strange intuitive and clairvoyant capacities is an old story and still a common finding in the related literature. Aware of this, the shaman would look into that abyss of death, bringing himself or herself closer and closer until the very powers of the dead were theirs. The same is true of the man or woman on their deathbed; the closer they come to their end, they are imbued with similar clairvoyance. Eshowsky once dreamed about a very large, tough-looking young man who, according to his dream, would be important in his current situation working with an organization dealing with gang violence. Eshowsky later "recognized him the minute he saw him."[18]

INDIGENOUS PEOPLES, SHAMANS, LAYMEN, AND SAINTS

In a biographical study of six Korean female shamans, we can read of a fascinating dream told by P'yongyang-mansin, one of the shamans. This woman dreamed of being at some Buddhist temple where the gates were bolted closed. Inside, there were "banner-carrying generalissimos of olden days riding away with fierce-looking, wide-open eyes." After leaving and returning to the same scene, a "handsome woman" was sitting on a divan and turned toward the dreamer. "Oh, you have come," the woman told P'yongyang-mansin, before offering her a very particularly curved and shining hair pin. Around three months passed, and she hadn't thought about the dream for some time when she went to attend a *chaesu-kut* (a rite for invoking fortune) that her mother was holding for her brother. "The instant I entered my mother's place," she told the author, "I recognized the handsome woman of my dream. She was the chief officiating shaman at my mother's *kut*. There was no mistake." Having heard of the dream, this woman later went on to suggest that they must have been fated to meet, telling P'yongyang-mansin, "You must become a daughter to me."[19]

On the planet's opposite end, Francis Mesteth, an Oglala Lakota Indian (originally of Minnesota and Wisconsin and later settling on the Great Plains), relates a similar incident in which a woman he didn't know approached him and his wife just as they were leaving for a meeting in Arizona. She told his wife that the woman sitting in the car behind them had dreamed of Francis sitting in front of her with a Peace Pipe (the most holy of Lakota religious sacramentals) and saw little round medicine balls off to his right. Among the Lakota, there is a known significance in dreaming of the Peace Pipe, so the woman was a little concerned. When they met later, after the woman had initially been driven off and Francis had gone after her, she told them that she didn't know him but that she had dreamed of him and wished to know his meaning. Francis told her he'd pray for her, and when they met again some time later, she was satisfied that nothing negative had come of the dream.[20]

Bavarian-born Karolina Gerhardinger (1797–1879) was a German Roman Catholic religious sister and founder of the School Sisters of Notre Dame. She was said to have "supernatural assistance" when choosing new school sisters. In one case of interest here, it was recorded that a certain Italian sister was "deeply moved" when she laid eyes upon Gerhardinger. As Dolorita Mast writes, "She recognized in her the Religious whom she had seen five years before in a dream and had asked for admission into her order."[21]

The Indigenous man or woman, the doctor to be, the shaman or the saint in training—all might be brought to their craft, or indeed their own masters, during a vision or dream. The same things, we must repeat, are still reported within and without that context. American anthropologist and educator Michael Harner speaks to accounts of this kind among Indigenous Shamans and Westerners alike. "Teacher" is the more general name he gives to "anthropomorphic deities and sacred ancestors in the Upper World" when speaking of these encounters with his students. While in the majority of these examples, the teacher met with was of another world, one of Harner's students, seemingly using techniques of sensory deprivation or something similar, met a still-living master. "For years," they write, "one of my main teachers had been an old man in the Upper World who inhabited a cabin in an unknown countryside. Then one day, while driving along a road in California, I came to a beautiful canyon and on impulse stopped there." The cabin was apparently "identical" to that in the other world, and the individual knocked on the door, after which a young man appeared. "I entered, and in the dim light saw an elderly man half-reclining on a couch. He turned his head toward me and smiled. It was a wonderful shock. I recognized him as being my teacher in the Upper World or, rather, being an aging ordinary-reality version of my teacher in the Upper World."[22]

Christina Donnell, PhD, in 2008 writes of a dream in which she found herself high on a mountain, struggling for breath as the sun beat down upon her. As she reached for a water bottle, a small man with cropped black hair, dark brown skin, and high cheekbones appeared from behind, carrying a jar of brown liquid. The man, with Asian features, sat down in the shade and offered some of the fluid to the Earth before offering some to Donnell. When he spoke, it was in a strange and guttural tongue she didn't recognize but could somehow respond to. After taking her leave due to the nauseating smell of the liquid, she fell down a rock embankment and suddenly woke. Two years later, Donnell visited the Sacred "Temple of the Waters" in Peru. While wandering down an alpaca trail, the dream bore its worldly fruit. There, she saw a small native man with high cheeks and Asian-looking eyes holding a jar of brown liquid, and who was sitting at the same rocky outcrop as Donnell's dream. The man was Don Martin, the most renowned sorcerer in the area and a friend of the Q'ero master shaman, Don Manuel Quispe, with whom her friend Ernesto had been working for years. Donnell continued to visit with Don Martin for shamanic training.[23]

In a dream, professor of history and Rupert Costo Chair in American Indian Affairs, Clifford Trafzer, once met an old Indian healer with long white hair falling to his waist.[24] This was a rather elaborate and meaningful dream in which certain knowledge was imparted and various scenes were visited, particularly along the Snake River (the Columbia's largest tributary that meets the ocean on North America's West Coast). Later in the fall, while visiting the Yakima Reservation in eastern Washington State, Trafzer attempted to track down a certain Palouse medicine man.* He had long been aware of this person's

*The Palouse are Native Americans, a tribe of the Sahaptin, who inhabited territories along the Columbia River and its many tributaries in the Pacific Northwest.

existence; however, he could never pin him down, and the man had become something of a mythical figure in that regard. When he arrived at the front door of the house he had been directed to, "the door stood wide open, allowing the cold wind to swirl around the tidy living room." A few moments later, an old man with long white hair emerged from the dark hallway. "This was the man from my dream," he writes before continuing, "the one who had taught me so much along Snake River, the one who had sung his song of thanksgiving while bending down and digging out the root."

More recently, an informant of Professor Susan Kwilecki claimed that a Reverend Stone "had appeared to her in a dream before she actually met him." She dreamed she was in her yard, sitting on a lawn chair, when a tall man walked out of her house. The man simply looked at her and walked away. "Later," as Kwilecki was told, "she identified the man as Reverend Stone."[25] While Kwilecki had previously expressed a little caution regarding this woman's faculties, this was not in relation to her dream life, and just as it is with the hagiographers, our own interests are as much why someone would tell such a tale in the first place as they are to discern that which may or may not be entirely reliable.

DOCTORS, ILLNESS, AND MEDICINE MEN

Whether the traditional healer, the medicine man, or even the modern practitioner, these persons are commonly the object of such visions and dreams. The association of experiences of these kinds with healers is an old one. According to Acts 9:10–19, the blind Rabbi Saul dreamed in Jerusalem of a man named Ananias who came in and spoke to him before restoring his sight. He awoke afterward and found himself still blind; however, he soon heard footsteps. A visitor was announced, and Saul's servant pronounced the unexpected guest's name, "Ananias." Saul found himself staring into the face of a fellow Nazarene, a Pharisee like himself. He was soon initiated into a new fraternity by the man.[26]

The fundamental and thematic similarities among these déjà rêvé–type experiences allow us to jump between greatly disparate people, places, and times. Among the Dakotan Sioux people, a young woman dreamed she was standing near a camp looking north and saw three crows fly by. This filled her with a feeling of dread, and she soon saw a middle-aged man standing with his gaze toward her, looking at the birds, and shaking his head sorrowfully. She was told that in three days she would be in danger. At that time while out picking fruit, she narrowly escaped the attack of three Arikara Indian men—those being primarily of North Dakota—and warned her tribe of their assault. Some years later, seemingly beholden to such strange happenings, this woman met the powerful medicine man called Saswe, "and identified him as the man she had seen in her dream."[27]

As described in his autobiography, the late Tendekayi Muzorewa—former bishop and prime minister of Zimbabwe Rhodesia—spoke of "happy days" as an "itinerant bachelor," where he would preach under trees and be greeted by chicken soup and other food by those he would preach to. During those times, Muzorewa had a dream that a sick woman was brought before him and that a voice commanded him to lay hands on her head. The woman was healed. "The dream was so real," Muzorewa noted, "that when I woke up in the morning it was difficult to dismiss it as a mere dream." Two weeks later, he and his colleagues were performing an evening prayer at the home of a sick friend. This scene instantly reminded Muzorewa of the dream, and he claims to have heard a voice tell him this was the person from that dream. After he had laid on his hands and apparently improved her condition, she told him, "Last night I dreamt a man was praying for me. Now as I think of it, this man who has just prayed for me has the image of the one I saw in my dream." Muzorewa didn't divulge the dream at the time, although he notes that if he did, he might have been considered a "faith healer."[28] Once more, it can be noted that the shared or double dream aspect turns up with notable frequency in these déjà rêvé–type accounts. Importantly, too, the dream in which the religious or other leader claims to have been the object of someone else's dream is one of curse, particularly open to abuse or fabrication. While this should certainly be kept in mind, it's conflation with a broader dismissal of all such visions is unhelpful, particularly considering the extent to which they indistinguishably occur outside of that context.

Kenneth Cohen, author and associate professor of history and director of the Museum Studies Program at the University of Delaware, describes an interesting related experience that he cited as a "turning point" in his life. A few days after being invited to lecture at a university in western Canada, Cohen describes a dream in which he saw the face of an elderly native woman. "The face appeared without background or context," he says. "I didn't know where she was or who she was." The woman seemed to have some sort of longing or need, which Cohen couldn't figure out. Cohen notes that the dream had seemed so "real" that when he woke up, he called a friend who had been house-sitting for him to ask if he had any calls from any Native Americans. Unknown to the author, an elderly First Nations political activist named Ann had come across his name in the lecture catalog on the same day as his dream. Her husband later called when Ann was ill, as he had seen the professor's lecture named "holistic medicine," and Ann had seen Cohen in a "waking dream" after seeing his name. When Cohen arrived some time later, he found Ann lying down, barely conscious, and remembered with certainty, "I recognized her from my dream. There was no mistake."[29]

Author A. P. Morris gives the account of Mathy, who was then recently bereaved and in much pain, and whose friend insisted she visit a man called Ricky who could help her. She had dreams leading up to the meeting in which she "clearly saw his unique physical features." When they arrived at his office, "he looked almost identical to the images she had seen in her dreams." It is interesting to note the qualification that it was an *essentially* identical match; however, Mathy later makes it clear, "It was the person from my dreams."[30]

While it is easy to assume these kinds of dreams and visions are found only in Indigenous or legendary stories that relate to larger-than-life figures such as the medicine man or the saint, it is patently still the case that they turn up with frequency in relation to broadly comparable figures in our own societies, and sometimes from surprising sources. In a document initially contracted by the University of California—and distributed only to U.S. government agencies dealing with approaching integrated care for breast cancer—a single related experience is tucked away. Forty-year-old Anne Abruzzi had woken up to a lump on her right breast, having dreamed the night before that she had been describing a pain there to a young blonde woman wearing a white lab coat, someone she didn't recognize. Having been later diagnosed with cancer and seeking another physician after refusing an initial mastectomy, a physician she did know recommended Dr. Laura Esserman (the very compiler of this government document). When Abruzzi first met her, "she felt Dr. Esserman was the woman she had seen in her dream." There was an instant sense of familiarity. As she puts it, "It was as if I'd heard all her questions before." "It was a very comforting feeling." Ultimately, Abruzzi became cancer-free and went on to conclude, "God brought me to the right people."[31] This attribution of the experience to a particular source is something we will return to in chapter 7. Similarly, Australian-born psychical researcher Richard Hodgson wrote an article in the political *The Arena* magazine, published in 1892, dealing with premonitions. Mrs. W, an informant of his, gave an account from 1880 in which she dreamed that the family doctor, Doctor R., could not make it due to a storm while her daughter Ada was giving birth. Her daughter was actually expecting soon and a great storm had brought some telegraph wires down. Still in the dream, after begging her daughter's husband to get another doctor, they are soon called for and arrive. He was described as a "tall, young doctor, having brown eyes, dark hair, ruddy, brunette complexion, and dressed in a black coat, gray trousers, and gray vest, and wearing a bright blue cravat, picked out with coral sprigs." Not long after, events similar to the dream unfolded. Ada was about to give birth and no doctor could be contacted with the wiring down. Soon, Mr. Chan went himself to seven different medical offices before bringing a young doctor to the house. He seemed immediately familiar to Mrs. W. Regarding the moment when her daughter pointed out the cravat the doctor was wearing, Mrs. W writes, "In a moment I knew he was the man whom I saw in my dream." The doctor's clothing, down to the details, were also "exactly" as she had seen it in the dream. Hodgson makes the following interesting observations of this case:

> I am not discussing these experiences just now from a teleological point of view, but some of my readers may be disposed to think that Mrs. W. was vouchsafed a vision from a "higher source" in order to increase her hope and confidence in the emergency before her. If so, it would seem curious that the vision should have so singularly failed of its purpose, since Mrs. W. never thought of it at the time until the crisis was over.[32]

According to physician Julia Crafts Smith who claimed to have spirit guides, she was once called to a Mr. N. who had been unwell for a decade. She later found that he had a dream before they met, in which he saw a lady hold out a bottle toward him upon which the words "Behold I come to bring relief!" were written. Being of "strong will," the man sent for multiple physicians in order to try to find the one from his dream, to no avail. When Smith was called for, however, the result was different. "As soon as he saw me," she writes, "he said, 'this is the one I saw in my dream. I shall be cured.'" As it happened, he was better within a week.[33]

In his 2016 work on cancer survivors, Mark Evan Chimsky gave the case of Caryn Hartglass. The afternoon before leaving for India, she stood in front of the Adele Bloch-Bauer painting, and it brought her to tears, something she couldn't explain as it wasn't usual for her. She soon saw the same painting in the movie during the plane trip. She returned home after being diagnosed with ovarian cancer during a hysterectomy, and some time later she dreamed of a "very tall, slim woman" holding her one-year-old niece. Three days later, and in her words, "I went to Memorial Sloan Kettering for a consultation with one of their top gynecologic oncologists. I was sitting in the waiting room with my mother and saw a woman who looked like the tall person in my dream! I got up to take a closer look. She had a purse with the Adele Bloch-Bauer pattern on it! It blew my mind."[34]

A very novel account of this kind was given by *New York Times* best-selling author Francesca Gould. Claire Sylvia, an American who became housebound with an incurable heart disease, was forced to wait for a heart and lung transplant. She survived the operation but began to notice small changes in her personality. She had new food cravings, became attracted to women—especially blondes—and had strange and vivid dreams about a man she didn't recognize. When she later met with the donor's family, according to Gould, "it was confirmed that her new personality traits matched those of the donor and that he was the man who had appeared in her dreams."[35] Author Alissa Lukara writes of something related in her work, documenting her twelve-year quest to reclaim her life after years of chronic illness and overcoming childhood trauma. A friend pointed her in the direction of a Native American healer named Sue. "The night before my first appointment with Sue," the author writes, "I dreamt I was in a school classroom with a woman who was teaching me about shamanism. When I met Sue in the lush garden outside her office the next day, my heart began to pound. The tender smile, the sensitive brown eyes, the thick, shoulder-length, dark hair. I had already seen her. Sue was the woman from my dream."[36] Like some of the previous informants, Lukara also notes that this wasn't the first prescient dream in her life, and they often seemed to herald major life events for her.

Echoing certain Eastern traditions regarding reincarnation (likely unknowingly), Joseph F. Smith, sixth president of the Church of Jesus Christ of Latter-Day Saints, spoke to these very kinds of connections formed in previous lives as "spirit memories."[37] According to former member of the United States Congress George Q. Cannon, these memories might specifically cause individuals to have spiritual compatibility with one another. He wrote the following on April 7, 1889:

> I was a boy when my people gathered with the Saints of God. I was very curious to know the Prophet Joseph, having heard a great deal about him. I happened to be in a large crowd of people where the Prophet was, and I selected him out of the large body of people. There were no means of recognition that I know of which would suggest him to me as the Prophet; but I recognized him as though I had always known him. I am satisfied that I had known him and been familiar with him. There were instances which all of us doubtless have known which have proved to us that there has been a spiritual acquaintance existing between us. We frequently say, "How familiar that person's face is to me." In this way kindred spirits are brought together. We are drawn together by this knowledge and this acquaintanceship which, I have no doubt, was formed anterior to our birth in this state of existence.[38]

It seems clear that such experiences might even engender reincarnation beliefs in the first place.

I MUST FIND YOU!

In all but one of the accounts in this chapter so far, the visionary has *incidentally* met with the object of the vision out in the world. Recalling our first chapter, however, there are numerous examples in which the individual finds themselves so affected that they must set off in search of the object of their vision. The individual, having dreamed or otherwise envisioned some man or woman of interest or esteem, finds themselves then compelled to locate them. They might go greatly out of their way, entirely assured of the dream's truth telling, and travel as far and wide as they must in order to locate the object of their vision. This is an old, well-attested, and ongoing reality.

A Pakistani man dreamed in 1946 that he was in a long, narrow basement room.[39] There was food on the table, and he seemed to be waiting for guests to arrive. Two people came; one was apparently his master—though he didn't actually know him—and the other was a tall and fair man with a white turban. They beckoned him to sit with them, and the *pir*, or spiritual guide, said to the saint, "This is my son, take a good look at him," before he ate from their hands and felt "longing and love." "Ever after that," the man recalled, he searched for the man in his dream. Whenever he heard some saintly person or scholar was coming, he would go, but he was always disappointed. In 1947, while taking a friend to visit a pir in Pakistan, he saw a man sitting on a prayer rug. "When I looked at him, I knew that this was my pir." "You have taken a long time coming," the pir told him, "but you are here."*

While these dreams among Muslims and here specifically among Pakistanis are said to have a "recognizable common structure" and potentially follow a "cultural template,"[40] it is hard not to note the fundamental simplicity of these dreams and their similarity to those still dreamed, both in cultures far separated from these recognized traditions and those not involving a healer or similar teacher. These dreams are considered to be the result of an external agent, a guide, or a teacher

*Among Pakistani Muslims, dreams often inform decision-making and action. See, Ewing, "The Dream of Spiritual Initiation and the Organization of Self Representations among Pakistani Sufis" (58.), who speaks to these dreams of "spiritual initiation," and makes some interesting comparisons between these and their ancient counterparts in this regard.

sending dreams to the receptive agent, another theme we have seen in the Native American accounts and others.

Similar was a story surrounding Swami Ramananda, the fourteenth-century poet saint recognized as the founder of the Ramanandi Sampradaya, the largest monastic Hindu renunciant community in modern times. During this time, the Muslim ruler Malik Kafur was spreading a "regime of terror," so Swami sent two accomplices south in order to bring him to the right path. One of the two, Sursuranand, purposely appeared in Malik's dream and advised him on the matter. The dream so affected Malik that he began to look for the person in the dream. When information came to him of someone matching the description, he went and remained in the service of Sursuranand and granted his wish that the atrocities be halted.[41]

Once more we note that among certain Native American tribes, the idea of locating a distant stranger upon the authority of a dream or vision—and specifically in a healing context—is often a rather expected capacity and turns up across the legend and lore of innumberable tribes. In one Lakotan example, it was known that a man might have a vision of someone they should or would later help, something we have already seen in more recent accounts.[42] Chokecherry Gall Eagle, a Lakota informant, said, "I have walked up to complete strangers and handed them an eagle feather because of visions. They always say what I said when I got my first feather. How did you know to give it to me?" Earlier in life, Eagle had a rather elaborate dream in which he saw "various people from some distance away" before noting, "later in life I would recognize them as good or bad people, accordingly. I also saw a solitary man atop a distant mountain," he then said. "He was a very old Sioux Holy Man, and he also saw me."[43] They met later in life.

Walking Thunder, the Diné Indian born in New Mexico (their lands stretching into Utah and Arizona), says that her people historically learned their medicinal skills from the Wing Singing Man. She herself noted that "Sometimes I saw a medicine person in my dreams, and then I went to find the person who appeared."[44] From the folklore in the Ozarks, this capacity is referenced in passing of a woman who was known for curing warts. She would simply "dream of a man, then seeks this fellow out."[45]

In many traditional societies, volumes could be produced on these dreams. It is by no means only the supplicant who might dream of and later meet the healer. In the South Pacific, for example, in the Polynesian nation of Tuvalu, it is also expected that a spontaneous dream "causes an affected person to seek help from a traditional practitioner." These are rarely vague intimations, either. They usually "pinpoint the sorcerer fairly explicitly."[46] This same capacity was well known among the ancient Druids, too, with all their magic and clairvoyance. The *Tarbhfhess*, or "bull sleep," was a ritual in which a chosen individual would eat only bull flesh before being chanted to sleep by four Druids. The idea was that while he slept, he would then dream of the person who was to be the next rightful king of Ireland. This information would be relayed to those watching over him upon waking in the hope that he would then be found.[47] It is similarly said of Paul, the first Hermit (c. 227–c. 341), that his god sent him a dream in which he showed him the location of a servant of his and that he should seek him out. Having traveled for some time, Paul saw a light that "revealed the abode of him whom he was seeking."[48]

These ideas even come out in Shakespeare's *Macbeth*, wherein Macbeth is given an apocalyptic prophecy by eight witches in which he sees a line of eight kings, with the last holding a mirror and reflecting even more kings. These were to be his heirs. Of great interest here, this itself has been speculated to have been based on a supposed event that occurred in the life of queen consort and regent of France, Catherine dé Medici (1519–1589). There had been a report in aristocratic circles that she was shown an apparition of France's future kings in a mirror, one after the other, before she fainted.[49]

Movers and Shakers

As recorded again in an 1889 issue of the psychical and spiritualist *Light* publication, English journalist, spiritualist, and founder of the National Press Agency, Edmund Dawson Rogers, told of a lady who looked into a mirror he had given her.[50] After gazing into it, she "minutely described a scene in which a lecturer, apparently an Englishman, was addressing an audience, while behind a chair stood the spirit of a North American Indian." Some months later, this woman was by chance introduced to the United States consul in Turkey, a man whom she "recognized as the subject of her vision, and who believed it to refer to some occasion when he had given an address in that town."

An importantly related although otherwise entirely disparate experience is remembered in the *Legend of the Wizard Clip*, a ghost story regarding an incident said to have actually occurred (with a transparently edifying bent, however) in Middleway, West Virginia, in 1820. Adam Livingstone, a Pennsylvanian man seemingly dealing with paranormal domestic disturbances, dreams of climbing a mountain. At the summit, he sees a man dressed in long black robes and a voice telling him, "This is the man who can relieve you." Interestingly, having set out to Winchester to find the dream man based on his knowledge of the clergy clothing there, he found that the "Episcopalian clergyman did not come up to the description of the person he had seen in his dream," so he returned. Later in Shepherdstown, a robed priest appears in the church, after which Livingstone is said to have fallen to his knees in tears, crying, "This is the very man I saw in my dream; he is the one the voice told me would relieve me of my troubles."[51]

Reported in 1997, a Louisianan woman, an informant of author Robert Thurber, dreamed one night of a "very old and wise"-looking man with a white beard and hair. This man told her to go to a specific bookstore in the city and that she, who had been looking for a higher purpose in life, would find what she sought there. While browsing the books, she overheard talk of Sant Thakar Singh who would be in town shortly. Following up, she asked who this was and found that there would be a meeting tomorrow where he would be discussing the "path of inner Light and Sound." This woman, now convinced this was important, went to the meeting, and as she was listening to the people speak, "the man who had appeared in her dreams walked in the door and sat down beside her." This was Kirpal Singh, a Pakistani spiritual master in the tradition of Radha Soami. She stayed for the initiation and later found that this man was already dead.[52] Another informant of Thurber, dejected and similarly uninspired in life, searched tirelessly for meaning in books, biographies, and conversation. One night, she dreamed of a copper engraving of the Last Supper, which resided in her parents' house. Christ began to move in the painting and gave her a loaf of pulsating bread, which eventually transformed into a nugget of gold. When the dreamer stretched out to grab it, it disappeared. Christ's face apparently began to take on features she did not recognize. Some days later, a friend they hadn't seen in a long time told her she had been to India and found a "master" who could connect her to God and that he, Sant Thakar Singh, would be traveling through her home country of Germany soon. That September, our informant—finally standing in front of this man—wrote, "For a moment, time stood still and held its breath. Then His eyes met mine and I recognized Him immediately as the face in my dream."[53]

Among the Shakers, a millenarian restorationist Christian movement, Mother Samuel walking home one day suddenly found herself unable to speak and later fainted. "When I fainted," Samuel explained, "my spirit traveled to a mother named Mother O'Hara." Having awakened, fainted once more, and met this woman again, the informant tried to say the name of the lady she had met in the dream, but the words only barely came out. Her mother picked up on it, and Samuel ran out of the house over hills and over paths, seemingly guided by a voice. The woman she had visited in her dream emerged from a church, "She was the woman I saw in my dream," Samuel told, before noting that she suddenly seemed healed.[54]

Another account from among the Shakers was Archbishop Pompey, who became a Spiritual Baptist in 1955. Pompey speaks of a "mourning room," a room one is called to in order to have visions where things might be revealed to the individual. In one vision, as he tells it while speaking of his god, "He sent to me a man whom I didn't know, in a village unknown to me. In the spirit I saw the man and saw his place. After the dream, I left to go find the man." They met later, and this experience is what led Pompey to his role as archbishop.[55]

In traditions ranging from East to West, the saint—like the shaman—may either be made or met in a dream. In a work related to nineteenth-century Indian mystic and saint Subodhananda was the dream of Charubala Guha, in which the saint appears in the dream of the latter. "I dreamed that a saint was giving me spiritual initiation," Guha told the author. "I hadn't seen him before, nor was I familiar with the process of initiation. All I know is that I felt very peaceful after seeing that saintly person in my dream. After I woke up, I felt a great eagerness to meet him. Something told me that I would find him in the Ramakrishna ashrama." Later, when they finally met, Guha, as he told it, "immediately recognized him as the saint who had initiated me in my dream!"[56]

In the Jewish tale, "The Prince Who Was Made of Precious Gems," a certain king despaired at his inability to bring an heir into the world and spent much time consulting wise men and doctors on the matter.[57] On the advice of his ministers, it eventually was decided that one of the Thiry-Six Just Men, a hidden saint, would be sought out, although no one knew where they could be found.* After some time, "three rabbis in three different cities in that kingdom had an identical dream" in which they met one of those hidden saints in a cave deep in a forest where a waterfall could be heard. The dream was recognized as a miracle, and search parties were formed in the belief that the details described in

*This is a reference to the Jewish legend of the Lamed-Vovniks, in which thirty-six righteous men are considered to exist in each generation, upon whom the existence of the world is said to depend.

the dream would help them recognize the location. At some point, they heard the sound of a waterfall and, at last, discovered the last cave. "When the three rabbis entered the cave, they recognized it at once. There too was the same old man with a white beard whom they had first met in a dream."

MESSENGERS, HELPERS, AND HEALING

That some mysterious event or supernatural entity reveals the location of another of great importance to the visionary or dreamer is a thread that runs widely through the world's legends, tales, and other literature, turning up strongly among the lives of the shaman, the saint, and others. The contents of the messages are myriad, although here we are only interested in a particular kind. The author and founder of the Order of Christ Sophia, Father Peter Bowes, for example, was visiting Boston to meet a certain priest he had been recommended to speak to. Arriving late, Bowes decided to wait till morning to make his acquaintance and dreamed a "very powerful dream" in which he saw a stranger offer him instructions, explaining something of interest, when suddenly thugs approached them with various weapons. The man placed Bowes behind him and defended him against them. The following morning, as Bowes explains it himself, "in the morning, I went to meet the priest we had come to see. When I was brought in to see him, I was stunned to see that he was the man from my dream."[58]

In an old Chinese tale, *Hsieh Yün and the Entrapped Tiger*, Hsieh Yun, while attempting to clear his name of wrongdoing related to war after being a captive of the household of Chiang Feng, dreamed of a woman who told him, "It is easy to come in here, but difficult to get out. You have a compassionate heart. I shall deliver you." Traveling to Wu-Tang mountain after his release and meeting a Taoist who seems to have been aware of his coming, Hsieh Yun enters the mountain and fasts for three days before seeing the master. "Upon seeing him," the author Kao relays, "he realized this was the man who had appeared in his dream."[59]

In the thirteenth-century *Uji Shui Monogatari*, a collection of myths, legends, folktales, and memorates, we read of a woman searching for her lost brother in a tale speaking to the belief in the possibility of such things. She hadn't seen him for many years and made inquiries all around the neighborhood of Tojaiji, but no one knew of him. The woman resolved to pray before the Great Buddha of the Todaiji and ask for the man's location. Later in a dream, the Buddha said to her, "The priest whom you seek lives on a mountain southwest of here. Go there and look for him on the side of the mountain from which a cloud is trailing." She later set out and found the man exactly there.[60]

While for the ancient Japanese the appeal might sometimes have been made to their Buddha, among the lives of the European saints, the very same was asked of other mysterious messengers. Despite the difference in what are often culturally appropriate supernatural messengers, the questions and answers seem to speak clearly to an extremely similar if not indistinguishable kind of experience. According to *The Legend in Nine Lessons of S. Daniel, Bishop of Bangor*, the Cathedral Church of Bangor, Wales, became vacant and needed a new bishop. As the tale goes—and very much recalling the *tarbhfhess* of the Druids—"the grace of the Holy Spirit was invoked, and it was revealed from heaven that they should send without delay into Pembroke, and choose a certain eremite dwelling on a mountain in the southern part of Pembroke, to be bishop and pastor of their Church." That man, Daniel himself, was later found exactly "in the place we named before."[61]

Among the Pima Indians of Arizona and New Mexico are "speeches"—those being portions of their cosmology recited—among which there another deity, Talking Tree, gave information. "In a vision," the speech describes of a certain man, "the location of the enemy was revealed." While he does not subsequently go to the man, the idea comes out similarly and more pointedly when a Californian shaman, during his initiatory dreams, encounters a deity who, in his own words, "showed me one of the people who live on high peaks, a *mumolno'm* or *huchatat* (mountain person), to be my helper in curing disease."[62]

This messenger dynamic, as it specifically relates to these déjà vu–type experiences, is not relegated to these more fantastical, literary, or legendary tales. According to the memoirs of Utah pioneer John R. Young, in 1845 an Italian sailor by the name of Toronto had a strange dream of this kind. He had been greatly concerned as to where to deposit the few hundred dollars he had managed to save when, just before reaching his destination of New York, he dreamed that a certain man stood before him and told him to leave his money with "Mormon Brigham." Toronto had no idea what to make of this and made inquiries, and after some effort he was told of a man by the full name of Brigham Young, who was the president of the Mormon Church and lived in Nauvoo, Illinois. Toronto made his way there and not only met with Young but became friends with Young, describing that he became a "permanent member of the family."[63]

Finally for this chapter, and given in an 1824 issue of *The Telescope*—a New York newspaper that ran between that year and 1829—was a letter written by a dying soldier after the battle of Bunker Hill. John Randon wrote to his wife that his Christian God had guided him to a man he "had no knowledge of" beforehand. Randon writes that in a dream he was "directed" to a man, including by name that of Samuel Pierce. "The dream made so strong an impression on my mind," he writes, "that next morning I inquired if there was such a person and was greatly astonished to find him." They soon began a close friendship. Indeed, as Randon explained it, "he became my spiritual father."[64]

Déjà rêvé, as the apparent fulfillment of a previous dream, turns up commonly across various and geographically disparate tales and traditions. The more general idea that a dream might locate a person, either known—or more specifically, unknown—is similarly not hard to find and as we have seen among the likes of the Druids and the ancient Chinese, a very important one. While in the legends and the lore, they are commonly tied to doctors, healers, masters, and other persons who will play a beneficial role in the dreamer's life, the same visions and dreams occur in modern settings. These shared dynamics between the ancient past and the most recent present will come into even sharper focus as we move now into the heady realms of poetry, romance, and love.

4
Divination and Dreams

Rhyme, Verse, and the Folklore of Finding Love

Legends may embroider the truth, but they seldom invent it outright; they grow from a seed of what was once real to those who told them.

Sabine Baring-Gould

We have seen and will continue to see how far and wide it has been believed that another may be met in a dream or vision before meeting in life. Doctors, healers, shamans, saints, mystics, and ordinary people alike. Such things are certainly experienced and then believed; however, they are often believed first in the hope of being experienced later. This comes out particularly in the area of love, accounts of which will now be brought in among the others we have seen and will continue to see featured. Whatever its literal truth, whatever even the importance of such a thing in the realms of romance and matters of the heart, there can be no doubt that it has long been believed that one might dream truthfully of, or otherwise envision their future spouse. This was often no passive superstition either, but was widely acted upon using a variety of rituals and divinatory magical rites. Whatever the source of these beliefs in each case, be they literal experiences, attempts to re-create some legendary tale or idea, or something entirely novel—and however many specifically adhered to the authenticity of the magic itself—this has been one of the major concerns of all times. Here, a nod to the kinds of lore, divination, rituals, and incantations that speak to and express these beliefs as they relate to our interests is offered in order to further contextualize the many more accounts, adventures, and tales that will then follow. A greater sense of how ubiquitous this notion itself has been, the belief in the possibility of these dreams and visions—and the often rather complex means of attaining them—will be helpful in understanding not only how widespread these kinds of visions and dreams are but also the dedication sometimes required in order to attain them.

While the following quote is usually misattributed to Plato, it is nevertheless often the case that, as the quote goes, "At the touch of love, everyone becomes a poet." If the visions, dreams, and rituals that precede them are to be believed, it seems the opposite is also true. Poems, indeed, might lead one to love in the first place. This, as will now be explored, has been commonly held.

UPON A STAR

According to old Greek traditions later imported and carefully preserved among Greek Americans, a single woman will dream of her future husband if a *koufeta*, a kind of traditional treat, is placed under her pillow. The chances improve if the koufeta comes from a tray of them laid out at a wedding.[1] Also Greek is the custom by which relatives and friends give wedding guests gifts of sugared almonds wrapped in a veil cloth.* Custom tells us that young and unmarried women would take these almonds and sleep with

*Of relevance here, almonds have long represented fertility among the Greeks.

them under their pillows so that they might dream of their future groom.[2]

In examining these superstitions, their ubiquity and idiosyncratic similarities quickly become apparent. These facts, in part, are explained geographically and as they relate to the movement of traditions with the movements of people. This, however, is not a universally applicable solution. With that said, the wedding connection brings up an old Irish tradition that had the individual sleeping on a bride-cake in order to "dream the apparition of a future wife or husband." More specifically, a young woman might place numerous emblematic objects beneath her pillowcase, such as a prayer book or pack of cards, before reciting a verse to the moon. Only then, it was thought, might their future husbands be dreamed of.[3] Such a fitting and romantic song to the moon as a means of attaining knowledge of one's future spouse finds us also among the folklore of Nebraska. There, if one sees the new moon over their right shoulder, they must utter the following words;

New moon, true moon, pray let me see
Who my husband is to be.
The color of his hair, the clothes he is to wear,
The happy day he weds me.[4]

The moon, and especially the new moon, appealed to as some magical mediary, turns up commonly in these rituals. Much farther north in Nova Scotia, one of those says that a person should look over their left shoulder, pick up whatever is underfoot, and recite the following while gazing at the moon:

New moon and moon of truth,
Tell me without falsehood in what direction my
love lies.
The clothes that he wears
And the color of his hair.

The item should then be placed beneath the person's pillow that night in order to dream of a future lover.[5]

Here—and foreshadowing more of our upcoming and fuller accounts of dreams in which lovers meet first in a dream—folklorist Joe Neil MacNeil offered an example more specific than these more general statements, in which a man went outside a house on Halloween night to pick up a clod while someone else plucked a hair from a dog's back and held on to it.[6] The clod was then divided among everyone there. One of those men told MacNeil that they had gotten a hair, put it under his pillow, and dreamed of a certain woman. "He didn't know her at all." Sometime later, he saw her at a dance and recognized her from the dream. They married soon after.

Something particularly novel, either a behavior or some important object, often turns up as an important requirement in these divinatory rituals. For some American pioneer women, it was thought that to sleep under what had to be a new quilt would be to dream of her future husband.[7] Something similar comes from among certain other North American communities. There it was said that among some other steps, one should "sit on something upon which you have never sat before" in order to dream of their future husband.[8]

Coming again to more of a narrative example, Thomas F. Pendel, White House doorkeeper for almost forty years—from the Lincoln Administration to the turn of the twentieth century—gave something related in his *Thirty-Six Years in the White House*. Regarding the marriage of Miss Nellie, daughter of President Ulysses S. Grant, to American diplomat Mr. Algernon Sartoris, Pendel writes that after presenting the wedding cake to the bridesmaids, they would cut it up and put it in boxes between three and six inches long. These would then be slept with in order for those singles to dream of a future husband.[9]

Victorian-era writer Ellen Emma Guthrie (also E. J. Guthrie), who compiled *Old Scottish Customs* after fifteen years of travel across Scotland, gave a very old custom called "Eating the Herring," in which one would eat a raw or roasted salt herring in order to dream of their future spouse, the idea being they would appear to quench the person's thirst.[10]

A poem from Scotland intended to foster a dream of one's future spouse, which would be chanted after three knots were tied in a garter, goes as follows:

This knot, this knot I knit, to see the thing I ne'er saw yet,
To see my love in his array, and what he walks in every day,
And what his occupation be, this night I in my sleep may see.
And if my love be clad in green, his love for me is well seen,
And if my love be clad in grey, his love for me is far away,
But if my love be clad in blue, his love for me is very true.[11]

On the Isle of Man at Hollantide, a remnant of the old Celtic new year, one should take a salted herring from a neighbor's house by darkness and without their consent. Having prepared it, it should be eaten in silence before retiring to bed backward before undressing in the dark. They should have the future husband appear in a dream, presenting a drink of water.[12] Commonly, in fact, these charms and incantations are said to have a rather ancient and seemingly pre-Christian pedigree. The following "old charm" would be used by the maidens of Rome in "ancient times" in order to "see" their future husbands. After attaining nine small keys, they should plait a three-plaited braid of their own hair, tie them, fasten the ends with nine knots, fasten them with their garters to the left wrist upon going to bed, and bind the other garter around the head and say:

St. Peter, take it not amiss,
To try your favor I've done this;
You are the ruler of the keys,
Favor me, then, if you please:
Let me then your influence prove.
And see my dear and wedded love.[13]

The Danes believe that on *Wassailing* or *Twelfth Night*, yet another tradition with pagan roots, girls will dream of their future husbands.[14]

Timing Is Everything

As with other kinds of magic, and as we have seen regarding the divination related to the new moon, timing and accuracy are often very important in these rituals. A tradition from Ontario collected in 1918 says that if one wishes to see their future husband or wife, they must sing the entire eight stanzas of *Solomon's Song of Songs* for nine nights in succession. The individual might then see their future husband or wife engaged in the trade in which they will then be employed. The author Waugh heard a more specific example in which a young lady of Scottish Highland descent from Manitoulin Island carried this out and saw her husband in a dream carrying a bowl of water. They would meet, and he would later be a municipal waterworks employee.[15] A likely Irish-influenced tradition from eastern Ontario in Canada says that a woman should boil a hard egg, remove the center, fill it with salt, and eat it on Halloween. She would then go to bed backward, speak to no one, and at midnight her future husband would appear in a dream, holding water in his hand.[16] Likewise, on Maine Island it was thought that if one was to eat a portion along the back of a dried salt fish, what they called the "dream-line," their future partner would appear in a dream offering water.[17] Something notably similar and very old—around a millennium older, in fact—comes from Wales. "The maiden would cut and prepare a pullet's egg in just the right way, make a cake from it, and eat one half. The other half was put at the foot of her left stocking and beneath her pillow. Falling to sleep thus with romantic thoughts, it was that "the future husband should be seen, in a vision of the night, to come to the bedside bearing a vessel of water or other beverage for the thirsty maid."[18]

A book of charms published in 1690 says that in order to guarantee a glimpse of their future husband or wife, they should go to bed on

Halloween night, place a sliver of wood in a glass of water, and place it on the bedside table. One was then said to dream of falling from a bridge into a river. The person who rescues them in the dream would be seen clearly and would be their future husband or wife. The following charm is related to this belief:

> *Last Hallow Eve I looked my love to see,*
> *And tried a spell to call her up to me.*
> *With wood and water standing by my side,*
> *I dreamed a dream and saw my own sweet bride.*[19]

In certain parts of medieval England, it was believed that putting an acorn under the pillow, specifically beneath the bottom right portion, would cause a dream of the individual's future husband.[20]

In North America, untangling the Indigenous beliefs from those imported was a particular challenge for the earlier American folklorists. These kinds of superstitions involving the placing of something under a pillow toward a prophetical and romantic dream are nevertheless widespread across that continent too. Indeed, the idea of magic and divination related to the placing of an object beneath the sleeper's pillow was clearly not a solely imported one, as there are many examples in the traditions of Native Americans.* In North Carolina, one should place some stolen bride's cake beneath their pillow toward this very end.[21] It was not always such palatable things that were to occupy that seemingly magical space beneath the dreamer's head by night; other traditions made use of some rather less appealing things. An old tradition from Ireland, for example, has a woman taking some skin from a corpse and

*Among the Lipan Apache, for example, there is a tale in which a man placed a switch (a tool used by Apache riders to control their horses) beneath his pillow each night. The author relays in Clark, *They Sang for Horses*, 165–67, that this was specifically in order to attain a dream encounter with a guardian that would teach him a ceremony for power over horses.

placing it under her pillow, which was supposed to make the future husband appear in a dream.[22]

FLOWERS, SAINTS, AND SPELLS

Commonly, certain flowers or herbs were considered particularly conducive to attaining this kind of knowledge. In these cases, too, associations with particular times of year or particular saints are often found. In both counties of Donegal and Derry in Ireland, for example, *Achillea millefolium*, or yarrow, used to be gathered by young people on the eve of May. Once more here we see a reference to something over the shoulder. After ten stalks were pulled and a charm was spoken over them, the tenth was thrown over the left shoulder. One must then say nothing until the following morning, and the sleeper will dream of their future husband or wife. The relevant charm follows:

Good morrow, good morrow, fair yarrow,
Thrice good morrow to thee; I hope,
before this time to-morrow,
You'll show my true lover to me.[23]

These kinds of charm-rhymes, in fact, were rather widespread throughout England in those times, particularly in rural areas, and often had an old Anglo-Saxon heritage. Although even the authors collecting them may have sometimes turned up their noses at these superstitions in the nineteenth century, these practices—symptomatic of broader, deeper, and much older magical beliefs—nevertheless persisted throughout rural England.* On Saint Luke's Day, there was

*For the interested reader, historian of religion Carlos Eire, in *They Flew: A History of the Impossible*, speaks brilliantly and more generally on how such beliefs persisted powerfully during and relevantly after the Enlightenment, despite the progress of rationalism.

a method by which girls were to anoint themselves with a combination of thyme, marjoram, and wormwood that had been ground to a powder before being simmered with honey and vinegar. That night, they would wish to dream of their love by repeating the following lines three times:

St. Luke, St. Luke, be kind to me,
In dreams let me my true love see.[24]

The saint was commonly appealed to in order to attain various kinds of special foreknowledge. The saint being dead, therefore, conforms to the ancient and widespread notion that the dead often know more than we do and may offer either solicited or unsolicited pragmatic advice and secret knowledge of various kinds. This is a belief with relatively few exceptions. In England, the mythical and magical *allium cepa*—or far less romantically, the humble onion—was sacred to Saint Thomas. At times, the onion would replace mistletoe atop the doorways. Girls would cut them into pieces, whisper the names of the ones they loved, and appeal thus:

Good Saint Thomas do me right and send me my
true love come tonight.
That I may see him in the face, and him in my
kind arms embrace.[25]

The girls were then required to be asleep before midnight if the appeal was to be successful. Welsh folklore similarly tells us that sleeping with the equally unremarkable leek beneath one's pillow will cause a woman to dream of her future husband.[26]

Returning to Scotland, the roots of the early purple orchid had magical properties and could also be used for divination. The large main root was representative of a desired husband, and the smaller root was a desired wife. If either was powdered and placed under the pillow, the person would see his or her future husband or wife in a dream.[27] Such divination was particularly widespread in eighteenth- and nineteenth-century Europe, where women were primarily encouraged toward the duty of raising a family and where a future mate was an early concern. A charm divination of the same kind was practiced in England at least until before the second half of the nineteenth century, in which on St. Faith's Day, three girls make a specific kind of cake that is baked in a Dutch oven while no one speaks. It must then be divided equally among them, each slicing their piece into nine parts before each piece is pulled through the wedding ring of a woman married for seven years. The cake must then be eaten while the girl both undresses and repeats the following verse:

O good St. Faith, be kind to-night,
And bring to me my heart's delight;
Let me my future husband view,
And be my visions chase.[28]

Such a practice, of course, was to bring about a dream of the girl's future husband.

Among Cornish families and neighbors, large apples called Allan Apples were thought to bring good luck. If an unmarried girl were to sleep with one beneath her pillow, she would dream of her future husband, although she must eat the apple the next morning for the divination to be fully effective. She may then flick an apple pip into the air, observe where it lands, and say:

North, south, east, west,
Tell me where my love does rest.[29]

While walking through London as long ago as 1694, antiquarian John Aubrey noticed multiple young women who, as a young man told him, were looking for coal under the root of a plantain. This they would place beneath their pillows in order to "dream who would be their husbands."[30] Aubrey notes that these were old traditions even then, and several had been handed down. Another woman he knew used another method relating to St. Agnes, the accompanying rhyme of which goes as follows:

This knot I knit,
To know the thing I know not yet,
That I may see the man that shall my husband be,
How he goes and what he wears
And what he does all the day.

A couple of years later, according to the author, she sees a man at church and cries out to her sister, "This is the very face of the man that I saw in my dream."[31]

Outer Regions

Moving farther from the regions most commonly associated with magic of this kind, in 2014 Marko Dragic presented a number of love-divinations from Croatian, Bosniac, Serb, Polish, and Italian sources, opining the extent to which they had at that point been fading into oblivion. Here, too, many of the divinations are related to Christian feasts. One tradition from Croatia stated that if a man were to fast on St. Andrew's Eve, "then he will behold his future wife in a dream."[32]

In Bosnia and Herzegovina, Dragic found as recently as 2008 that on St. George's Eve, certain girls would pick buttercups, daisies, feverfew, and others, holding them while they would say:

Daisy, don't daisy me,
Feverfew, don't feverfew me!
Rather tell me who my intended one is.[33]

It was then believed that they would later marry the man who appeared in their dreams that night. During the Festival of St. John in parts of Germany, St. John's herb (*Liebeskrant*, or "love herb") is used similarly. If they put a branch of it under their pillow, they would dream of their future lovers.[34] In parts of southwestern Germany as well as eastern Switzerland and Alcase, it was believed that if a widow cut an apple in half on St. Andrews Eve and put the other half beneath her pillow, she would dream of her next husband.[35] Historian George Coulton noted of Germany, that during the middle ages—particularly at Stommeln, a village (Stadtteil) in North Rhine-Westphalia, Germany—the idea that girls might dream of their future husbands on certain days was an idea that was very much "in the air" at the time.[36] The Germans, like so many other Europeans, took these ideas with them across the Atlantic. Among the nineteenth-century German communities in New Hamburg, Missouri, belief in witchcraft was common. Spells were cast and charms were worn; despite the march of rationalism, this was nothing out of the ordinary. If one wanted to dream of a future love, he would sleep with nine different kinds of leaves beneath his pillow.[37] In Poland, people would put "various items" under their pillows in order to divine similarly on the night of Katarzynki. It was believed that "W noc swietj Katarzyny pod poduszką sa dziewczyny" or "In the night of St. Catherine the girls are under the pillow."[38]

In Belgium, girls would lay their garters crosswise at the foot of their beds and place a looking glass under their pillows in order to see their husband in a dream, in which he would appear in the glass.[39] *Gergyovden*, or Georges Day, was one of several days considered particularly conducive to prophecy in Bulgaria.[40] In one of those, a girl would place wheat or a small piece of Gergiovden bread under her pillow in order to discover her future partner. In Bulgaria, too, girls would build little bridges of willow, oak, or cornelian cherry sticks tied with red thread that they would place over the gutters and water channels in the village and recite:

May he who is my fate,
take me across this bridge tonight.[41]

In Macedonia, a girl could take wheat from a church, place it under her pillow, and expect to dream of her future husband.[42] On December 21, St. Thomas's Day in Austria, single girls in the village of Flachgau would say a traditional rhyme before they went to sleep in order to see their future husband's face that night.[43] Moving to early twentieth-century Armenia, it was believed that young lovers should eat salty bread before bed on St. Sarkis Day. They may then dream of their future spouse bringing them water for their dry mouths.[44]

Serbian statesman and historian Chedo Miyatovich noted that every girl in Serbia believed that her future husband existed as a predestined entity somewhere out there in the world and that there existed magical ways to discover his identity. One of those methods took on a communal role, wherein priests would distribute handfuls of wheat that were to be boiled after consecration. This would be placed under the pillow and slept on in order to "gain a vision of their future husbands or wives." "I have done it myself as a young man," Miyatovich offered, before continuing, "everybody believes in it." Miyatovich offered a more particular reminiscence of the past in which he visited with the Queen of Serbia, who told him that she had a premonition of the fact she would marry her then current husband, King Alexander I of Serbia (1889–1903). She carried out just such a charm as the previous mentioned, and "that night," as she tells it, "I dreamt I saw a large picture lowered from the sky. It came before my eyes and looking at it, I saw a portrait of King Alexander smiling at me." "It cannot be," she later said to herself. "Surely I am not going to marry King Alexander." The prediction, of course, "as everyone knew," was fulfilled.[45]

Given in the *Connoisseur Journal* (published between 1754 and 1756) was another more specific example from a correspondent who gave an account of her own Valentine's Eve: "Last Friday," she began, "was Valentine's Day, and the night before, I got five bay leaves, and pinned four of them to the four corners of my pillow, and the fifth to the middle; and then if I dreamt of my sweetheart, Betty said we should be married before the year was out." After carrying out further rituals to be sure, Betty claimed they worked and that the following morning she met the man from her dream.[46] This is in reference to the tradition that the first member of the opposite sex you meet the following morning will be one's lover. Much later, a correspondent to the *Daily Mirror* in 1971 gave truth to the survival of these traditions, writing that she had put her shoes in the shape of a "T" and said "goodnight" out loud seven times before climbing into bed backward with her eyes closed. This was supposed to bring a dream of her future husband. That night, the woman claims she dreamed of the writer Douglas Fairbanks Jr., and ten years later, according to her friends, the man she married was his double, a complete look-alike.[47]

British author and folklorist Jennifer Westwood (1940–2008) also spoke to the age and survival of these kinds of traditions when she wrote, "Country people, and people in isolated work groups such as fishermen and miners, have been less touched by outside influences than the rest of the community and have remained more conservative. Consequently, divinations known in sixteenth-century England were still practiced in the nineteenth, and even in the twentieth century old divinatory formulae may be part of our daily lives without our knowing it."[48] While the rituals and rites themselves are less carried out, we will see that the same beliefs that underlie them very much are still held or even engendered by dreams and other experiences today.

MIRROR MIRROR ON THE WALL

Cakes, the skin of a corpse, the magic of the moon, the flower, or the herb—there are many magical means by which one might have discovered their betrothed. One other of those worthy of some mention is the mirror. Historically, mirrors and other reflective surfaces have been used toward various magical ends. Keats memorialized this tradition in his 1820 poem, *The Eve of St. Agnes.* Pushkin, another literary giant, also implemented the date of January 20—the eve of St. Agnes—in his poem *Eugene Onegin.* It is on this date that his character Tatiana places a mirror beneath her pillow in the hope of seeing her future husband.[49] Far from there in Massachusetts, an "old superstition" says that if a girl were to sleep with a mirror beneath her pillow, she would surely dream of what her future husband looked like.[50]

According to Spanish folklore collected in Florida, "If a girl puts a mirror under her pillow, she will dream of the man she is to marry." Likewise, if she were to look over her left shoulder into a mirror, he would be there too.[51] In Texas, it is thought that the man who sleeps with a mirror under his pillow will marry the first woman he sees the next day. This might come by way of a dream, although this is not necessary to the success of the ritual.[52] The same belief is widespread and can be found elsewhere on that continent, such as in Florida, Newfoundland, Illinois, etc.

On Skalohori, on the island of Lesbos off Greece, there is a custom that takes place on Candlemas Eve in which the women place a mirror upside down on their pillows in the hope of dreaming of a future husband.[53]

Twentieth-century Anglican minister and hobby folklorist Harry Middleton Hyatt found that in Illinois, if a girl were to count nine stars for nine nights in a row and then place a mirror under her pillow, her future husband would be revealed on that final night.[54] Among the Acadians (those who were descendants of English-speaking Acadians expelled after the loss of the French colony in 1755), it was said that young girls might put a mirror beneath their pillow in the hope of dreaming about their future husbands.[55]

In Romania, if a girl stepped naked into a body of water, she would see the reflection of her lover's face.[56] Cassandra Eason noted that as late as the nineteenth century, single girls would visit certain holy wells, often associated with a particular saint (the saint having replaced the original otherworldly guardian), in the hope they would dream of a future husband.[57]

Circling back to Macedonia, we can see that some of the more complex elements of these rituals return alongside the mirror. There, on the eve of ἀνήμερα (Baptists eve), parties of girls entered darkened rooms with the intent of spotting a future husband in one of the mirrors. More elaborately, a maid should undress in front of the mirror in her own room, utter the following charm, and then sleep with the same mirror beneath her pillow in order to dream of her husband to be:

> Παιέρνω τὸν καθρέφτη καὶ τὸν θεὸ περικαλῶ Ὅποιος
> εἶναι τῆς τύχης μου ἀπόψε νά Τον διῶ.
>
> *I take up this mirror and God I beseech, whosoever is to*
> *be my fate, may I see him this night.*[58]

It could be speculated that the rather elaborate nature of some of these rituals may have been designed in order to tap further into the placebo-type effects that may be required in order, at least in some cases, to *actually* engender such a vision or dream. This truly would be a form of magic, and considering we know these dreams do really occur, it is not at all unreasonable to assume the possibility that they could be induced using such techniques—that these are not all or only mere superstitions, despite the extent to which they might be remembered, ridiculed, or even carried out as such. Jennifer Westwood spoke to this, specifically in relation to these kinds of divinations across Britain when she wrote, "Darkness, secrecy, silence, the expectations raised by performance at the witching hour and on special 'ghost nights'—all played a part in creating the right context for these ceremonials."[59]

APPARITIONS AND AMORE

Rather than a dream or some kind of vision as such, other traditions attempt to conjure the actual apparitional form of the future lover. While in the folklore, wraiths often portended bad news, this was clearly not always the case. Numerous old methods of this kind of divination made use of a ball of yarn and often involved the same kinds of strange elaboration we have seen in some of the other methods. One of those called for the yarn to be thrown into a lime kiln and wound up until "invisible hands" caught it. This should be performed in complete silence and only at the witching hour. The individual should then ask aloud, "Who pulls my yarn?" In reply to these actions, either a voice would then reply the name of the future husband or wife, or their appearance would materialize.[60]

In Ireland and various regions throughout the British Isles, it was believed that if a woman entered a barn at midnight and used a kind of sieve called a *riddle* three times to separate grain from chaf, an apparition of her future husband might materialize. This may have a sting in the tail, however, as if a coffin appeared it suggested the death of the woman herself would occurr within the next two months.[61] In Wales, specifically on St. David's Eve, people would walk around a bed of leeks three times without making a sound in order to hopefully summon the apparition of a future husband or wife.[62] According to another tradition from the British Isles, two unmarried girls must sit for thirteen hours together in a room without speaking a word. During this time, they must take the number of hairs from their heads that they are years old, mix them with the true-love herb, and burn each as the clock strikes one, saying;

I offer this my sacrifice
To him most precious in my eyes
I charge thee now come forth to me,
That I this minute may thee see.

This was then meant to conjure the apparition of the future spouse.[63]

Another custom from Wales had a rather darker tone. Certain maidens should place a shoulder blade of mutton under her pillow, stab the bone at midnight, and repeat:

Tis not this bone I mean to prick,
But my love's heart I wish to prick
If he comes not and speaks to-night,
I'll prick and prick till it be light.

The figure of the loved one was then thought to appear.[64]

From a collection of Kentucky superstitions, we read that one should go to a deserted house at midnight and light a candle before placing a pin in it. When the pin falls out, someone's future husband might appear.[65]

There is an interesting reference in a Scottish story given in *The Christian Lady's Magazine*, a periodical published between 1834 and 1848 that suggests that on Halloween, on the Bay of Mora in Scotland, maidens might lay out a feast of some kind specifically for the "spectral apparition of a future partner for life."[66]

WORLD OF MAGIC

While the kinds of European, pagan, early-modern, and particularly English charms, divinations, rhymes, and other magical methods we have seen have been separately reproduced ad nauseum in collections of various kinds (if not often compiled), rarely—if ever—do either their specific or general counterparts further afield come into the conversation. There is much work to be done here; a number of suggestive examples, however, are worthy of consideration and a worthy avenue of inquiry for others. Just as we have seen the New Year cited as a time conducive to such rituals on the Isle of Man, for instance, the very same was true as far away from there as Azerbaijan. At *Novruz*, a traditional Persian holiday that celebrates the coming of spring and the new year, putting ten apple seeds under a girl's pillow was considered to be a sure way to have a dream of her husband.[67]

MacKenzie expressed that "many of these rituals and spells can be found in similar forms in places as far apart as Hungary and Ireland, Spain and Norway."[68] Yet further afield in Tell Touqan village in northwestern Syria, however, the very same kinds of rituals are found. There, tattooing is carried out by the *Qirbaat* (Dom) women, and many hailing from pastoralist traditions are extensively tattooed. These are often cosmetic, although others have specific "love charm" purposes. Girls begin to acquire the relevant customary designs early on. Regarding one of those, the *ib camm* design (father's brother's son, the preferred husband)—a triangle with appendages tattooed on the inner right forearm—it is said that "when a girl sleeps with her head on the design she will dream of her future husband."[69]

Among the Ilocanos—the third largest Filipino ethnolinguistic group living in the northwest—a man sleeps with a dipper of water near his bed in order to see the reflection of his future spouse, needing to wake at exactly twelve o'clock in order to be successful. Likewise, looking into a mirror with a lit candle at this time of night will have a similar effect. Among Filipinos, all the most common European forms of love divinations of this kind are present. An Ilocano may therefore also learn of his future lover by placing a flower beneath his pillow. The woman he dreams of offering it to will be his future love. While we have seen that we should not assume it as the only explanations, one wonders to what extent colonial influence may have been a factor in instances specifically similar to some European customs. The Tagalog Filipinos, for example, would throw an orange peel over their shoulder in order to help attain knowledge of a future lover. Similarly, the number nine turns out to be important, just as it does in America and Europe. The Visayan Filipino man, for instance, should count nine stars on nine consecutive nights before going to bed in order to dream of his future better half.[70] With this said, these capacities—often of the spontaneous kind—are implied as possible in many of the beliefs and traditions that may be found in these regions and may speak, in fact, to how readily they are taken up even when they are partly or fully related to diffusion. It is notable just how seriously the shared dream is taken in certain Polynesian cultures. As it relates more specifically to such experiences involving love, Gillison found that the Gimin of Papua New Guinea's Eastern Highlands are of the opinion that "future marriage partners should first view each other in dreams."[71]

Although referencing lovers known to each other, it is interesting to note that in Japan, a woman should sleep with her night robe inside out and over her pillow in order to dream of her love.[72] The pillow and the idiosyncratic ritual are surprisingly similar to those we have already encountered.

While we have seen traditions relating to the use of a cake under the pillow from Greek, Roman, and other sources, Emily Gwathmey notes that "the custom of giving a piece of the cake to everyone present and saving some for those not present—who might then put the cake under their pillow to inspire a dream of a future mate—began with the Chinese, who were certain the cake itself stood for good fortune."[73]

Something more specifically similar to the early-modern accounts comes from the Karanga of primarily southern Zimbabwe who speak rather carefully of dreams and their different kinds. Some of them are wish-fulfillment dreams, the author Aschwanden noting with tongue in cheek that Freud may have been a student of theirs. Then there are the dreams that come from their dead ancestors, which may be of as good or bad a kind as those people. Among them, however, are those "extraordinary dreams which predict the future," a perfect example of which the author describes. "Sometimes one will understand such dream-pictures only later, as when, for example, a man sees a girl in a dream who is a perfect stranger to him, but whom he will later marry."[74]

If we were to include the wider gamut of love magic that extends beyond just dreams, the cross-cultural approach could be even further extended. Among certain Aboriginal Australians, for example, we could reference the *munji-minji* game that involved arranging leaves upon the ground in a certain manner that women used to attract men. In one example, they managed to attract a group of traveling South Australian Dingari to their camp.[75] Far off in parts of Paraguay, during the *Fiesta de San Juan*, a girl should place a cross of laurel leaves under her pillow in order to bring a dream of her future love.[76] In Texas, one may see their future lover in a dream if they do not chew their food well, perhaps speaking to ancient ideas regarding the extent to which diet may affect dreams.[77] In this case, however, the person will appear faceless! Finally, in Turkey it was believed that one could dream of their future lover by following certain steps. They should first sleep somewhere new, and then they should place their house key under their pillow. One might then hope to catch a glimpse of the one they desire.[78]

If we have seen the idea that one may locate another, known or unknown, in a vision or dream or recognized later from either, it seems the same is true regarding the locating of a future lover; this would naturally follow. As seriously as these beliefs and their related rituals were often taken over long periods of time, those documenting them were often somewhat derisive. While speaking to their historical importance, Philpot describes the kinds of beautiful and succinct poetic charms we have seen as "doggrels whispered by foolish country girls."[79] British journalist and academic Norman MacKenzie (1921–2013) wrote that "the readers of such books were simple people, often living in the country and buying chapbooks from peddlars who went from village to village selling ribbons and fairings." MacKenzie went on to opine that "country people clung to old beliefs about the importance of dreams."[80]

Regarding the ubiquity of these kinds of divinations and beliefs, MacKenzie wrote that "all kinds of different sources seem to have been drawn upon for such rituals—some from antiquity, some from medieval magic, some from local folklore, some plainly the invention of the author; they seem to contain both pagan and Christian elements, and even the pagan elements in Europe are a mixture of Roman, Greek, Egyptian, Teutonic, and Celtic traditions."[81] It seems, though, that such beliefs may have been bolstered by—or perhaps even had their origins in—experiences of the kinds we have already seen, and especially in those we have yet to see in which people still claim to have actually met their future love in a dream. Furthermore, the kinds of more legendary stories, romances, and tales that now follow would surely have been a point of reference in some of those cases. They would have spoken to the possibility of such things in the first place and been an impetus for their implementation where they were popularly read in later periods. Perhaps some of those, too, had their origins in such experiences—we can only speculate. Those very romances, poems, and adventures we now come to, however, speak strongly not only to the past, present, and future of these beliefs and traditions, but are representative of a very real phenomenon, whatever the exact connections between the two.

5
Dream Visions and Real Decisions

Love and Déjà Rêvé in Antiquity and the Middle Ages

Nothing is sweeter than love, nothing higher, nothing stronger, nothing larger, nothing more joyful, nothing fuller, and nothing better in heaven or on earth.

THOMAS À KEMPIS

Despite the many pitfalls in ascertaining it, folklore sometimes tells truth. These truths are often either missed or assumed not to exist in the first place, even by their collectors. Legend, lyric, and lore carry this truth through long ages, each apprehended with various systems of belief and interpretation, until when it is finally analyzed, it may not be recognized for what it is. Later, however, in other places and times, it may again become known. Folklorists often disregard experience-centered comparisons between the old and the new, although valuable insights are left behind. Already, we have seen the truth of this. The visions we have presented—in which people have dreamed of others before meeting them—and the lack of voluminous and historically syncretic work in this area—particularly by spiritualists and parapsychologists—seem to speak to the importance of remaining open to such connections. As will continue to be explored, these visions and dreams are as much a part of the legendary and literary annals as they are the biographical, historical, and others. As they relate to love specifically, however, the following chapters will now similarly attest. This "Love at Second Sight," as we call it, is an old, widespread, and popular notion. Here, then, we will examine the déjà rêvé phenomenon across a sampling of both the most renowned world literature and others more obscure.

In medieval literature, the dream vision was an incredibly popular genre and was commonly centered around love and romance. Prophecy abounded in those often widely read texts. Here, we are concerned only with one kind of prophecy, those related to the future lives and loves of the visionaries themselves, and in that we are spoiled with riches not just from the Middle Ages and most certainly not just from Europe. Far too many, in fact, for our purposes, which by no means relate to anything comprehensive regarding an overview of the type and others of the kind. The idea here is simply to offer the reader some context, an idea of how widespread these tales and beliefs are, and as will become apparent in later chapters, how similar they are in their fundamental aspects to those still being lived and recorded. Especially apparent in these tales is the extent to which the potentially truthful nature of the dream is believed. We will continue to see that just as some of the most renowned characters in the legends have been moved to action—in this case, to romance—in light of these strange experiences, so too have our own contemporaries and others in more recent decades.

LOVE MOVES MOUNTAINS

It is fitting that the other world and its strange timelessness are so often entwined with the romantic tales. After all, for lovers time is certainly set apart—the world itself often takes on more numinous or elevated qualities under its influence. Poets and singers are born. "How I would like to be sitting beside you on Our Beach!" wrote American playwright Eugene O'Neill in a letter to his wife. "It was only three days ago that we were there and yet it seems like three centuries. It was only the night before last that I said good'bye, and yet I seem to have languished through years of bitterness since then."[1] Time passes differently for the lovelorn in reality as much as it does for the heroes of the tales, such as Oisin from Celtic lore who, famously stepping foot in the waking world after being away in the otherworld with his love, Niamh, found that hundreds of years had passed upon his return. There is no escape from the relativity of time. Love, however, seems to bring this especially and often painfully to light. Here, in beginning, we should mention an ancient, powerful, and renowned dream: *The Dream of Maxen Wledig* from the *Mabinogion* (the earliest Welsh prose stories compiled in the twelth and thirteenth centuries). To an extent, the dream is based on factual events and certainly people, but fictionalized.

Maxen, having been hunting in the valley of a river flowing to Rome, lay down in the heat and dreamed this most famous dream.[2] He seemed to be flying through those valleys in an out-of-body state and reveling in the most beautiful sights. Mighty rivers and vast mountains eventually led him to a resplendent city the likes of which he had never seen. Nothing like home, full of vast castles and bright, astonishing colors. The palace was especially extraordinary, and Maxen beheld many people in strange and unfamiliar dress. He saw a maiden sitting in a chair of ruddy gold. "Not more easy than to gaze upon the sun when brightest, was it to look upon her by reason of her beauty," were his words. Dressed in silk and covered in red gold, she was the "fairest sight that man ever beheld." They embraced, and all too soon he awoke, saddened so much that he couldn't eat. Gloomy and downtrodden, he did not go with his men to celebrate or hear music as usually he would that week. Maxen eventually consulted his wise men, who recommended he send messengers for three years to the three parts of the world specifically to look for his dream woman. After Maxen himself led them to the point of his dream, they followed the path he took and confirmed each of its details until eventually they found the city, with its maiden "sitting in a chair of ruddy gold." "If the emperor love me," she said, "let him come here to seek me." Maxen then conquered both men and lands in the name of love until he finally held her.

The Irish *Aislinge Oengusso*, or *The Dream of Aengus*, is a tale first mentioned in the twelfth-century *Book of Leinster*, and its full form is found on a 1517 manuscript. The piece is similar in this way to an *Aisling* (literally *dream* in Irish), a kind of Irish dream vision poem dealing with the appearance of an often symbolic maiden in the dreamer's mind. While in our own times and for some previous centuries, we may not take these experiences seriously when they are reported, pieces of prose and art of extraordinary beauty have nevertheless been made in honor of their kind.

Sleeping one night, Aengus sees a woman, "the most beautiful woman in Ireland," at the end of his bed (where apparitions, as it happens, are still so likely to appear). When he reaches out and tries to hold her—just as had been the result for the likes of Achilles and Aeneas in the writings of the classical world—the form lacks substance, and she simply vanishes.* Aengus falls ill after the episode, and she appears again, this time holding a cymbal and playing him to sleep with a song. She continues to visit Aengus, and he continues to fall ill until Fergne, the physician of Conn, understands his problem and sets out a search across the entirety of Ireland in order to find this maiden, a venture initially unsuccessful. The *Dagda*, a king and Druid in Irish mythology, is called upon, and enlisting the help of a fairy king, the maiden of Aengus's dreams is located at Loch bel Dracoon at the Harps of Cliach.

*Patroclus, the mythical hero of the Trojan War, in his famed appearance as Achilles in the nearly three-thousand-year-old *Iliad*, lacks substance. Achilles cannot grab his old friend (Il. 23.99–101). Similarly, Aeneas cannot embrace Creusa's ghost in the *Aeneid* (Aen. 2.792–94). These examples are myriad.

Aengus recognizes her as the exact woman in his dreams, despite the search for her taking a total of two years. The woman was the daughter of Ethal Unbual, a king of the province of Connacht, and the two ended up happily together.[3]

The related Scottish tale of *Angus and Bride* has Bride, the beautiful young princess, being held captive by Beira, the jealous and envious goddess of winter. Day after day, she felt the wrath of her captor, being made to perform odious and drawn-out tasks. The reason she had been taken prisoner was that the son of Beira, Angus-the-ever-young, had fallen in love with her, having "first beheld Bride in a dream." "Last night," he told the king of Green Isle, where he stayed, "I dreamed a dream and saw a beautiful princess whom I love. Tears fell from her eyes, and I spoke to an old man who stood near her and said, 'Why does the maiden weep?' Said the old man: 'She weeps because she is kept captive by Beira, who treats her with great cruelty.' I looked again at the princess and said, Fain, would I set her free. Then I awoke. Tell me, O king, who is this princess, and where shall I find her?" This very meeting between Bride and the old man had actually occurred earlier in the tale, speaking already to the perceived potentially truthful nature of the dream. After many tries, they finally rendezvous in a beautiful and scenic forest near the castle of Beira, where violets and primroses are blooming and where the birds are described as raising their voices in song to the sun. Angus, finally united with her, tells Bride of his dream, and Bride tells him that she too had dreamed of his coming.[4]

In most lands from which these examples have been plucked, many predecessors and successors could similarly be laid out from various sources and genres. In *The Bailie's Daughter*, too, a later Scottish tale, a man sees in a dream "the most beautiful lady that there was in the world, and he dreamed of her three times, and he resolved to marry her and no other woman in the world." The dream spurred this man to action, as he immediately set off and traveled the world looking for the literal woman of his dreams. After much trying and much failure, the man eventually came to London and one day, while taking a walk in town, "he saw a woman at a window, and he knew her at once, for she was the lady he had seen in his sleep." They later marry and live happily together.[5]

In *Fljotstdaela hin meiri*, the longer version of the thirteenth-century Icelandic *Droplaugarsona saga*, speaking of events from 1000 CE, we can read something similar about the character of Droplaug. When she was young, Droplaug was taken from the court of her father, a *jarl* (Norse or Danish chief), by a giant named Grettir. The following Yule season, a man passing through her town named Thorvald dreams strangely that he was walking by the sea until he came to a cave beyond a fjord in which a fire was burning. "I saw an iron pillar under the roof of the cave," he said, "and to this pillar a woman was bound; her hands were made fast behind her, and her hair was wound about the pillar; iron chains were on her hands, and there was a lock at the other end, with which she was fastened; methought I undertook to free her, and I was able to do so." Speaking later to the jarl, he discovers that Droplaug's father had promised her hand to any man who could find her. Thorvald, on the authority of the dream and the jarl himself, "sets off and discovers the maiden in the highly uncomfortable position of which he had dreamed." They eventually live rather happily ever after.[6]

More ancient still was the tale according to Lucian, in which Medea, daughter of King Aeëtes of Colchis in Greek mythology, first saw Jason, the ancient Greek mythological hero and leader of the Argonauts, in a dream.[7] This "motif," according to Dronke—so often found in the songs of the troubadour—struck scholars as so "remarkable" that "it seemed necessary to 'explain its occurrence' by the influence of Arabic poetry."[8] Such attempts and connections are of course important; however, it does seem to go unmentioned by most in these areas that essentially indistinguishable dreams are still dreamed and with surprising frequency. Furthermore, they occur in such numbers that this should absolutely be factored in during etiological and related analyses.

Spanish dramatist, poet, writer, and knight of the Order of Santiago, Pedro Calderon de la Barca's seventeenth-century Spanish play, translated to English as *The Schism in England*, deals with Henry VIII and Anne Boleyn. Early on in Calderon's rendition, Henry dreams of Boleyn before he has ever met her, the pipes playing dramatically at this point as a curtain is drawn back over the sleeping king. She speaks to him in verse, and later again she comes in his dreams:

> *She came towards me, and I was perturbed*
> *At seeing her, and contemplating her*
> *I could not go on writing—to be precise,*
> *however much I wrote and noted down*
> *With my right hand, my left hand would erase*

As Carole Levin explains in her analysis, "Soon after his dream, the king meets the actual Anne Boleyn, a lady-in-waiting to his queen, and he recognizes her as the woman from his dream."[9]

Moving now to the folklore in eastern Spain, Anglo American Jason Webster, writing of his time living with his wife on the slopes of the sacred peak of Penyagolosa, collected multiple tales. One of them, "The Story of the Three Lemons of Love," tells of a prince who dreamed one night of the most beautiful girl in the world and involves exactly the kinds of divination we had seen in the previous chapter. Immediately after the dream, he told his father he would be setting out to find her. After traveling for some time, he met an odd and wise old woman who offered him lemons after learning of his quest. "When you find a spring, cut it in half, and the woman you seek will appear before you," she told him. "But make sure to give her some water to drink if she asks for it." Not long after, he carried out the ritual, and "no sooner had he done so than the girl who had appeared in his dreams suddenly stood before him." Twice he was so awestruck that he forgot to offer her water, and she disappeared, so the third time he filled a goblet before she appeared, and upon offering it to her she stayed. They quickly fell in love and eventually lived happily ever after.[10] Similarly, in Wagner's romantic opera *Lohengrin*, first performed in 1850, the character of Elsa, who falls into the arms of Lohengrin to sing their duet, saw him in a dream before he came to her: "He was led by love to her side."[11] The English epic poem *The Faerie Queene*, first published in 1590 by Edmund Spenser, has a knight of the Red Cross dreaming likewise of a maiden, who had also dreamed of him before they finally met.[12]

A Love from Afar

Huon of Bordeaux is the title character of a thirteenth-century French epic poem with a romance element and is a favorite of the Middle Ages. Poems like those of German poet and writer Christoph Wieland have been written about it, and Weber's opera *Oberon* has taken its inspiration from there. Shakespeare's *A Midsummer Night's Dream* even owes some amount to the work. The hero Huon, having been given an important errand and having already come through multiple trials on his journey to Baghdad from France, rests at one point under a tree. Here he has a "wonderful dream, in which he beheld his future lady-love," whom exactly he later meets.[13]

An earlier legend tied to the sixth-century Saint Herve of Brittany reads similarly. In the times when Childebert was king of France, a young and handsome minstrel, Hyvarnion, spent his days writing and playing beautiful songs for his king. He was also said to be very wise and nicknamed "the little sage" at school. Four years into his time with the king, he one night dreamed of a beautiful maiden picking flowers who smiles at him and offers one of the blossoms, saying, "This is for my King." Three more nights he dreamed the same, and on the fourth, Hyvarnion set out with the resolve to find her. As the heroes so often do in these particular tales, Hyvarnion made his way through a dark and menacing wood until he finally emerged into a beautiful and almost otherworldly meadow. There, he saw "the very maiden about whom he had dreamed, but much more beautiful than any dream." She, too, had dreamed three times, "and it was of golden-haired Hyvarnion that she had dreamed."[14]

Such dream visions were immensely popular in medieval Europe and later. *Le Roman de la Rose,* a thirteenth-century medieval allegorical love poem written in old French, is such an example. Although less of a romance in the traditional sense, this work—one of the most widely read during the Renaissance in France—has a man seeing a woman, Rose, first in a dream, and typically he sets off to overcome many trials and obstacles before eventually discovering her.[15] Jaufre Rudel, prince of Blaye, France, and a troubadour of the early-to-mid-twelfth century, is particularly noted for developing this *amor de lonh,* or "love from afar" theme in his songs. While aspects of his life are in dispute, he is an important figure in the movement of this idea through the ages, having himself sung of "a lady whom he has never seen."[16] Such a tale and the more broad idea of falling in love at a distance (by myrid means even beyond visions and dreams), were favorite devices of the troubadour, and dozens of instances could be cited. An ancient example of such amor de lonh comes from Ovid's *Heroides,* in which Paris (Alexander), a mythological figure of the Trojan War, declares that this was exactly the kind of love he had for Helen of Troy. He tells of how he had loved her and dreamed of her before he had ever set eyes on her:

> I longed for you before I met you, my mind beheld your presence sooner than my eyes. Your renown was the first envoy of your face. . . . My eyes saw you by day, my mind by night, when the eyes are overcome by serene sleep. You who thrilled while still unseen, what will your presence do? I burned, though the fire was far away![17]

It is very clear how widely recognized it has been that such dream visions are useful literary devices. This is not in dispute. Consider just one example: a dream from the German poet, dramatist, and novelist Heinrich von Kleist's play *Das Katchen von Heilbronn oder die Fuerprobe. Ein grosses historisches Ritterschauspiel.* In this "double dream," Katchen "sees her future husband in a dream," seeing both his "form and face."[18] That man, Count Wetter vohn Strahl himself, "has likewise seen his future wife in a dream." Blankenagel makes the following point:

> Kleist motivates the heroine's affection, which outwardly seems love at first sight, by basing it on her vision of Strahl. The attraction which the Count has for her by virtue of this dream is like an irresistible, magic power. It is mysterious and, after all, about as inexplicable as romantic love at first sight. But for Kathchen, the dream is born of heaven and carries divine assurance, for with childlike faith she believes that in answer to her prayer God has allowed her future husband to appear to her in a dream.[19]

That such things actually occur and in surprisingly large numbers again goes unmentioned. We will also see these appeals to the individual's religion, as guiding their ideas regarding the source of the experience, turning up again and again beyond the curated confines of fiction.

In a shortly summarized Serbian folktale, the daughter of an emperor was married thirteen times, but each of her bridegrooms died on the night of the wedding. Another prince, however, set out of her castle after he had "fallen in love with her through a dream."[20] Across Europe and farther East, these visions are widely found. Just as the *Hikaye*, a shared dream that "has two lovers meeting in a dream before later meeting in life," is a long-recognized trope in eastern European folklore, the same was true much further afield.[21]

In the Jewish tale *The Angel's Daughter*, Yoel, the youngest of seven sons, dreamed he was in a strange city in a land unknown. Crowds lined the streets, apparently waiting for the "daughter of an angel" who lived in a palace on a golden mountain to ride through the city. She came once a year, and the people looked to see if she still had her dove, as they considered it a blessing. Yoel saw her, a woman of astonishing beauty dressed in white, perched atop a similarly heavenly horse. Suddenly, thunder and lightning came crashing down, the horse reared up, and the dove took flight. Yoel took it upon himself to search for the dove so he could bring it back to the princess. Making his search, he eventually tracked it down near a tree overgrown with white flowers. Just as he was within arm's reach, he awoke from the dream. That day, his mother said to him, "Your six older brothers have each married beautiful brides, and now it is time for you to be wed." But Yoel, still remembering his dream, told her, "The only one I will marry is the daughter of an angel, the one I saw in my dream." Needless to say, after many challenging adventures, travel, and toil, Yoel tracked down the real dove after entering the lair of Azazel, the fallen angel, and snatching it from his grasp before finally finding and marrying the princess.[22]

LOVE IN THE EAST

According to the old Persian tale *The Story of Ashraf Khan*, one night Ashraf dreams that he is mounted upon a white horse and ascending toward the sun. He finds himself in a garden "beautifully green and fresh" and sees impressive structures of white marble. Like Maxen, he enters a place where he sees a "maiden of surpassing beauty," whom he instantly falls for. Ashraf dreams of her again, this time with her seemingly asking for his help that she is kept in bondage. Ashraf can no longer wait and travels into the sunset on horseback for twenty days in pursuit of his dreams. After a long and perilous journey full of marvels and treachery, even suffering "a thousand tortures" in his quest for love, Ashraf reaches a mysterious city populated by strangers speaking in tongues. Here he is told by a voice that his dream showed him a real person, Shamsa Banu, the daughter of Karywan Sham. After many further trials and almost falling dead in the desert, Ashraf, with the help of a *peri* (a winged spirit known for their beauty), arrives at the paradisiacal abode of his dreams and sees her. "For long I have beheld you in my dreams," she tells him, "and the good tidings of your coming have been with me." He and his new wife live happily together from then on.[23]

Another ancient example from the first century CE *Histories of Alexander* has Zariadres (212–188 BCE), king of the Caspian countries, and Odatis magically meeting in their shared space (466–67). The marriage is a cross-cultural one between a Median (ancient Iranian) and a Scythian (ancient nomads who came from farther east to eastern Iran). Zariadres dreams of a girl of the Marathi people, close to the northern borders of Media. According to the narrative, she dreamed alike and "saw Zariadres in a dream and became enamored of him, while the same passion for her attacked him in the same way." It is made very clear they have not seen each other in real life, and makes the important point that "presumably descriptions of their dreams are enough for the two families to realise who they are and enter into correspondence."[24]

These, in fact, are truly old ideas. In Genesis 2:21, Adam is put into a deep and ecstatic sleep, during which time God is said to have taken one of his ribs and created Eve. However, as laid out by psychoanalyst and former student of Freud, Theodor Reik, "Almost all commentators agree that in his dream Adam saw God take a rib from his side and close the wound. Then he saw the woman and immediately, or 'after a time the woman he had seen in his dream is brought unto him,' he recognizes her."[25] The legendary love story of *Yusuf and Zulaikha*, a general title given to many versions of a tale told in the Muslim world, has similar themes. This tale is old, and despite taking on its own life and identity later, developed primarily from an account in the Qur'an. The great Persian poet Nur ad-Din Abd ar-Rahman Jami, one of the most celebrated intellectuals of his age, had his own take on this tale in which Zulaikha "first sees her lover in a vision so powerful that lust impedes her from loving him truly."[26]

In the Arabian epic *Kitab Qissat al Muqaddam Ali al Zaibaq*, Adashir, son of the king of Isfahan, tells his father Babak that he does not want a wife. He had "fallen in love with a girl whom he saw in a dream." Later, an old woman tracks her down and discovers her to be Sara, the daughter of Babak's Jewish banker.[27]

In the thirteenth-century Byzantine love romance *Livistros and Rodamne*, the prince dreams of the beautiful princess Rodamne of India in the palace of Eros. He is so taken with her that he makes a long journey to India, finds her, and wins her hand after taking part in a joust. According to the tale, she had dreamed of him too and had been in love ever since. Schlauch, making a comparison between this tale and some others, makes the note that "it happens that both falling in love through a dream and the rescue of a stolen bride are favorite themes in the *lygisogur*"[28] (Norse fictional and chivalric legendary sagas), later noting that the *Rémundar saga Keisarasonar* (medieval Icelandic romance) is, in fact, "built on them."[29]

In the Turkish tale *Husnuguzel*, we find a young warrior in training dreaming of a beautiful woman three nights in a row, the most beautiful he has ever seen. He falls immediately in love with her and neglects his worldly duties in his melancholy—food, drink, and all. Very much in the vein of Maxen, no one understands his illness, and none of their attempts to help him succeed. Eventually, he convinces his mother and father to allow him to search for her, and he is offered a sword for his journey, which was one of great distances. Husnuguzel has many adventures, battles, trials, and tribulations in his search for the love of his dreams and eventually finds an old man who tells him both of her location, in a palace by the sea, and that she was apparently searching for him too. After carefully following instructions regarding how to get there and which incantations to recite at the entrance, he finally finds her. When she sees him, "she knew at once that this was the man with whom she had fallen in love in her dreams." They eat, drink, and make love with each other for a week afterward. After many further adventures, they do indeed live "happily ever after."[30]

In Turkey, too, the physical or spiritual quest for a beautiful woman first glimpsed in a dream is a very common motif. In something of an early indication of the kinds of connections that have been and might be made between the tales and the experiences individuals still have today, Walker and Uysal fascinatingly gave a real-life example after their presentation of the tale. Having spoken to the theme itself in folklore, the authors mention that they knew of an actual person "so beset by this obsession that he gnawed away most of his upper lip in his frustration at not being able to find again the girl glimpsed in his dream."[31]

Another related shared experience was given in the *Kathasaritsagara*, an eleventh-century collection of Indian legends. Padmavati told her friends that while staying in Meghavana, she dreamed of a man wearing matted hair coming from a certain temple and telling her that she should be reunited with her husband soon. Later that morning, she saw with astonishment her husband, Muktaphaladhvaja, bathing at the temple she had seen. Muktaphaladhvaja was later heard describing that he, too, had seen this temple in all its features in his dream and, upon seeing her, was told that she was the very woman he had seen in the dream.[32]

Tales of this kind may be found in impressive numbers across Indian literature, and at times they rather vividly and very particularly echo the European stories. One of those is from the *Dasakumaracharita*, a Sanskrit prose romance in which Prince Pramata, lying down under a tree, fancied himself "transported to a palace where he beheld a lovely maiden with whom he immediately fell in love."[33] Wondering upon awakening if this had been an ordinary dream or something more, a nymph appears and confirms the reality of the vision and that the woman seen by him was Princess Navamalika of Sravasti, to where the prince then left with haste. Later, disguised as a woman and with the help of a Brahman he made friends with on the way to the palace, he wins the affection of Navamalika. It is hard not to think of the adventures of the thirteenth-century laird and poet, Thomas the Rhymer, who, having lay dreaming beneath a tree, was similarly come upon and transported away.

Another tale seems to come from the ancient Indian epic *Brihatkatha*, known only by the references to it, the earliest being that of Subanhdhu in the seventh century. The handsome prince Kandarpaketu falls passionately in love with a maiden he "saw in a dream." He then sets out to find her. Princess Vasavadatta, the woman from his dream, had herself rejected every suitor to that point until she herself saw her heart's desire, Prince Kandarpaketu—likewise in a dream. They eventually do unite; however, this is not without first overcoming various treacherous adventures, obstacles, and drama. Such dream visions are "typical" in these kinds of tales.[34]

The moment in which love comes through a vision or dream is truly a convention common in both Persian and Indian romantic tales. Just like in the European dream visions and stories, the hero must often fight demons and other evils and pass other trials of strength in order to attain his lover. Such tales, too, are often modeled on Persian spiritual quests.[35] In *Gulshan-i 'Ishq*, a Sufi Indian romance from 1657 and based on older sources, we find Prince Manohar completely set on attaining the princess Madmalati—who lives far off in Maharasanagar—after falling in love with her in a dream. Having drifted off to sleep on a moonlit night after celebrating his coming of age, fairies carry him away to distant Maharasanagar and show him Madmalati. After some beautiful descriptions of the palace from above and the surrounding night scenes, and having found Madmalati, a similarly detailed description of her extraordinary beauty brings the dream to an end. After waking, Manohar, like so many of his European counterparts, travels over sea and land in his search. Like the heroes of medieval European romance, he comparably traverses dense jungles and wastelands before arriving at the palace of his beloved and finally uniting.[36]

Farther East

We continue farther East now, where such visions and dreams are myriad and feature in abundance right across the genres of literature. According to a Korean legend relating to Taejo of Goryeo, founder of the Goryeo Dynasty (918–1392), Yonggon, one of two sons who later changed his name to Yung, dreamed alike. A woman appeared who was "too beautiful for words," and he became fascinated by her and couldn't keep her from his thoughts. Soon after, on his way to the castle of Yongansong from his home in Songak, he met a beautiful maid. She was the "very woman with whom he tied the nuptial knot in his dream." Yung at once took her as his wife, and people called her "Lady Dream" owing to his having met her there first.[37]

Featuring something of a less romantic ending, *The Peony Pavilion*, or *The Return of the Soul*, is a romantic Chinese play written by Tang Xianzu in 1598. While resting at a hot spring, Xianzu's protagonist dreams of a handsome young man, who carries her off to a garden where they share some short-lived passions. This woman, in something of an extension of the kind of illness we had seen overtake Oemgus, died in her pining. Later, the very same man from her dream turns up, a young scholar who himself had "dreamed of a maiden who is none other than the protagonist."[38]

In a fantastical Chinese tale set during the Chin Dynasty (265–420) and hailing from Canton in the south, a young man named Pony dreams of a maiden who tells him, "I am the daughter of Hsu Hsuan-fang of Pei-hai, the previous magistrate here." She tells Pony she died four years ago but that a mistake was made, that they were destined to be together, and that he could help her return to life. She gives Pony the time and date of her next appearance. When that day came, hair mysteriously covered the floor near his bed. He soon realized that "this was the girl from his dream," after which she fully emerged. They later married and had children.[39] In *Huan-hun chi* (*The Return of the Soul*), a Chinese drama completed in 1898, Tu Li-ninan and the scholar Liu Meng-mei "fall in love in a dream." So strong, however, was Tu's passion for the man that she actually dies of lovesickness, "even though she has not actually met Meng-mei in the flesh." Later, however, she is resurrected and marries the scholar.[40] Something of interesting relation can be found in a Japanese *Kwaidan*, a kind of ghost story, that has the two woodcutters Mosaku and Minokichi taking shelter from a fierce storm in a ferryman's hut. Minokichi, by far the younger of the two, lay awake, disturbed by the "awful wind, and the continual slashing of the snow against the door." In the midst of the creaking and swaying hut, while Minokichi shivered beneath his raincoat, he saw by the snow light, the door having been flung open, "a woman all in white." She breathed, seemingly with malicious intent, over Mosaku and turned to Minokichi, who saw that she was of incredible beauty. "You are a pretty boy, Minokichi," she said, "and I will not hurt you now." The woman, seemingly sharing the same ethereal qualities as the apparition who we had seen appear to Aengus, then passed through the door, warning him that she would kill him if he spoke of her presence. While it took five years for Minokichi to realize who she was, he met and instantly fell in love with this very woman soon after, bumping into her on one of his routine excursions.[41]

While a comprehensive overview of such tales is not our purpose here, many more could be found in Japan, and this will not be our last stop there as the chapters continue to unfold. In the fairy tale *The Eight-Headed Serpent*, Susano finds himself walking by the river Hi. Lying down to sleep in a thicket of bamboo, he dreams of a beautiful maiden floating down the river and a great monster about to kill her. Later that evening, following the sound of voices, he finds the very same girl. Susano saves her from the predicted fate by killing the serpent that owned the land, which would have killed her like he had her other sister, and later unites with her.[42] While something as simple as a name may not reverberate through time, it is nevertheless fascinating that the legacy of such a dream would be remembered in this way.

OCEANIA AND BEYOND

The same dreams are dreamed in Polynesian tales too. In *Laieikawai*, a heroic romance from Hawaii, "Companion-in-suffering-on-the-plain," a beautiful woman of Kohala lives under strict taboo until the age of twenty. Once, while stringing *lehua* (pompom blossoms) in the woods, she has what seems to be a kind of dream vision in which she is carried away by the elepaio bird in the form of a handsome man. He brings her to be the bride of Kalamaula, the son of Kawaihae's chief, and asks for thirty days to consider it. For each night after, she dreams of "a handsome man, with whom she falls in love." Later, she runs away and wanders in the uplands of Pahulumoa until she is found by Puuhue, who brings her home to his lord Puuonale, the king of Kohala, "who turns out to be the man of her dream."[43]

According to one version of another Polynesian legend, after hearing strange music the fire goddess Pele "dreams" of traveling across the water encircling her island of Hawaii to Kauai and standing on the peak of Haupu. There, while "hovering unseen" out of her body, she sees that the sound she had followed for so long was that of the hula drum beat by Lohiau, the handsome young prince of Kauai. The beach is filled with dancers and musicians, with him being the center of attention. Pele takes the form of a beautiful woman to walk among them and eventually falls in love with the prince. This, however, was not her body. Her body has been "carefully watched by her brothers and sisters, who had dared not disturb it." With some striking parallels to the European visions, Pele then organizes a search party to find the prince. They travel through forests and encounter demons, gnomes, fairies, and other obstacles. When they arrive, they discover that Lohiau has died, and now they set out to retrieve his spirit, a quest that is successful. They later restore it to the prince's body.[44]

While this version does not end quite as happily ever after as some of the others we have seen, the analogous imagery and concepts are patently clear, and in some sense, the outcome is more comparable to the contemporary visions—which by no means always ultimately end so ideally. Our contention that the mere existence and popularity of such tales might speak to a connection between them and the kinds of actual experiences we have seen and will continue to see seems to be particularly valid among Polynesians. With their widespread belief in the movement of a literal and clairvoyant soul during sleep, they would have no issues in accomodating such ideas. It should not be surprising that the Polynesians, and myriad others, would offer many examples of déjà rêvé. Their beliefs that the soul literally separates and moves around the world during sleep mean that later seeing what one has dreamed would naturally follow as a possibility.

Shared Romance

While there isn't room here to flesh them out, there are no doubt far more relevant visions from broader Oceania. The belief in shared dreams may be found widely there. British anthropologist Beatrice Blackwood, in her work on the Melanesian Solomon Islands, noted "several instances" of "reciprocal dreams" among the Indigenous Melanesians. Relevant here is the type she recorded, in which "a man may dream of having connexion with a woman and the woman with the man. The next day the man will say to the woman, 'I dreamed about you last night. My skin wants you.' Then if the woman is willing they go to the bush (implying that they have sexual intercourse there)."[45] Very similarly, among the Gimi of Papua New Guinea, it is agreed that "women dream first" and that their power to dream often grants them the initiative in marriage. While it seems they knew each other beforehand, the following example is entirely relevant in that it seems to be implied that the same can occur in the opposite case.[46] Gillison heard that one named BohaEha married his wife due to a dream. He saw her come to his garden, asking to follow him. He threw a lighted firestick at her, and it stuck to her arm, burning her. He put it out with water, and the next day he met Revakione and spotted a sore on her arm. "What hit you?" he asked, to which she replied, "You burned me last night." "That's how she revealed herself to me," he said. The marriage was arranged soon after.* While it comes to mind that such a belief might be taken advantage of, the fact that such things would occur or were believed possible is an entirely reasonable extrapolation, particularly considering the extent to which dream clairvoyance is taken for granted there. Blackwood herself offered an instance from the Melanesian Solomon Islands, where a man noted that "sometimes my dreams come true." He dreamed of a man walking about with his arm around the neck of a certain girl. He went to the man who told him, "True, I did walk about with my arm round the girl's neck."[47]

Moving beyond Oceania from southern Canada and south through Montana, Native Canadian writer and member of the Blackfoot Indian confederacy Beverly Hungry Wolf gave a Blackfoot Indian legend in which a beautiful young woman was turning down all potential suitors because "her dreams had shown her a certain man who was to be her husband." Other details were forthcoming, including his light-brown hair, light skin, and a buffalo robe. Some days later, while out gathering firewood, "there suddenly appeared in front of her the man she had seen in her dream," every detail being duplicated. They married quickly after, although the tale doesn't entirely end so happily.[48]

One tale, "Ishka-Maatuk and the Thunderbird Boy," from among the Ojibways tells of a powerful medicine man and his beautiful daughter, Ishka-Maatuk. One day, a sorcerer of considerable repute, Limping Bear, arrives at the shores of their home at Ontario's Kasshabog Lake. Some weeks earlier, "he had dreamed of Ishka-Maatuk, whom he had

*As an aside, one of the oldest reciprocal, shared, or double dreams of this kind is to be found in the ancient Greek novel *Daphnis and Chloe*, in which both future lovers, despite never having met, dream of making love. See, Moxon, *Peter's Halakhic Nightmare*, 472. We will see in the next chapter that these reciprocal dreams of lovemaking, attested in the ancient world, still widely come to lovers to be.

never seen." He was so taken with her beauty that he decided to travel the long distance to Kashishibog Village and find her. He "recognized Ishka-Maatuk immediately from his dream." After failing with an offer of gifts, the sorcerer successfully attained her hand using a rather potent potion on her father. Not being exactly like the romantic tales we have seen, Little Bear was clearly a ne'er-do-well, and his new wife escapes and lives with another. Limping Bear himself was later punished with death.[49]

In a folktale from Panama, *The Louse-Drum*—said within to be from somewhere "far away,"—a king holds a banquet for princes to come and vie for his daughter's hand, as was done in those days. There would be a game wherein the princes who guessed what the rum was made from would have her. No one, however, succeeds. When an old man guesses correctly, she runs away. Traveling through forests, over rivers, and past villages, she eventually comes to the city of a king and comes into his employment. When she finally sees the prince of that city, he recognizes her, saying, "You look like the princess my heart has dreamed of." If the suggestion might be that he simply pined after one as beautiful as her, the princess makes clear what has occurred when she states in reply, "You've seen your princess in dreams. Now see her in life." They later marry.[50]

Although with a slightly less directly veridical bent, there is value in offering the following African tale that begins with a king staring up at the stars.* One in particular kept his attention, and he said, "If that star were a woman I would marry her!" In his dreams that night, he saw that same star come down to where he stood, "like a white crowned crane onto a lake." That evening, his chief minister announced to him, "There is a lady to see you your Majesty. She says you asked her to marry you." The king was particularly astonished to see that the girl

*Country of origin is not given; however, Zimbabwe seems the most likely candidate based on the name Nyachero being most popular there.

coming toward him "shone like the stars in the Milky Way," suggesting the connection between her and his dream experience of the previous night. This is confirmed when she tells him, "I am Nyachero, daughter of the star. Last night you said you wanted to marry me," which they did that very same night![51]

There is a related reference in the mythology of the African Mvet, or Fang people, from Gabon in which the daughter of Angone Endong tells her father she had a dream in which a certain Zong Midzi appeared to her (by magic) and that now she wanted to marry no one else.[52]

LOVE IN LITERATURE

Many more of these legendary, poetical, romantic, and folkloric dreams and visions could be presented here, although the point has been made. The idea itself is also very commonly found throughout a broad range of literary works, even in the present century. Just as the experiences persist, so too does their representation in literature. Although this is not the primary aim of this chapter as we approach its end, numerous examples could easily be given. Samuel Coleridge-Taylor, who played a role in the British and American civil rights movements around the turn of the twentieth century, collaborated with playwright Paul Laurence Dunbar on an operatic romance entitled *Dream Lovers*, which was performed in 1898. The story has a Madagascan prince and a woman of mixed race who "first meet in a dream." They later "recognize one another in real life, immediately fall in love, and wed."[53]

Former British prime minister Benjamin Disraeli, in his somewhat autobiographical *Contarini Fleming*, included a related kind of dream vision that begins in a Venetian church. His character was in the habit of spending time here, and it was full of tombs from his family line. While becoming entirely enamored with the swells of a beautifully singing choir, seemingly to the point of entering a visionary state, Contarini's mind "wandered in delightful abstraction." The music stops—in his mind, at least—and he beholds a most beautiful woman kneeling at the altar. Lowering a black veil from her face, she wears a great melancholy on her features. At some point the scene overwhelms him, and he falls into something of a deep slumber in which he sees nobles passing him, then later his father—who eyed him severely—and eventually the lady from the altar. She held a crucifix of ebony, and tears came down her face. He wished to go to her; however, he awoke and found no woman, and nothing but puzzled looks as he asked if anyone had seen her. After wandering looking for her, simply convinced this was no ordinary experience, Contarini spends time wondering and asking around, but to no avail. Sometime afterward, at the Malbrizzi Palace, he "instantly recognised the kneeling lady of the church." Later, she says that she hadn't been to that church in that time period. Contarini concludes that it must have been a dream, and yet, it was due to this dream that he recognized her.[54]

These examples could be multiplied a hundredfold as they are represented in popular, obscure, and even pop culture–related literary genres. The likes of George Orwell's seminal *Nineteen Eighty-Four* could be pointed to, wherein the protagonist Winston dreams of his later lover, Julia, before he has actually spoken to her for the first time.[55] Similarly, Rudyard Kipling's *Brushwood Boy* has both protagonists dreaming of each other for many years before they finally meet.[56]

It is true that many works of literature look to the past for inspiration. It is true that dreams and visions of these previous kinds are implemented in myriad literatures toward very particular ends. It is also true, however, that some of those ideas, such as the poetical/romantic dream, vision, or shared dream, *actually do occur* among the general population, and often entirely divorced from those traditions. Scholars commonly elucidate in great detail the relationships between visions, spend time distinguishing between types, and attempt to ascertain the character and motives of the visionaries and their authors. They often seem set on assuming such an experience must have an antecedent, literary or otherwise, as indeed they often do. The idea that such visions and dreams are so fundamentally part of the human experience that, of *course*, they would turn up among unconcerned cultures is rarely acknowledged. It is undeniably the case, however, that visions and dreams that are entirely indistinguishable from those found in those renowned texts are still ongoing. The same visions that came to the heroes of those medieval romances and from other sources still come to "ordinary" people—the very same visions we had seen the ordinary folk try to elicit so widely with their divinations and their magical poetry. If this seems overly speculative up to this point, these next explorations will attempt, at least to some degree, to more convincingly bridge this gap.

6
Love at Second Sight
How Lovers Still Meet in Their Dreams

> *Romantic dreams, say the skeptics, are for poets and the love starved. But are they? Couldn't they also be the result of still unknown vibrations sent across time and space by the deep emotions of compatible humans?*
>
> VINCENT GADDIS

The folklore and the legends, the divinations and the ditties; the records are in agreement on one thing. For an impressive amount of time and across a wide number of cultures, often entirely unconnected, people have come to believe that dreams might truthfully reveal the location of others—people either known or unknown to the individual and either alive or dead. They have come to believe that one may be met in a dream before being met in life, and this refrain often comes to the dreamer even before the meeting takes place. Why is this so? Among the uncountable traditions and "superstitions," which may or may not have an experiential basis, certain of those stand out in the extent to which they are seemingly still reported and recorded. While there may be many other kinds that speak more powerfully to this reality, very little has been written in this light about the kinds of accounts we have seen so far and those that now follow, especially from the cross-cultural and historical perspective, and certainly within the context of déjà rêvé. We tread here on fertile ground.

Just like the renowned romances, poems, and dream visions we have seen, and just as we have already noted correspondences between the old and the new, people in surprisingly large numbers *still* claim to have met their loved ones in a dream before meeting them in real life. Whatever the links between these two facts, however important or incidental, it would seem to be unlikely that there are none. In speaking to the links between the old and the new, we will see that these widespread experiences may be related to the kinds of archaic and endearing traditions and beliefs we have encountered to this point. Indeed, in some cases we will see the reality of this, and at the very least we might ponder the part that the recognized déjà rêvé phenomenon and its visionary relatives have played in the engendering of beliefs, traditions, lyric, and art. However many other questions that may arise, this alone is surely a worthy endeavor.

Like the previous accounts in which dreams informed of another's location, it soon becomes apparent that some of the most important connections between, for example, the oldest Greco-Roman and medieval romances and the kinds of scattered accounts later collected by folklorists among ordinary people, are in their capacity to impel action. This is perhaps what comes out most strongly in the stories. These visions and dreams have been and continue to be agents of change in the life of the individual. And where other than love might such a change be felt so powerfully? These are no mere records of disparately experienced and collected anomalous occurrences that may or may not be explained "mundanely," or dispassionately filed away, but a record of often life-altering events in the lives of the individual, his or her wider community, and beyond. It is to these strange and mysterious synchronicities between lovers that we now finally come.

DESTINY, DREAMS, AND THE POWER OF LOVE

Irish poet and polemicist Bernard Shaw, in one of his letters to his lover, Mrs. Patrick Campbell, about halfway through their romance, wrote, "I saw you first in a dream forty-three years ago. I have only just remembered it." Mrs. Campbell was to play the role of Eliza Doolittle in Shaw's *Pygmalion*, a play that he wrote for her. In another letter, he tells her, "You are a figure from the dreams of my boyhood; let me have my dream out."[1] Shaw's *Pygmalion*, then, owes its very existence to a dream he had as a boy.

Born in 1641, Swedish chemist and geologist Urban Hjärne, in his autobiography, described how he first met his future wife in a dream he had while staying in Cologne, Germany. Profoundly, Hjarne had initially been set on a plan to marry into a rich family in order to secure his financial future; however, this dream experience changed all that, showing him rather that he would marry a "young and virtuous but poor woman." A number of years later, in 1676, Hjarne met the woman from his dream in Stockholm and stated that "everything happened exactly as predicted by the dream in Cologne."[2] The same reluctance we had touched on earlier that people have had to share such experiences is an old one. Speaking to the relation between Hjarne's uncanny experiences and his professional exploits, Hjalmar Fors said, "let himself be guided to his choice of spouse by a precognitive dream. It would have been inopportune for Hjarne to talk about such subtle matters as precognitive dreams and little spirit-men in the context of the commission on witchcraft."[3] Miss Mercy, co-founder of the Frank Zappa–produced band the GTOs, expressed the same sentiment when she was asked during an interview where she met American singer-songwriter and musician Shuggie Otis. She replied simply, "I met him in a dream, I really did. It was in Los Angeles. I met him in a dream and they said you're gonna marry this person and I did. It was crazy."[4]

Finnish American writer and sociologist Mavis Hiltunen Biesanz, writing of her childhood in Finland, recounted something her grandfather had told her while they were fishing together on a lake. The author wished to know more about him, a man who was later to die at the age of just thirty-eight. He told her that one evening in 1893, the night before he met his future love, after coming all the way to Michigan some months apart, he "saw her in a dream." She was "rosy-cheeked and lively." "I knew her the minute she stepped off the train," he told her. "She was the girl in my dream even to the clothes she was wearing. I never again thought of going back to Finland."[5]

We have seen these dreams may bring the individual to move, to travel, to leave their lives behind; it is made clear here too that they may similarly convince them to stay. The grandfather of Scandinavian author Selma Lagerlöf, who was the first woman to win the Nobel Prize in Literature, was similarly moved and affected, though not strictly by his own visionary experience. He himself was entirely against marriage; however, when his sweetheart "revealed to him that she had seen him in a vision before their meeting," that had apparently "settled the matter."[6] Even the visionary experience of another was enough to move this man to action very much in opposition to his frame of mind before the experience.

One informant told psychiatrist Bernard Beitman that she dreamed of the one she would marry before they met. He was older than her and had "salt-and-pepper hair." Exactly as we had seen in the legend and the lore, she described him to her mother the following morning and shared that she was now convinced they would marry, despite the fact that he was unknown to her. "Two weeks later," she told the author, "I met the man I'd dreamed about. He looked identical to the person in my dream." They married after two months, and the informant interpreted the experience as speaking to the reality of "destiny."[7]

Herein lies the intrigue, the power, and the importance of these déjà rêvé and related experiences. As with the old tales, decisions are made, lives are altered, and destiny is set into motion. *The Christian*

Herald—a weekly American newspaper that ran between 1878 and 2006—offered the case of Bella Cook, an invalid who was apparently confined to her bed for thirty-five years. According to the story, around the time her illness began, she met Mr. Cooke while she was in Hull, a man who was later to become her husband. Cooke told Bella's sister that "some time before, he had dreamed that Bella was to be his wife. Now he saw her for the first time, and she was identical with the woman he had seen in his dream." They were married later.[8]

Notable rock climber and author Pat Ament wrote briefly, although not without a sense of great import, of his own experience of this kind. "I met my wife in a dream several years before I met her," he wrote. He explains that he might not have recognized her if it weren't for the dream. The overall message of the dream seemed to be that they would eventually be together, and Ament came away with the sense that certain things are, in fact, predestined in some way. "Do I comprehend the mechanics of such experience? Not likely," Ament wrote, before concluding, "I sense, however, that the relationship of any person to any given day is in effect and perhaps was formed prior to the living of that day."[9]

Another account speaking to how brief these references often are, comes from the *Adair County News* newspaper that ran weekly in Kentucky between the years 1887 and 1987. Tucked away in an issue from 1901 is a single paragraph that states: "W. W. Carter, aged fifty-eight, and Miss Ermine Rains, aged eighteen, of Maupin, Clinton county, were married recently. The strange fact about the wedding is that Carter found his wife in a dream, so to speak. A short time ago he had a dream in which he saw the girl. He did not know, he says, that there was a girl by that name until his dream. He lost no time in making her acquaintance, and as a result, they were married."[10] Author Carol Chapman recorded something similar in her dream journal in 1990. "I first met my husband in a dream that told me he was the man I should marry," she recorded. In the dream, Carol saw the man on a stage, with a spotlight upon him. Very soon after, she noticed a man from behind in a cafeteria whom she thought she recognized. After seeing his face, she says, "It was the man in my dream. It was very hard for me to approach him when I first saw him in my waking life." They were married for seven years at the time of the anecdote's publication.[11]

In his book, *A Gift of Barbed Wire*, Robert McKelvey—a former marine who served in Vietnam—briefly recounted his own dream, dedicating just a single paragraph to what was clearly a rather moving experience. McKelvey writes the following, having first recounted a rather dark dream he would have while living in New York in 1963: "I also dreamt about my wife before I met her. When I later saw her I was stunned! We met in Da Lat. A friend of mine introduced her. After we had gone out together a few times I told her that I already knew her from my dream."[12] Rob Ellison, in his memoir dealing with his journey through grief after the death of his wife, also gives short shrift to a dream in passing. Tena, a Franciscan bath lady who worked in a hospice, reminded him of his wife when she was younger. He says he dreamed of a girl like her when he was starting high school and that, even then, he wondered if he would actually meet her in life. "I sure did," he concluded himself, "and when I first saw her, I knew she was the girl in my dream."[13]

Roger Garfitt, a freelance writer and winner of the Gregory Award in 1974—who has held many prestigious positions, such as editor of *The Poetry Review*—writes very briefly in his memoir of a related dream. Garfitt, in fact, gives us a rather fitting analogy regarding his friend Ron, who "had a story straight out of the troubadours' chronicle, of a girl with Pre-Raphaelite hair, long twisting strands of a brown so light she might have been spun out of the air." According to Ron, "He had first seen her in a dream." She was standing at the top of a temple staircase. Later, standing on the opposite side of a London pub, he saw "so clearly the girl from the dream that he hardly dared to speak to her." They had been together ever since at that time.[14]

Francis and Bridges, in their work *A Golden Love,* note that "many golden couples reported feeling the presence of their future partner, seeing them in a dream, or receiving a vision about their future sacred partnership." In one of the examples they received, a woman wrote the following:

> In this dream we were united soul-to-soul. From that second, over the next several months, I felt he was already with me. I had a complete knowingness, not just a hope or even a belief, but a rock-solid knowingness that he was on his way. I even knew how we would find each other. Sure enough, he showed up as he promised in that precognitive and highly spiritual dream.[15]

Similarly, author Kathleen Vande Kieft writes of a couple she had known who were "introduced by their guidance in a dream before they ever met." Kieft goes on to note that "many other friends" have been led to each other through similar means.[16]

It is clear, then, that the initial experiences themselves may sometimes be extremely powerful and moving and affect the individual's life. As with the tales, this may come even before the later "confirmation" magic is set into motion. It is very clear that if accounts were dispersed among people similarly in the classical world, the Middle Ages, and certainly the early modern period, there would have been more than enough raw material to suggest connections between the literary and the literal. If such ideas are no longer "in the air," they are certainly there to be found just below the surface and explicitly comparable to their historical counterparts.

THE OLD LOVE AND THE NEW LOVE

One of the stories attached to the history of the famous Tuscany galleon, *Admiral of Florence,* tells of an *infanta* (a daughter of the ruling monarch of Spain or Portugal, especially the eldest daughter who was not heir to the throne) who dreamed she was to embark on the galleon when a person appeared to her with the distinct features of a foreign nobleman whom she was apparently to marry when the fleet arrived at its destination. In light of this experience, she decided to sail on the *Admiral* despite "all the remonstrations of her relations." Later, when the galleon came to Tobermory Bay in Scotland, a Spanish commander was invited on board, and "immediately the infanta set eyes on him, and she declared that this was the man she had seen in her dream, and he was to be her future husband." The ship, however, came to a tragic end, and all but one perished.[17]

English war correspondent and author George Frederick Abbott, in his 1903 work on Macedonian folklore, gives the example of a woman who in her youth carried out exactly one of the kinds of divinations we had seen earlier involving a ritual and a lyric, despite being married at the time. That night, she dreamed of a young man she had never seen standing behind her husband. The dream soon came again, this time the youth wearing a snow-white kilt and holding a canary in each hand, one of which he strangled before handing her the other. Not long after, as she describes it, "her lover died, and in course of time she was wooed and won by the strange youth who smiled at her in her sleep, and whom she recognized immediately upon seeing him in real life."[18]

More lately, Rita Rogers—psychic to many, including Princess Diana—spoke to a number of accounts of this kind, particularly in the context of the possibility that the recognition between lovers might relate to their having known each other in a past life. In one of those, a woman named Carla said that when walking into a work function, it was "such a shock" when the man who was to be her future husband walked into the room, she "instantly recognized him." "I was about to go and say hello but I realized that we had never met," she told. "I realized that I had seen him the night before, not in the flesh but in an extremely vivid dream. He was wearing exactly the same blue cord jacket, navy shirt, and chino trousers." Carla notes that she had told her flatmate about this dream that morning, including these details, and for this reason, she was sure the event had merit and wasn't imagined.[19]

French physician and scholar Maurizio Macario, who explored topics related to sleep, dreams, and somnambulism (sleepwalking) in his 1857 *Du Sommeil, des reves et du somnambulisme*, investigated and gave the case of Angele Bobin, a baker's daughter from the small French town of La Charite-sur-Loire. Having had several aspirants for her hand in marriage, she refused them all and prayed for guidance. She afterward dreamed of a young man in traveling clothes, wearing a large straw hat, and heard an inner voice tell her that this was to be her husband. Based on this dream, she decided to tell her parents she would not be marrying the man they had chosen for her. Some time later, at a town ball, Inglis relayed, "What was her surprise when she met the young traveller who appeared in her dream!" They married soon after. Macario, intrigued by the tale, followed up, found the man, and proclaimed the case to be "of the most complete exactitude."[20]

From a collection of pioneer histories, we read the story of Tamar Loader Ricks, born in September 1833 in Oxfordshire, England. She was less than happy about having to leave England for Utah and leave her sweetheart behind. One night, while out on the plains, she dreamed of him and also of another man accompanying him wearing a slouch hat and walking with a limp. In the dream, her sweetheart faded away while the other man, this stranger, remained. When Mormon pioneer Thomas Edwin Ricks came to town some time later, she saw him leaning on a wagon wheel and smiling at her. Tamar took her mother's hand and said, "Mother, that's the man I am to marry—the one I saw in my dream." There was now "no doubt" in her mind that this would be her lover, and they married the following spring, on March 27, 1857.[21] Much later, author and medium Jodi Livon noted something alike regarding her own related experience: a dream she had six months before meeting her husband-to-be, Jason. "The dream," she writes, "before I met Jason, ministered to me on a purely unconscious level. It helped calm my fears about moving quickly before these fears could hit." This was in reference to the fact that the dream she had written about only came to light after they had met. "Each time a coincidence occurred, it felt like a hug from the Universe."[22]

Tuckahoe in Virginia was built between 1733 and 1740 by the prominent Randolph family, some of whom were soldiers and politicians. Thomas Mann Randolph, grandson of one of the original builders, married Harriet Wilson from Richmond after just such an experience. During a dream, he saw a young lady open his closet door and bring him a glass of water (recalling the earlier folklore). Randolph claimed that he had seen her face in such clear detail that he would recognize her if they ever met and resolved that if they ever were to meet, they would marry. Some years later, as it happened, they did meet, and they did marry.[23]

In the memoir of humorist David Ellis Dickerson, he writes of an episode in which, after failing to court a certain young woman, Jessica, she relates completely in passing a dream she had. To Dickerson's dismay on this occasion around three months after they had first met, she wanted his help to hook up with another man in the lettering department. "You don't understand," she said. "I dreamed about him last week. I didn't know who he was then. But then I saw him today for the first time—the guy from my dream. It's freaking me out. I have to go talk to him, but I'm terrified." Dickerson seemed to think nothing of it; however, the impact on Jessica herself seems clear. She and the other man were dating by the end of that week.[24]

Clinical psychologist Sally Rhine Feather gave the account of a woman who had a dream "so real," as she describes it, "I related it to my mother the next morning." She saw a tall man with dark curly hair and blue eyes and told her mother that was the man she was going to marry, despite having never seen him before. Six months later, she saw him. "I saw his face. He looked just like the young man in my dream, except that he had a cap on, and I couldn't see his hair. It later turned out to be black and curly." Three months later, they would marry.[25] It is interesting to note that in this case, the woman seemed to recognize the man a few days earlier from behind, and then she recognized him even without his characteristic dark curly hair. These kinds of observations may be important to note for anyone interested in conducting future studies on these topics, particularly as it pertains to the potentiality of the déjà rêvé explanation.

While in cases such as the following there are fewer particulars, the impact of the experience on those involved is plain to see and bears examination for this reason along with the large timescales involved. Bettine Clemen, an informant of nurse and psychotherapist Joyce Vissell, and her co-author told her that while living alone by Medicine Lake in Minnesota after separating from her husband, her friend Zanna visited her. "I had a dream about you last night," she told Clemen. "I dreamed that I was at your wedding." Zanna dreamed that she had been married to a man named Peter David Longley, although Clemen knew no one by that name. Five years later, while aboard the ship *Queen Elizabeth II*, she met the cruise director. "Can you imagine what I felt," she told the author, "when I learned his name was Peter Hovenden Longley!" Clemen noted that "naturally" she was curious, despite the middle name not matching the dream. "Two names out of three, I reasoned, was pretty darned accurate." Clemen composed a song for this man of her dreams over a year later and sent him the tape. It wasn't long before they married. The dream still remains written in Zanna's journal, and she still hopes to understand why his middle name was David in that dream, which ultimately changed her life and inspired her, as we had seen with the troubadours and their amor de lonh, to create art in its wake.[26] The author and Dr. Kleber Mbenuon offered a similarly "third-person" account. He noted that around seven months before he met the woman who would become his wife, his friend had an important dream to tell him. "In that dream, she saw my future wife and described her to me in an e-mail. The description fit, down to every detail but one." She was living in Cameroon at the time of the dream, and the author was in the United States.[27]

Returning to the work of author Kathleen Vande Kieft, she writes that one night she dreamed of a man she had never seen before approaching her. He was tall, with striking visual features, brown eyes, dark hair, and a "spirited, friendly personality." He walked up to Kieft, took her hand, and said, "Have we met? I'm Kevin." That same morning, Kieft awoke to a phone call from a close friend inviting her for breakfast. While they were having coffee, her friend announced she had met a new man over the weekend; his name was Kevin. "That's funny," Kieft told her, before relaying the dream. "I had accurately described her new boyfriend in detail," she writes, "including his direct, enthusiastic personality."[28]*

One experience that dealt with a vaguer identity, yet had a powerful worldly impact, was that of Richard, as given by artist and author Suz Andreasen. Richard dreamed the same dream for around ten years, in which he was at an unfamiliar high school and speaking to his friends. He would then sense a woman, look behind him, and see her. He could recall her long, dark, and straight hair, though not her face. With such vague details, one might expect him to correlate the dream with one of the many women of that description he would have come across in that decade; however, this wasn't the case. "Recently I began dating a woman and I fell in love with her," Richard contin-

*It should be made clear that in certain cases there is a suggestion that there is more than a simple visual confirmation involved in confirming the dream to the individual. It may not be as simple, that is, as some random individual out in the world matching the dream. This should be taken into account in any future scientific work in this area. Carolina Williamson, for example, dreamed of a "tall, handsome man with green eyes and dark hair" as a teenager. She imagined herself with this person, and, according to her, "When I was nineteen, I married a man who fit the physical description but didn't have the right character." They divorced three years later. See Vissell, J., and Vissell, B., *Meant to Be*, 58.

ued. "I realized she was the woman from my dream. How strange is that?" Whatever its ultimate origin or meaning, it was upon the basis of this dream that Richard was considering asking her to marry him; however, he felt that she might be skeptical of such reasoning if he were to forward it.[29] One our own internet informants had a similar experience:

> *I saw my husband of 10 years in my dreams before I met him. I knew the minute I saw him he was the one. I was engaged to someone else and eventually broke it off and moved in with my husband after dating 4 days.*[30]

Lore and Long Distance

As with the romantic dreams and visions we have previously seen, these experiences may truly be found in all quarters widely across cultures. In a biography of twentieth-century Torah scholar Reb Yechiel Mechel Rabinowicz, we read how his father had arranged the marriage of his sister, Perele, and another named Aharon Moshe Leifer. Perele traveled with her father from Lithuania to meet this man in Hungary, and then her father went back home. Having no mother and father with her, she felt very alone in this pivotal period of her life; however, that night she dreamed of them. They encouraged her not to worry and told her to "look at this." Her father opened a door, behind which stood a young man with long *peyos* (the Hebrew term for sidelocks), before continuing, "Here is your chosen." Later that same day, she met the prospective groom, "the [same] young man she had seen in her dream." They later became engaged.[31]

The life of Charles Puckett, an informant of Lewis and Hamilton, was similarly reoriented by a dream. In 1957, according to Puckett, "I had a dream about the girl that I was supposed to marry. It turned out NOT to be the girl I was engaged to." Later, traveling to St. Louis for work in 1958, Puckett walks into a restaurant in Missouri, sees a girl behind the counter, and, per his own words, "I had to do a double-take because she was the same person I saw in my dream!" This meeting would be the beginning of a forty-eight-year marriage.[32]

Gerald Cottingham of Houston, Texas, an informant of Ann Spangler, illustrated again of these experiences that even after meeting the woman he saw in his dream, he was not compelled to tell her or anyone this. Cottingham notes that in his sophomore year of high school, rounding a corner with an armful of books, "there she was—the girl from my dream." While they dated, Cottingham's being drafted meant they were to drift apart, and this girl, Evelyn Fleming, had engaged another. Just as the hero of romance might dream of a distant maiden but lose many hundreds of years of time during their otherworldly sojourn, Cottingham had to wait over forty years before he reunited with his dream bride. After the death of Evelyn's husband, however, they met and renewed their love. "She was the same girl I'd loved since I was twelve," Cottingham concluded. "Finally she became my wife."[33]

American historian and professor Andrew Burstein noted briefly that in the decade of the American Revolution, a certain fisherman along the Massachusetts coast claimed to have seen his future wife in a dream before meeting her. He said that he had recognized her because of the moles on her cheek, the details of which he had seen in the dream.[34] Rather than so brief, some of these dreams are sometimes quite elaborate and beautiful and as we had seen in the opening chapter, echo the legendary and literary tales in this way. American author and motivational speaker Chip St. Clair writes in his memoir of the most "vivid, wonderful dream" of his life and felt compelled to jot it down before the details escaped his mind. St. Clair dreamed he was on a ship, alone at sea, seeming to be sailing for weeks in search of land. A dolphin soon loudly pushed itself from the water and through the air, each time coming closer to his ship until it landed, with the dreamer stepping aside. "To my amazement," wrote St. Clair, "upon touching the surface of my ship, the dolphin changed shape. Now kneeling before me, it had become a young woman with flowing dark hair and eyes the color of the sea. I was speechless." With St. Clair enraptured and enamored, the woman took his hand, and they kissed before the dream ended. After abruptly leaving the subject, some time later in the memoir, the author—during one of his first days back at school—looked up the stairs and saw "familiar sea-blue eyes" staring directly into his. "She had long, dark hair that seemed to flow like cascading water when she walked. Her eyes glittered like sunlight off a serene lake. I stood dumbfounded as she came toward me, a slight smile on her lips. As mysterious winged creatures engaged in battle inside my stomach, a cold wave swept over me—she was the girl from my dream." They were later to marry.[35]

In the fascinating biography of TJ Kearney, a 107-year-old man from the southwest of Arkansas, his daughter, Janis Kearney, relates an incident from his life that occurred during Christmas 1936, culminating at a point in the book under the header *A Dream Come to Life*. Kearney's dream, which at the time of recalling he considered to be "as clear as if it happened today," had him driving to the Pine Bluff main station. Getting out of the car and heading to the terminal, he saw the girl standing there as if waiting for him. "I swear, in all my years of traveling," Kearney told it, "I hadn't ever seen a girl as pretty as this one." She had a head of "coal black hair" and shiny, light brown eyes that Kearney swore he could "never forget." The woman soon speaks to him. "You come to carry me home, James? I'm your wife." She repeated this multiple times while moving away from him, waiting for him to catch up. Later, at a friend's house for New Year's Eve, Kearney goes to speak with his friend Gracie, who has a friend with her. At a glance, he feels he knows her face. Soon, she is formally introduced to Kearney as Ethel Virginia, Grace's cousin. "I was sure I'd seen that girl's shy smile somewhere before," he said about the memory. "When our hands touched," he continued, "it was like electric currents went through me. I knew in one instance she was the girl from my dreams. She had the very same eyes and smiling mouth and the very same voice. I stood there shaking her hand with my mouth hanging open. She must've thought I was the biggest fool in Arkansas." Kearney explains that she had the same green suede shoes as in the dream. Kearney even specifically goes looking to confirm other aspects of the dream, such as the woman's coat. Although he didn't find the coat, Ethel herself later wore it: "Ethel's coat was as I remembered it in my dream, a light and dark green plaid coat, and I wasn't a bit surprised to see her in it." They married soon after. "I always wondered how my life might've turned out if it hadn't been for that Christmas Eve dream in 1936," Kearney concluded poignantly.[36]

MEN AND WOMEN OF OBSCURITY AND RENOWN

These visions and dreams manifestly alter the course of the experiencer's life. They have played some part in our individual and collective past and deserve attention. It is only when so many are collected together that their place in the record becomes clearer. Some of history's most renowned names, in fact, have claimed such things. The sixteenth-century Italian polymath Gerolamo Cardano, who wrote widely on subjects such as mathematics, astrology, and biology, recorded that he met his future wife in a dream.[37] Cardano, like some of our previous "seer types," claimed that numerous key episodes in his life were "heralded or accompanied by dreams."[38] Famed author and industrialist Arthur Edward Stilwell similarly believed that all of his important actions in life were somehow guided and that the information might come to him in dreams.* It isn't so hard to understand such a perspective when one considers that in 1974, at fifteen years of age, Stilwell dreamed that he

*According to the same *New York Times* article on Stilwell, only a "close-knit circle of friends" knew of his abilities, "which surfaced at the age of 4 when he could tell his mother which relative would be visiting them days before the person would arrive," something of great relevance to chapter 8.

would meet and marry a Genevieve Ann Wood in exactly four years. He knew of no such person, but he was sufficiently impressed that he put the experience to paper. Shortly after his nineteenth birthday, he met a "Jennie Wood" at church, and it was apparently mutual love at first sight. They soon married.[39]

Another German polymath and inventor of calculus, Gottfried Wilhelm Leibniz, wrote in 1765 that he had been "assured that a lady of a well-known court saw in a dream and described to her friends the person she afterwards married, and the hall in which the betrothal was celebrated and she did this before she had seen or known either the man or the place." While Leibniz was not convinced such things could not simply be explained by coincidence, he based this opinion on the unproven supposition that they were rare events.[40]

Pearl Tyler, daughter of the tenth president of the United States, John Tyler, married William Ellis, a member of the Virginia House of Delegates. Of interest here is that she "claimed to have seen him in a dream before they met." "I had the most amazing dream," she told her sister-in-law. "I know I saw the man I will someday marry. He was sitting on the porch of a cottage on the side of a hill. I walked up to him and he rose and came to meet me." The fact that she dreamed this exact dream two nights in a row convinced her of its reality as a vision of the future, which came to pass several weeks later while sitting in the state capital's public gallery. "I see the man of my dreams," she said to her sister-in-law as she pointed to one of the delegates seated below. They married soon after a "whirlwind courtship."[41] Martin de Lesseps (1730–1807), then French consul general at St. Petersburg is likewise said to have married Mlle Cayzergues, one of his ultimately two wives, "because she had seen him in a dream before they met."[42]

Professor of defense analysis at the Naval Postgraduate School, Anna Simons, spoke of Bashir, a thirty-year-old man from a long line of famous central Somali sheikhs. More specifically, she relayed of his father and his father's fourth wife that he reportedly "saw her in a dream before ever meeting her."[43] Something similar can be seen in the life of German botanist Georg Wilhelm Steller, a man who after extended travels through Siberia during the eighteenth century was said to know more of that land than anyone else. In 1728, he abruptly ended his studies and became obsessed with one Brigitta Helena Böckler, a woman "whom he believed to be the very woman he had seen in a dream while in Solikamsk" (an eastern Russian town).[44]

Returning to the realms of poetry for a moment, J. R. R. Tolkien, perhaps echoing a real event in his life, writes suggestively in his poem, *You and Me and the Cottage of Lost Play*, of his meeting with his wife, Edith, in dreams before their meeting:

> *You and me—we know that land*
> *And often have been there* [. . .]
> *In drowsy summer night,*
> *That You and I got lost in Sleep*
> *And met each other there*[45]

Twentieth-century Hungarian aristocrat and ballet dancer Romola de Pulszky dreamed three dreams that seemed to foretell her romantic future. In the first, she was backstage in the Budapest opera house when suddenly the door to the practice room opened, and a young man walked out, smiled at her, and left. The second had Romola sailing in the English Channel. Once ashore, she met three men, one of whom was the same slender young man from the previous night. The third and final dream had her in a baroque-style church filled with onlookers. She was walking toward the altar in a white dress when she saw the same young man from the last two nights standing and smiling at her. "A year later," she wrote, "the Russian ballet gave performances in Budapest. The instant I saw Nijinsky, I recognized him as the young man who had appeared in my three successive dreams." They married a year later in Argentina, in a baroque-style church, with de Pulszky dressed all in white. She often pondered these dreams and their nature, noting the "extraordinary clarity and detail and the great part that color played," later suggesting this could be an indication that the "signal was sent from some deeper part of the mind than the place of origination of ordinary dreams."[46]

American author Vincent Gaddis wrote an interesting article in a 1970 issue of the *Sedalia Democrat*, a Missouri-based daily, entitled *Romantic Dreams-Do They Ever Come True?* Gaddis offered a number of accounts, some of which we have seen, including that of prolific American actor Ralph Bellamy, who claimed to have had a premonition of his future wife when he was a young man. "That night," he writes, "I dreamed I was five years older and that my bride was alongside of me. She was blonde, beautiful, and talented. Her name was Catherine. It was exactly five years from the night of my dream that I married and went on my honeymoon. My bride was blonde, beautiful, and talented. Her name was Catherine. She fitted my dream picture perfectly."[47]

Relationship psychologist Susan Quilliam, in her work *Women on Sex*, which primarily deals with the sexual lives of women, has a mildly graphic dream from an informant in which a man came under her quilt and made love to her. She strongly and distinctly remembered certain details, such as his body odor, his chest, belly, and penis. "About a week later," she writes, "I met him and walked with him in some woods. We fondled each other and kissed, and his smell, his chest and belly and prick were exactly as in my dream. I already knew his body. We made love on later occasions, and he truly was the same as my dream."[48]

A well-known English Unitarian clergyman, Robert Collyer, relayed the story of a friend of his dreaming one night in the middle of a Pacific voyage. He saw a face in this dream, and it was mysteriously impressed upon him that this was eventually to be his wife. Seven years later, at a quarterly Quaker meeting in Bucks County, Pennsylvania, he "saw, in a Quaker bonnet, for the first time with his human eyes, that face he had seen in his dream." They married soon after![49] The author Dr. Donald

Schnell also made a reference to just such an experience in which he met his wife, Marilyn, author of *Fit for Life* and a pioneer in the vegetarian food movement, in 1992. "From the moment I saw her," Schnell writes, "I knew she was my soul mate. No words were exchanged, but I recognized her from my dreams."[50]

Time Waits for Some

Catherine Crowe, in her seminal *The Night-Side of Nature,* had an informant who dreamed of hearing a sound that attracted her to the window of a house in Edinburgh. Looking out (and in her haste) she dropped a ring from her finger into the whistling winds below. Donning her night clothes, she searched and searched, but she couldn't find it. Later in the dream, she met a young man at her front door carrying loaves of bread who presented her with the lost keepsake. According to Crowe, "some months afterwards, being at a party, she recognised the young man seen in her dream, and learnt that he was a baker." While it would be two years before the two would meet again, they eventually married.[51]

In contravention to the old platitude, time, it seems, does wait for certain men. There are an impressive number of accounts, some of which we have seen, in which the time frame between the dream and the meeting spans years, even decades. There may be an avenue of inquiry here for those interested, as it seems very unlikely that it would take such a length of time for something such as the déjà rêvé phenomenon to "kick in." Surely, one could assume the individual would have seen another who reminded them of that dream long before. Perhaps not, though. These are interesting questions to be pursued elsewhere. Dr. Michael Lennox, a practicing psychologist, gave the "remarkable" account of a woman who told in her fifties that a relationship from her earlier life "first appeared in a dream." She dreamed of the man very shortly before they met; it was she who assured him they would be together in the future. They did later meet in life and have a relationship for several years.[52]

Something else interesting that emerges in these accounts is that sometimes there are references to dreams in which the person dreamed of appears in the dream as they would be destined to look years later, as one of our own internet sources described:

> *Yes, I had the most vivid dream of my life where I met my twin flame. I was only twelve in real life, but she appeared out of nowhere. She appeared as she looks when I met her sixteen years later. We had a kiss, that was very reminiscent of our first kiss in real life. In my dream, I actually woke up. I felt the kiss as a real kiss. She just laughed and said 'I'll see you soon.' For years, I always wondered if I would meet that person in my dreams. About a month into separation, I finally realized that was my twin flame.*[53]

Another of our internet sources had a similar example and held on to the recorded dream for almost fifteen years until she met the person she considered to be the man from her dream.

> *I saw my future husband in a dream when I was 14. I still have a diary with a very detailed description of him. Met him when I was 30. In a dream he gave me a bracelet with a tiny wooden elephant. He gave me the same bracelet short[ly] before we started dating in real life.*[54]

Hypnotist Cliff Aguirre met his future spouse, Janis, in 1982 through Davina, a roommate of hers. Cliff would ask Davina every now and then if she knew anyone single, as he was looking for love, until eventually she introduced him to Janis. They were married the following year. "In truth, though," as Aguirre explains it, "I actually met Janis and her father and also visited her parent's home a year earlier in a dream." Aguirre notes that the dream, which occurred in 1981, included many details of her features, including her height, her Italian descent, and her Mediterranean skin color. Even the layout of the house remained familiar to him. In the dream itself, he is sitting on her bed when her father comes in and shuts the door, leaving him a little nervous. He asks him for his daughter's hand in marriage before waking up. "When I finally met Janis," he wrote, "she looked just like the woman in the dream." Aguirre also offered both that her father looked the same as in the dream and that the house layout was identical.[55]

Author and spiritual medium Marianne Michaels offers a potentially illuminating example in which she speaks of meeting her lifelong lover, Lucas. One evening, some time after they had already been together, Lucas turned to her and suddenly said, "It's you!" Michaels noted of Lucas that "he had a dream before we met," in which a woman came into his bedroom, made love to him, and left him with an image of her hair and smell. He had apparently awoken crying from this powerful dream. "That evening," the author offers, "he realized that I was the woman in his dream." There are a few things worthy of note in this particular case. Michaels stated that she later discovered that she and Lucas lived across the street from one another and frequented similar spots. While we have seen cases where such an explanation was either unlikely or impossible, certainly such a circumstance as this would suggest a more "mundane" explanation. Doubtless, a number of cases may be explained in this way. With that said, it is interesting in this context that it took Lucas a significant amount of time to recognize her. Most importantly for our purposes, though, is the impact of the shared experience on the two lovers. "We knew, in that moment," wrote Michaels, of the instant when Lucas shared this experience, "that we would spend the rest of our lives together."[56]

DOUBLE TAKE

Broadcasting to the San Francisco Bay Area, a KFPA radio folio (a program guide for their listeners), has a reference to two guests, Bruce and Jenny, who according to them, "first met in a dream." They had a similar message and conclusion as did Ament, eventually coming together after the dream "to celebrate the power of dreaming, trusting, and knowing there is something greater than what is sensed when we are blinded by suspicion, fear, and doubt."[57] Indeed, just as we have seen that both lovers-to-be might dream of each other in the legends, the same shared or double dreams are still recorded. *The Heart of Healing* is a book dedicated to the "spiritual odyssey" of professional therapists Bruce and Genny Davis, who "first met in a dream." Bruce had many dreams of this woman, so much so that he actively anticipated meeting her in the flesh on many occasions. One afternoon, in a scene that bears a fitting resemblance to so many romances, Davis falls asleep under an oak tree and dreams of a fair maiden, as it were: a woman with dark hair and hazel eyes who told her they would be together soon. From this initial experience alone, he was convinced it was true.[58] Bruce was about to leave for Germany when he went up to the Sierras, walked into the house of two acquaintances, and "she was there, the woman with dark hair and soft, hazel eyes. I couldn't believe it! It was really her! She was exactly the woman who came to me that day in the park."[59]

Gaddis, too, gave a shared dream worthy of any of the romances of old. Schoolteacher Ruby Carrol, on a moonlit spring night, dreamed she was seated alone in a crowded café when a young and handsome man approached and joined her. "I'm a schoolteacher," the dreamer told this mystery man, who replied with surprise, "Teaching is my job too." They discussed much and exchanged details when taking their leave. Carrol was so impressed with the dream that she recorded it the following day and later decided to write and find out if there was actually a Mr. Herschel Hughes teaching at St. Paul, Arkansas—the name and place given in the dream. As it happened, their letters crossed! Hughes had written to her and said that he had met a Ruby Carrol in a dream and wished to know if she existed. After a steady correspondence, the two met, fell in love, and married. The author also makes the seemingly accurate note that such shared previsions are far less often reported than those in which the future spouse is simply dreamed of on one side.[60]

Author Russ Michael claims to have begun dreaming, and rather elaborately, of his soulmate a full two years before they met. "The dreams were romantic, passionate, and like no other dreams I could remember," he wrote. "In the morning I would awaken with such greatly enhanced zest and vitality that the feeling would last through the entire day." About six months after his last dream of her, they met, and according to Michael, she was astonished as she had dreamed similarly of him. Michael worked from home on his locally founded newspaper, *The Virginia Beach Free Press*, and arranged to meet with a woman who wanted to place an ad. Speaking of the time that she arrived after the initial phone call, Russ noted, "Less than twenty minutes later, I looked up from my work to see what appeared to be the most familiar face I had ever seen in my life." After she greeted him, Russ said, "I know you." Their somewhat rocky adventure through life together began soon after.[61]

In a biography of Mabel Dodge Luhan, American patroness of the arts and associate of the Taos Indian art colony, we read of a strange experience she had after she impulsively and unhappily married a man in 1917. As she puts it, she experienced a vision of an Indian face "with wide-apart eyes that stared at me with a strong look, intense and calm." It was upon this basis that Mabel was not surprised to discover later that this man, who later turned out to be Tony Luhan, a man of the Pueblo Indians, "had also seen her face in a vision before they met." "Such magical appearances," writes her biographer, Winifred Frazer, "are granted to those who truly love." Tony later told Mabel exactly how she would wear her hair in braided coils over her ears, despite never having seen it like that. Again, we can see the powerful impact upon the life of the individual such experiences may bring. It was, after all, precisely these specific details that convinced Mabel that they had been "fated for each other long before they met."[62]

Scholars have consistently made the observation that as a literary device, the double dream may serve multiple purposes, one of which would be to add further weight to the idea that the dream was divinely inspired or truthful. Very rarely do they note, however, that the same dreams are still dreamed and that the same conclusions are reached. An internet source of ours gave the following such account from April 2023:

> *[I] Dreamt of my face against a girls face who I loved intensely, met her a week later. the dream came true exactly in the dream. insane intense love and instant connection. told her i dreamt of her and she said she dreamt of me the night before we met but more in a hazy way.*

Of importance here, the informant also noted of the dream that "it made me certain our meeting and relationship was divinely orchestrated."[63]

LIGHTNING DOES STRIKE TWICE

While in their own way, cases in which the dream is the only dream of its kind in the individual's life are compelling in that detail, there are nevertheless an interesting number of accounts in which these individuals have had many such experiences in their lifetime. If, as we have seen, the individual might be prone to seemingly extrasensory experiences throughout their life, they might better be able to distinguish between "ordinary" dreams and others. Victoria, from the United States, also told us that the same thing happened to her. That she had dreamed of a man multiple times before meeting him in life:

> *This happened to me!!! I used to dream all the time about a man with short dark hair and brown eyes, and we would meet in passing in my dreams. Every time he appeared in a dream, I knew it was my soulmate. The dreams were always very calming. When I was 18, I met him in real life. I saw him and thought immediately that he was*

the most attractive man I'd ever seen. We started dating when I was 20, planning to get engaged this year.

Victoria felt a great sense of recognition even during these initial experiences. She also noted that, while she had previously had "prophetic" dreams, this was the "first time" she had ever dreamed about someone before meeting them. Of great interest also, Victoria spoke further about the impact of the experience itself:

I guess it affected my ideas in that I realized the subconscious mind or spirit may hold more knowledge than we can access or understand with our conscious mind. Or that maybe the significant people in our lives are people we've met before some other place in some other time.[64]

As far as the experience being differentiated from other dreams on their own merit *before* the actual premonition (or event) plays out, we can look to the account of another gracious internet source, Rae, from the United States. She describes an experience that occurred a quarter of a century ago, something about which she had "never told many people about." Like a number of others we have seen, Rae, too, was otherwise romantically involved at this time, which, according to her, was "going nowhere."

I had a dream one night that I walked up to a house, a red truck parked outside, I entered the living room and it was dark except for the TV light, a man—my future husband—was standing in the living room and just opened his arms when he saw me. He hugged me and I just felt so loved.

Something else of interest turns up once more in Rae's account in that, as she explains it, she recognized more than just the man himself. Such details likely add a bolstering element in some cases.

> *At the time I was a little confused because I really thought I liked this other person. It wasn't until 6 months later that I met the man in my dream and his home looked like it did in my dream. He also had a red truck. I didn't tell him about it for many years because I was afraid he wouldn't believe me.*

Rae claims that she has "had other precog dreams over the years, but this one was so vivid and clear" and that this dream was "pivotal" in the sense she had that the romance was "fated."[65] While the resulting romance didn't last, another source, Joan, wrote oppositely of a dream in which she found herself at a hospital maternity ward and found herself being led to a particular room:

> *I walk in and lo and behold it's ME in bed cradling my newborn. I then wonder who the father could possibly be because I was single and in walks a Hispanic man in glasses who I'd never seen. Second time I was at the altar looking at the pews dejected because only 3 people showed up for me and being upset about it and my groom said don't worry about it. This is about us not them. 3rd dream I walk into what looks like a house in the front but a medical facility in the back and I'm led to the kitchen and introduced to the person who would be training me in food prep. Well fast forward I work at an RCFE and on my first day when I pull up I instantly recognize it's the house from my dreams and I walk in and there he is. Imagine how hard it was to keep a poker face as you stand in front of what is literally the MAN of your dreams.*[66]

An informant whose account was compiled by British author and former director of investigations with the British UFO Research Association Jenny Randles, going by the name of J, who had other seemingly paranormal experiences in her life, claimed that she "had a vivid precognitive dream" of her Persian husband before they met.[67] As recorded in 1896, Mrs. Vincent Bliss, a woman to whom many strange visions had come, claimed similarly to have "had a vision of my future husband some days before I saw him in the body." When she met the man, therefore, she was "not at all surprised" at his appearance.[68]

Finally, as recorded in the sixties by American journalist Martin Ebon, one Sybil Devon likewise claimed to have experienced a number of "precognitive dreams," one of which took place in 1953 when she rented an apartment in Pacific Heights, San Francisco, from a Dr. Spierel and his wife, who lived on the ground floor. After living there for two weeks, Devon had not yet met Mr. Spierel. She describes a dream in which she seemed to "melt through the walls of the building until I was standing at the side of a bed. In the semidarkness, the pale face of the man lying there was clear in every detail." That week, having gone to speak to Mrs. Spierel, she stepped into the living room on the ground floor and "realized" she had "been here before." "Dr. Spierel arrived while we were conversing and immediately I recognized him from my dream."[69]

In *The Natural History of Love*, psychologist and science writer Morton Hunt, in speaking on the extent to which such dreams—dreams in which lovers meet before meeting—were implemented in the Greek romances, notes that dreams of this kind were merely "set in the context of make-believe and mythology."[70] But is this so? Is it reasonable to assume that these experiences were always, and in every case, entirely contrived? Is it reasonable that an experience, so clearly a widespread and ongoing human one, existed entirely in separation from their literary or legendary counterparts? Taking a different tack, American author and professor for the United States Naval Academy William Oliver Steven, in his work, *The Mystery of Dreams*, spoke to this when he made a comparison between a literary example and those anecdotes he himself had collected, writing, "When George du Maurier wrote his romantic novel, *Peter Ibbetson,* he represented his hero and heroine as meeting each other in dreams. It is a beautiful story, but at the time it was published it seemed the height of fancifulness, a sort of adult fairy tale. And yet these examples of reciprocal dreaming are nothing less than that, brief as those encounters are in actual experience."[71]

Steven, at least, having collected many experiences from among his contemporaries, was sure of the reality of such things, while Hunt was entirely unimpressed. In the realms of the paranormal, or otherwise less accepted and non-ordinary areas, this, in fact, is often the dynamic between experiencers and bystanders. On the part of the latter, there is commonly a lack of understanding regarding the extent to which such experiences are actually reported. We have already seen the incidence of déjà rêvé seems preliminarily to be rather high. We have also seen strong similarities between the anecdotes and the tales. This alone should give us pause. Clearly, and particularly in light of the number of accounts we have seen and will continue to see, a more balanced approach would be the most suitable for moving forward, and biases regarding their ultimate origin, if even that is a singular one, should be left aside. This, particularly in light of the lack of research in the area, speaking with such authority among such a dearth of research may, in the final analysis, be a mistake.

7
God of the Gaps
Finding Religious Meaning in Déjà Rêvé

> *The greatest of all collectors of Celtic folk-tales (F. G. Campbell) propounded in 1890 the theory that all folktales carefully sifted would provide a residuum of facts—facts arising out of true human experiences, put into impossible relations of time and space, confused and garbled perhaps, but facts in the last analysis none the less.*
>
> Fritz Kunz

Psychiana was a New Thought denomination, a religious movement, created in 1928 by Frank Bruce Robinson. Directly related to its origins was a dream, the meaning of which Robinson had no doubts. This dream, this eventual déjà rêvé, was the very origin of the word *psychiana* itself. One night, Robinson had a "realistic" dream of a large, dark room, in the middle of which was a cot. There was a corpse within, and over its head, moving his arms up and down, was a man who Robinson had never seen before. Seeing these strange movements in the dark, he asked the marauding figure, "Now what do you call that?" The figure turned, looking astonished, and said, "Why, you don't know? Well, this is 'Psychiana,' the Power which will bring new life to a spiritually dead world." Robinson, upon awakening, wrote the name down and knew this was what he had been looking for. Importantly here, too, he had also considered the episode an example of "how the Power of God works."[1]

It has become apparent that sometimes these experiences, real or contrived, are specifically identified with a source. Often, the individual's religious persuasion offers the scaffolding upon which to contextualize these different experiences. This, of course, will vary between individuals, cultures, and times. While it is by no means the intention here to offer anything conclusive in this regard, and while this has been no religious endeavor, there are enough examples of this kind that they warrant their own treatment. Furthermore, as is the case for the remaining chapters, a number of the kinds of visions we have seen to this point fall under this category—those in which either lovers or people more generally are mysteriously brought together.

LOVE FROM ABOVE

Pastor and author Phillip Porter, in his memoir about his experiences growing up as a Black man and later a pastor in Denver, Colorado, writes that when he met his bride-to-be, at nineteen, she was quite literally the girl of his dreams. As he explained it, "I realized she was the girl the Lord had shown me in a vision at the age of twelve." In the dream, he was a middle-aged version of himself driving to a church in a large black car. Climbing out, he looked across the seat and saw the woman who was "obviously" his wife. They agreed to marry nine months after meeting.[2]

Author Zipporah Bennett writes of a time in her life in 1980 when, above all things, she wished for a partnership in which she and her significant other could focus on a committed relationship with God. At a lower point, Bennett took a trip down to the breezy seaside atmosphere of Netanya, Israel, where two of her friends lived. After voicing her woes to one of them, Ruth told Bennett that she was sure she'd be married and that she had dreamed of her just a few days before, seated at a great feast—her own wedding, in fact. "And there was a man," she told Bennett, "seated next to you who was obviously your husband. I saw him so clearly I know I would recognize him anywhere. Even as I awoke, his face stayed with me." Ruth soon clarified that she didn't recognize the man as someone she had ever met. Bennett would later pray that God would bring this man to her, despite the story not initially making a deep impact on her. Back at home and teaching again, Bennett got lost driving an acquaintance into the city for a home meeting as they looked for a certain address. Eventually arriving, there were many faces, but, as Bennett notes, "one in particular caught my eye. A good looking-fellow was seated practically opposite from me. He appeared about my age, and a further discreet glance revealed that he was not wearing a wedding ring." They later became acquainted, and the man's name was Ramon Bennett. They only met once more casually over the summer, although she apparently put him out of her thoughts. That October, they met again at a music conference, which Bennett was attending with her friends Yatsuk and Ruth, her friend who had the dream. When Ramon wandered off on his own, Ruth asked Bennett, "Who is that man?" She soon grabbed Bennet's hand and said, "That's the one! That's the man I saw in the dream!" Bennet had forgotten the entire thing at that point, asking Ruth what dream she was talking about. As it started to come back to her, Ruth said, "That's the one, that's the man I saw in the dream, that's your husband!" They would eventually be married. Bennet later makes her beliefs on the matter crystal clear. "Until this day," she said, speaking about Ruth's dream and its role in their romance, "we have taken it as a seal of the Lord's approval upon our marriage."[3]

Author Jenny Swindall, in her work *Freedom From Depression*, recounts how in 1999 she had a dream that she similarly attributed to God. "In the dream I saw a kind man with short, dark-brown hair smiling at me," she writes. The man's kindness and aura, more than anything else, stayed with her, and the dream itself had felt "totally real." Kevin, the man she was to marry, and in her own words, "matched my dream exactly." Swindall concluded that "the Lord revealed to me in a dream the man I would one day marry."[4] Camille, an informant of Chevaneeze Howell, wrote of a dream in which she saw herself preparing for a wedding. She, too, saw the man she was to marry. "It was after two years," Camille explained, "that I met the person I saw in the dream, and it was unbelievable." Camille considers there to have been many confirmations from God even after the initial meeting.[5]

Just like those ancient Asclepian temples where dreams were incubated and celebrated, like those young women of the ancient, medieval, and early-modern past who recited their rhyming words and slept in the hope of a vision, still the same wishes are put into the universe. Blanche E. Ferguson tells us that after his first two years working in a New York mission and the death of his mother, Methodist minister and civil rights activist Frederick Asbury Cullen then "turned his thoughts to the selection of a wife." According to Ferguson, "He talked this problem over with the Lord, who sent him an answer in a dream where he saw a picture of the woman he would marry." Soon after, while attending a musical concert in Atlantic City, "the voice of an angel wakened him from his apathy." He looked at the stage, and there she was, "the very woman he had seen in his dream. She had the same pompadour of red-brown hair, the tall well-proportioned figure, the printed challis dress, and the glorious singing voice." He is said to have fallen in love with her there and then. They married before the end of that year.[6]

While for Cullen the picture of the woman he had seen was interpreted as having been sent by God, for another—such as the following informant—the attribution plays out a little differently. A student in Southern California told Joseph Murphy, having been studying such topics, that she had a "dialogue with her Higher Self" and asked of it: "You are all-wise; you know everything. Bring into my life a man who harmonizes with me perfectly and who is right for me. Now I go off into the deep of sleep." She dreamed of a man, tall and handsome, with books under his arm. She "knew immediately" they would marry, this stranger and she. Two months later, she attended a religious service, "and the young man who sat next to her was the man she had seen in her dream two months before." They married the following month. Despite the fact that the experiencer herself had not specifically attributed this experience to any particular god, the author seemed to want to make that link.[7] The same was true in another example sent to Francis and Bridges. After an encounter in a dream that led to a meeting and eventually love, the recipient had no doubts as to its greater meaning. "When first connecting with him, I experienced an overpowering love that was beyond any personal will or attachment. Our relationship was and is orchestrated."[8]

Robert, an informant of author Marlene Lindenburgh, told her that at thirteen years of age, his youth pastor would encourage them to pray for the man or woman they would marry in the future. "I did," Robert writes, "and one time while in prayer, God showed me in a vision a cross pendant that my future wife would be wearing. It was so detailed, so ornate, so beautiful! A delicate, scroll-like design was etched into the silver, while it elegantly displayed both garnet and aquamarine gems. The pattern was so unique, I felt it had to be a custom design. Since there are many pretty, but ordinary crosses that people wear, I though[t] that if I ever saw that design, I would surely know that the woman wearing it would be the one." Even by his thirty-third birthday, Robert still wondered about this dream and about that ornate cross. Visiting a new church, he got talking to the secretary. When she asked him, "May I help you?" he noticed, as he put it, "*she wore the cross*!" He found it was an heirloom she had from her grandmother, and her name was Christa. "She became my beautiful bride only one year later." According to Robert, he later found that Christa's grandmother had attached a note to the cross that read, "This cross holds a special meaning and promise which will directly relate to your future husband. He will be very drawn to this cross."[9]

Anthropologist Loudell F. Snow, in his 1993 work pertaining to southwestern American folk medicine, gave the case of Anna P., who like a number of our previous percipients had done, makes her own beliefs regarding the origins of her experience clear. "God chose this last husband of mine" are the account's opening words. This would seem like a reasonable conclusion for Anna, as she happened to have made just such a request of him. The connection was an intuitive one for her. On that summer night, she dreamed, or rather "had a vision," of two men standing side-by-side. One she recognized, Reverend Roberts, and another who was wearing a gray suit, she didn't. Four years later at a party, the door opens, she walks in, and, as she explains it, "I knowed 'im right away; it was the man from the vision. So we got married. And do you know, when he come to the weddin' he was wearin' a gray suit."[10]

An issue of the *Chicago Daily Tribune* from 1903, referencing a Mr. and Mrs. Thomas Brace, has the headline, *Young Man Sees Future Wife in a Vision and He Meets and Marries Her as Depicted in the Mental Picture*. Brace, formerly a mason contractor in Chicago, had described sitting in a church as a member of a choir in his dream. "I could see her coming from the choir loft and knew that I was being introduced, and that she was to be my wife." Brace was so impressed with the dream that he told his sister in the morning before going to church with her. "I recognized the girl as soon as the choir rose to sing," Brace told it of his walk to church that morning. "After church, I was introduced to her, as I knew I should be, and, well, there is a golden wedding today, and my wife is my dream wife."[11]

Near-death experiencer and evangelist Richard Madison claims to have first come to the attention of his wife, Laura, in a dream and ascribed the revelation to his god. "The Lord gave me a dream of my wife before we were married," as he tells it. Madison references a dream he had after they first met. During that meeting, however, Laura herself revealed to

Madison, as he states it, that "God had revealed to her that we would be married," which indeed they later were.[12] Similarly, Anthea, a near-death experiencer from the sample of Cherie Sutherland, reported having a clairvoyant experience of her future husband when she was a child and in her words, "when I saw him in real life I recognized him straightaway."[13]

Like some of the previous accounts, it is again striking how commonly these experiences are described very briefly without much context, almost in passing. Author John Webb Kline, in recounting how he had met his wife, notes in just one paragraph of a larger work that "Stacey and I fell in love and she became my wife two years later. God had shown her that I was the one she was to marry in a dream, five years before we ever met."[14] Once again we see experiences that aren't fulfilled for long periods of time and experiences that are told to others ahead of their fulfillment. Holistic healer Vianna Stibal claims that for years she dreamed of the man she was later to meet in life. She "knew that this person would be from Montana." She "knew that he was a rancher and a farmer," or at least one of the two, and apparently became aware of other details, such as the color of his truck. Years later she met the man, with him and his surroundings meeting every one of the details of which she had dreamed, and she attributed the experience to her god.[15]

German-born choreographer, dancer, and educator Sandra Harnisch-Lacey married Rob Lacey, a poet, actor, and award-winning author of *The Street Bible*, after dreaming of him. "I saw Rob and loved him for six months before I knew of his existence," she wrote powerfully. "I fell asleep and then fell in love with a man who, quite literally, turned out to be the man of my dreams." Sandra was very clear that she thought God had gifted her with this experience. In the dream, Rob was a young man with curly hair and round glasses cycling on a red racing bike wearing a striped shirt and blue dungarees. "And that was it," she wrote. "Simple. Clear Uncomplicated. It was sharply focused and very filmic. As I was having the dream. I realised that this was my husband to be and I was getting a sneak preview." Lacey claims that it wasn't until after their honeymoon that she realized the connection. "All the facts fell into place," she writes, "and every one of them, except one, was true. During Rob's year at Desmond Jones, he did cycle on a red racer down a tree-lined route through Ealing Common to Shepherd's Bush in West London every day. The hair, the eyes, the glasses, the striped shirt were absolutely perfect. Rob's jaw dropped when I told him. The laughter of amazement when he corroborated the facts was matched only by the hoots of derision at the mention of dungarees. No way would he have been seen dead in dungarees!"[16]

A dream of exactly this kind was included in a casual recorded discussion held between Mormons Price W. Johnson, Rhea A. Kunz, Mark Baird, and Helen Hull in June of 1971 in Salt Lake City, Utah. Johnson recited a dream related to his then-wife, Helen Hull. Asking Helen first for permission to retell it, Johnson opens with, "I had never seen her before." He then speaks of a dream in which he was down at "Lee's Ferry" and dreamed of whom he would later come to know as Helen, and it was apparently shown to him that she would be his wife. On the authority of this dream, Johnson goes to Salt Lake City and enlists an acquaintance, Nathan Clarke, to help him find the woman of his dreams that he knew was here. He doesn't initially come to success; however, later, having been invited out with another acquaintance, Dayer LaBaron, he was told of three sisters, one of whom was spoken for and the others single. When they went to a meeting they would be at, Johnson recalls the moment, saying, "We watched and when I saw her she WAS the one I saw in my dream—Helen. She evidently knew me for she immediately came in my direction. . . . The result was that we were married. Well, she's the one I saw in my dream." It is made clear that Price related to this guidance from his lord in "seeking how to live the holy law of Celestian marriage."[17]*

*Celestial marriage (also called Celestian marriage, the New and Everlasting Covenant of Marriage, Eternal Marriage, or Temple Marriage) is the doctrine that marriage can last forever in heaven. This is a unique teaching of the Church of Jesus Christ of Latter-Day Saints (LDS Church) and branches of Mormon fundamentalism.

Finally for this opening section, an informant of Rob Campbell, soon after having been released from prison to Wimberley, Texas, found himself at Cypress Creek Church. At this particular service, as the man describes it, "God showed me my wife to be." He then goes on to tell us, "In a few years, I married this beautiful woman."[18]

GOD, GUIDANCE, AND GIFTS

Gustav Scheller, author and co-founder of the Christian Zionist organization Ebenezer Emergency Fund International, related a déjà rêvé in his book, *Operation Exodus*. Scheller, sitting for breakfast in a Jerusalem hotel, had Baptist minister Bill Styles looking at him intently. "I had a dream two months ago," Styles began. "I was standing in a huge terminal surrounded by many people, old and young, poorly-dressed, with their luggage at their sides. I realized they were Jews. Nobody seemed to know what to do. Then I noticed a man came in dressed in a business suit. He had white hair and was carrying a briefcase. He knew what to do." Styles went on to tell Scheller, "As soon as I saw you this morning, I recognized you. I can tell you, it was you I saw in the dream." Scheller considered this to be the workings of his lord.[19]

Bruce Van Natta, having had a near-death-related out-of-body experience and founding a Christian ministry, claims to have met someone in a dream before their actual encounter and was similarly convinced as to its origin. Van Natta dreamed he was among a line of people near a pickup truck where someone was handing out bread. After taking their bread, people would enter a large open pavilion full of picnic tables and eat. While Van Natta was eating his own helping, a "tall bearded man" came through the line and, after looking at everyone's plates, seemed to find something of interest in his. The man ate his bread, and the dream soon ended. Some weeks later, Van Natta was vacationing in New York when to his surprise, and in his own words, "up walked the bearded man from my sweet bread dream!! He was even dressed in the exact same clothes I had seen in the dream."[20]

While these experiences might often be attributed to "God," or the "Lord" in many cases, it is clear that the events themselves don't always necessarily present in that way, and it is the individual's cultural understandings and frameworks that are what prompt this response. So it could be said of Christian minister Shawn Bolz, who wrote that the day before meeting his closest friend in life, he dreamed of him. "It wasn't a parabolic dream; I literally saw him. I felt like God was showing me friendship." Bolz didn't quite understand the dream in its entirety at the time, as he explains, "I didn't know what that meant, but when I met him the next day, he was the exact person from my dream."[21]

Despite the evidence not necessarily going beyond the statement of belief in most cases, it is perhaps unsurprising how commonly these attributions are made, particularly within religious groups, considering—among other things—their existence across the lives of various saints, mystics, and monastics. The earlier presented déjà rêvé–type vision in which Adam had seen Eve before their meeting is unlikely to be unimportant in this regard either. Often, too, the authors of their lives or works relating to them make these very conclusions and connections. For example, French Roman Catholic nun Mary Euphrasia Pelletier (1796–1868), foundress of the Congregation of Our Lady of Charity of the Good Shepherd in Angers, France, once dreamed relatedly of something "extraordinary." "One night," she writes, "when I had fallen into a calmer sleep than I usually enjoyed, I seemed to see a prelate who was unknown to me. He was dressed in the robes of a Cardinal; his countenance bore the stamp of gentleness and sanctity; his whole appearance inspired me with respect. He said to me: 'Fear not, my daughter, your work will be approved. I am chosen by God to be its protector.' After uttering these words he disappeared, leaving me filled with comfort and consolation. My astonishment was indeed great, some years later, on my first visit to Rome, when I recognized in his Eminence Cardinal

Odescalchi, the very prelate who had appeared to me." The author, A. M. Clarke, was of the opinion that this "vision" was "encouraged" by the "special providence of God."[22]

Quietism was a set of contemplative practices that came to prominence at the end of the seventeenth century, practiced by a number of Catholics, and was condemned as heretical by Pope Innocent XI. One of those accused of advocating this Quietism was Jeanne-Marie Bouvier de La Motte Guyon, a French Christian mystic who was imprisoned for eight years between 1695 and 1703 after publishing a related work. Of interest here, when she first met French Catholic archbishop and polymath François Fénelon, he was somewhat cold toward her, although the effect on her was entirely the opposite. There was no question in her mind "that this was he." She had seen him eight years before in a dream, which she was sure God had given her. "It seemed to me," she wrote, "that our Lord united him in a most intimate way with me."[23] Anne of Saint Bartholomew (1549–1626), born Ana Garcia Manzanas, was a Spanish Discalced Carmelite who led the founding of multiple monasteries in France and elsewhere. Before becoming a Carmelite, however, she had to travel to a newly established monastery at Ávila in order to be interviewed and accepted. "For my part," Anne said after having arrived for interview, "I experienced great content to find myself with them, and I recognized those I had seen in my dream."[24]

While we have noted that in the lives of the saints and other mystics or monastics, such visions might serve the function of speaking to their sanctity, in the previous example the vision is barely mentioned. Something similar was related in nurse Beka Serdans' chronicle of the rare disorder dystonia (a neurological disorder involving sustained or repetitive muscle contractions), wherein she writes of her best friend who had just survived a dangerous surgery. She describes spending much time with her throughout this period, during which, as Serdans writes while speculating regarding her friend's experience, "She relates seeing me in a vision before we met." "It was God speaking to her," was the conclusion. "She had been asking Him for a 'best' friend. Well, she certainly got one. Me."[25]

In other cases, however, the reasoning as to why the dream or vision was interpreted the way it was is more clearly established. In his 1851 autobiography, former minister of Cave Adullam Chapel in London, William Allen writes of a dream in which he was preaching to a woman who was undergoing some great despair. After his words to her, she became somewhat lightened of being, took ahold of his hands, and began to "bless and praise God." One morning after, as he explains it, while taking a solitary walk out of his way through a churchyard, "I met the very woman I had been preaching to in my dream the night before." While the origins of such experiences—if they are external as such—are of course challenging to define, Allen makes his own beliefs on the matter along with his reasoning plain. "My not having any previous knowledge of her and being confident it was the same person I saw in my dream, I was compelled to believe it to be of God, and I have often thought since how wonderfully the Lord works."[26]

Pioneer Baptist preacher and frontier historian John Taylor (1752–1833) gave the case of a "backwoods woman" from Lunies Creek in West Virginia who dreamed something alike a little before she saw Taylor himself. The dream thus takes on something of a self-aggrandizing and perhaps even indulgent character; however, its historical interest and others of its kind persist. Why one would choose to potentially utilize this particular type of vision toward an end is, of course, an intrigue in and of itself. The woman dreamed, in any case, that she was before Christ, and he was preparing to cast judgment on many who were present, handing each a book to read. There were two others showing how to make use of these books. According to Taylor, "When I rode up to the meeting where was a great assembly gathered, she knew at first sight that I was one of the men she had seen with the Saviour in her dream."[27]

At the age of sixteen, Jeanette Beale, an informant of Cheri Fuller, described a "vision" she had during prayer in which among a sea of brown faces, one came "sharply into focus." It was a girl about his age with long black hair and a braid wearing a pink sari with roses woven in. Two months later, while traveling in India to perform for the villagers, the informant notes that they saw a familiar face. "It was the girl from my vision, with a long black braid hanging down her back, and she was wearing a pink sari with burgundy roses." The experience was attributed by Jeanette to God.[28]

Steven Musick, founder of financial firm Destiny Capital, wrote of a gathering he had arranged at his home relating to the Christian faith of he and some friends. "I had just had a dream about the wife of one of the members—even though I had never seen her or met her before," Musick began. "In the dream I saw that something about her was broken. Simply broken. What came to my mind was that God wanted to set her right. As I said, I had never met her, knew nothing at all about her or her history. When she came into our house, I recognized her immediately and exactly as the woman from my dream." Musick later found that the woman had a rather serious back problem and that she was quite uncomfortable that someone had apparently dreamed about her.[29] Here again, we note that the faith of the individual often determines their ideas regarding the origins of such visions. Musick, being a devout Christian, had ascribed such things to his god. Again, however, these are not steadfast rules.

Given by Joseph Heinerman was an interesting account from Australia in 1853 involving the Chittendens, who had just lost a son after only a few weeks of life. Mary Chittenden dreamed that two men came to the foot of her bed, one carrying a satchel in one hand and a cane in the other. She woke up within the dream, a false awakening as it were, and saw these men again, their faces "indelibly" impressed on her memory. One summer day, some time later, two tired, dirty, and hungry men arrived with a satchel and a walking cane at the Chittenden farmhouse. "And what saw Mary, when she came to the porch? With a queer throb, she saw in her door the very man who came to her bedside in her dream. She even noticed the lowcut vest showing the white shirt underneath." The story is attributed to inspiration from God.[30] In another work, Heinerman also relayed what he called the "miraculous vision" in 1837 of a Latter-Day Saint, Mrs. Taylor. She saw five men who told her to believe in Christ. They began to sing a hymn. Three years later, the American religious leader of the Latter-Day Saints, Wilford Woodruff, called at her house, "and she instantly recognized him as one of the five men" from her vision. She also recognized two others, and a note was made that the men were not in England, where she was at the time of the vision, and that the hymn she heard had not yet been published.[31]

Seventh-Day Adventist evangelist Kenneth Cox writes of a dream he had in Russia in which he saw a dark-haired young man with Italian features walking into the room where he and his colleague Steve Gifford were. A voice then said, "He speaks English." He and Steve laughed at the dream the following morning; however, as they arrived at Sabbath School that morning, just as church service got underway, a dark-haired young man with Italian features walked in. "I nudged Steve with my elbow," Cox wrote. "There he is! He's the one I saw in my dream!" When the man started speaking English, they couldn't believe their eyes and ears. The man suggested he didn't really know why he had come today, with Cox making the interpretation to him that "The Lord sent you today."[32] Cox and many others who are so inclined would likely attribute many of even the more relatively mundane events in their lives to the object of their religious devotion, so it shouldn't be surprising how common this refrain is when these remarkable dreams arise.

DÉJÀ RÊVÉ AND CONVERSION

Oftentimes, and across numerous religious traditions—or upon the individual's path *to* those institutions or a generally more spiritual path—these experiences are specifically cited as being the catalyst for spiritual change or religious conversion and deserve further attention in this way. According to a French anecdote given in the *Ensign* periodical founded in 1971, a young man in 1989 lay in a coma after a serious intestinal issue. "I strongly remember envisioning a man in white standing next to me after my operation and telling me it was time 'to return and wake up,'" he wrote. Seemingly having had a near-death experience, the strange man then tells the informant they have died and that he can either go back or stay here. After this experience, dreams recurred in which strangers he had never met persistently appeared. This man specifically searched for two years to understand who these strangers were who kept appearing in his dreams. Later, having been handed a book dealing with Mormonism and being intrigued enough to meet with some missionaries, he claims he had his answers. "When I met the missionaries, I was astonished to see that one of them was someone I had seen in my dreams." The French informant claims to have later met the others from his dreams and took a religious path thereafter.[33]

Publications of the Latter-Day Saints and other related groups saw fit to publish many of these visions over the decades. These déjà rêvé–type visions often recall episodes from the lives of various saints and would have bolstered and inflamed zeal within those following the LDS or perhaps those yet to adhere to their doctrines. One of those was printed in *Improvement Era*, an official magazine of the LDS church that ran between 1897 and 1970. Taking place in 1871, a Mrs. W. told Taylor Nelson, then president of the Oneida Stake of Zion (which consists of the Latter-Day Saints residing in the north part of Franklin County and the south part of Bannock County, Idaho), of a dream in which two unfamiliar men were apparently teaching the gospel. One was middle-aged, the other a youth. As Mrs. W., living in Preston, Ohio, described it, "When I saw you elders from my window the day you were speaking with my husband on the roadside, I recognized you as being the men I saw in the dream, and said to my daughters, 'There are the men I have been waiting to see for twenty-seven years.'" Later, it is made clear that the truth of this dream, including other details such as the accuracy of the men's clothing in the dream vs. reality, helped settle the matter for her as to whether or not Mormonism itself was true.[34]

Exactly as we had seen with the Sufis and others, these same visions seem to be relatively common among various Mormon groups and often speak directly to the authority of the individuals involved or the related religious institutions themselves. Norman Ruoff had the case of Mormon George B. Franklin, who once dreamed he was attending service at a church he didn't recognize where he saw three ministers mount the rostrum to begin services. One stood out, a very short, plump man wearing a "neatly trimmed goatee." One Sunday some time later, after Franklin had banished the dream from his mind, someone came in late, and he was curious who this latecomer was, so he cashed seats in order to take a glance. "To my astonishment," Franklin writes, "there was the man I had seen in my dream, the man with a neatly trimmed goatee." Franklin makes it very clear that "I was sure our heavenly Father was revealing to me through my dream and the visit of his servant that this was the true church of Jesus Christ."[35] We come now to an account from a collection of Mormon experiences published in 1983. Here, the informant notes that one day while traveling, a man called Jimmie Hughes had left work specifically in order to come and meet her. "He told me that he had seen me the night before in a dream." The man also seemed to know she was hungry and invited her into his home and offered her food. The informant's conclusion was that "thus, the Lord watches over his faithful servant."[36]

In the work *Becoming Muslim: Western Women's Conversions to Islam*, one Fatimah tells the author of an "incredible" dream from which she awoke instilled with the sense that she should convert to Islam. She went to tell someone who worked at the spiritual center where she was then staying and was directed to visit with two Muslims who had arrived, one of whom's son had fallen from a tree and broken his arm. "So when I went in after lunch and into the room," Fatima said, "there was the boy who had broken his arm and he was the boy that had been in my dream the night before. There had been two children in my dream and he was one of them. And in the dream he had been carrying a white sword. He came into the room with his arm in a sling carrying a white plastic sword." Based on this correlation between the dream and life, Fatimah concluded, "So you know I thought this is definitely what I need to be doing."[37]

Given in the Christian magazine *The War Cry*, a Salvation Army monthly, was an account from 1714 involving a renowned Methodist preacher named Whitehead, and a girl dangerously ill of fever. This girl's father asked Whitehead to pray for her before and after his sermon. One morning, the girl woke up and spoke to her attending mother. "Oh, mother! I have been dreaming! I saw a man lifting up his eyes and hands to Heaven and fervently praying to God for my recovery! The Lord has heard his prayers and my fever is gone: and—what is far better, the Lord has spoken peace to my soul and sealed His pardoning love on my heart!" The girl recovered soon after and was able to return to her normal affairs. Some weeks later, she met Whitehead for the first time and told him, "Sir, you are the person I saw in my dream when I was ill of fever. I beheld you lift up your eyes and hands to Heaven and most fervently pray for my recovery and conversion to God. The Lord, in mercy, heard your prayers and answered them for the healing of my wounded spirit and the restoration of my body to its former health and strength. I have walked in the light of His countenance from that time to the present, and I trust I shall do so as long as I live."[38]

In her memoirs, British Wesleyan Methodist preacher Mary Taft (1772–1851) recounts being the object of such a dream herself in 1803. Taft, while praying at a chapel in Sandwich in southeast England, meets and speaks with a woman who was herself praying and in tears at a pew. After Taft approaches her, this woman speaks eventually saying, "I have three children, and when I was big of my first, I dreamt that I was walking down a fine broad road, and all appeared pleasant about me,—but there came a woman and clapped her hand on my shoulder, and said, 'this is the broad road that leads down to hell.'" The woman then said, "Oh! what shall I do? or whither shall I fly?" The answer came that "there is a narrow road here on the right-hand,—it is but rough, but turn into it, for it leads to heaven." This woman, according to Taft, then grabbed her hand and told her, "You are the very person I saw in my dream." The vision is later credited with certain intriguing aftereffects, her husband being apparently "astonished at the change in her."

While many of these accounts *have* clearly occurred, whatever their origins and meaning, it is very likely that in many cases—perhaps such as the present example—the details were contrived in order to imply a certain sanctity regarding either the object or the subject of the vision. With that said, in this particular account, the focus is entirely on the girl's seemingly spontaneous recovery and its attribution to God. The girl's vision of Whitehead takes a backseat, and furthermore, such veridical visions at the bed of those dying and ill are not uncommon. This account then, at the very least, has the ring of being related to real knowledge.[39] The same was true in the life of Mormon missionary Serenus "Rea" Gardner. The following account was given extremely briefly in a diary of his and wasn't mentioned again after. At face value, and unlike many others of this kind and in this context, it also gives the impression of being related to something that actually occurred. A certain Mrs. Bish bought three books from Gardner and as he simply writes, she "stated she had seen me before—in a vision—and knew me immediately."[40]

While again not speaking to whether or not such things actually occur, one can certainly imagine the same implementation in the following vision that occurred among Jesuit missionaries in China. After they came to visit the lieutenant governor of Xaucea,* headed

***Xaucea* is likely a romanized transliteration of a Chinese place name used by Ricci, reflecting the kinds of phonetic conventions of sixteenth-century European missionaries. Records place him in Shaoguan (historically Shaozhou) there around this time, which may provide a clue as to the intended location.

by Italian Jesuit priest Matthew Ricci (1552–1610), the official was "bewildered and remained for some time without saying a word." Eventually recovering his composure, he told one of his other governors, "What does all this mean? Only last night, in a dream, I saw several strange gods, such as we are not accustomed to see in our temples. I have no doubt but that these foreign priests are the persons I saw in my dreams." From that moment on, they had good relations.[41]

It seems then that such visions are found to be indicative of the worth of a religious leader or others of importance. The dream is something of a mandate, speaking to his or her authority, piety, and esteem. Indeed, in the following account, this dream type turns up twice. Mirza Husayn-Ali Nuri, or Bahá'u'lláh, was the nineteenth-century founder of the Bahá'í Faith, which initially developed in Iran and teaches the basic worth of all religions and the unity of all people. It is related that one of his earliest disciples, Mirza Muhammaa-Taqu, having been badly beaten and tortured during a struggle against the government, dragged himself to the edge of the Persian city of Nayriz. He fell asleep and dreamed about the "Ancient Beauty," a reference to Bahá'u'lláh, even though he had never seen the man before. The dreamer then proceeded to have a conversation with Bahá'u'lláh in which he was invited into Baghdad where Bahá'u'lláh was, after which he awoke and saw a caravan had set up camp on the banks near the river by which he had fallen asleep. One of them invited Mirza into their tent, where he saw a man of "striking appearance," who told Mirza, "During the night, I dreamed that the Imam Husayn had entrusted to my care a person with the same appearance and features which I behold in you." They both later traveled to Baghdad, and when Mirza himself eventually came into the presence of Bahá'u'lláh, he spoke as follows: "I recognized Him as that same holy Personage Whom I had seen in my dream, and I was favoured with His limitless grace."[42]

Returning to the work of author Richard Madison, he offers a dream that he claims diverted a woman from her path of suicidal ideation. In the dream, he saw a lady whom he emphasizes he had never seen in his life appear to be weeping. Speaking to her gently, he then saw her face more clearly. The following day, in a Birmingham restaurant that was forty-five miles from his home, he writes, "I walked into the restaurant, I saw the same woman who had been in my dream the night before. I introduced myself. I told her that Jesus loved her and wanted to give her peace from the tragedies that she had faced recently." The dream and the entire book within which it is found were attributed to his god.[43]

An older account from Ireland was given by County Meath-born Reverend Matthew Lanktree (or Langtree) (c. 1770–1849) in a carefully and meticulously crafted biography of Methodist minister Gideon Ouseley (1762–1839). The night before Lanktree (then a junior preacher) visited Boyle, a small town in County Roscommon, he had a "most impressive dream" regarding a man he had "never known." He had a "solemn aspect, and a defect in one of his eyes." During the course of the dream, Lanktree saw how this man overcame Satan when the latter was attempting to negatively influence Lanktree's sermon. "When I saw Ousley next day," he writes, "I was quite surprised. His face was familiar. [including the defect, which was related to an injury Ousley had taken in a bar brawl.] He was the man I had seen in my dream."[44]

In his biography of his wife, Reverend Horace Moulton—a Methodist preacher who died in 1873—wrote of a dream that came to a young man he was later to meet. Before Moulton came to Oxford, where he would be offering his services, this young man as Moulton describes it, "dreamed that we were appointed to preach in Oxford." This dream was apparently "deeply impressed" on this young brother's mind. He was apparently "so sanguine of this fact" that when he laid eyes on Moulton, he said, "That is the man whom I saw in my dream." Of interest here, however, is that Moulton does not exclusively connect this dream to anything regarding his religious beliefs.[45] In other cases, too, no interpretation is necessarily made; however, the context such as the following—being printed in a Christian magazine—suggests either the individual involved or the editors may believe something similar regarding the origins and significance of the experience. Mary Frances Williams wrote to the spiritual magazine *Guideposts* of a dream in which she was visiting with an older woman named Pearl in a room that had an old cedar chest. Frances Williams was a volunteer services coordinator and arrived at a local hospital to greet a choir she had arranged when, to her disbelief, she recognized one of the group, writing, "There was the woman from my dream!"[46]

The late author and reverend Colton Wickramaratne claims that in 1957, he had a night vision in which a hand seemed to come through his bedroom window multiple times. This frightened the man, so he set to prayer, and so the window became like a "big screen" through which he saw eight distinct faces. In the vision, a being that Wickramaratne interpreted as Jesus told him he would encounter these people in the coming years. Ten years later in 1967, while attending the U.S. Assemblies of God in Long Beach, California, Wickramaratne was sought out by Brother Hogan, who told him that Pastor Syvelle Phillips had come and that he wanted Wickramaratne to speak at his Sunday school, which he accepted. After the class, as Wickramaratne explains it, "A man approached me after Sunday school. I realized I had seen him before; I looked at him closely trying to remember where we had met. Then it suddenly came back to me—I had seen him in the vision God gave me in Kandy in 1957. It turned out that he was Pastor Syvelle Phillips. Pastor Phillips's face was the first face I saw in the vision." According to Wickramaratne, over the years Phillips was gradually introduced to the others he had seen in his vision a decade previous. It was their belief in this vision that caused them to support him for years to come.[47]

Finally here—and drawing again from the *Zion's Landmark* journal from 1867—was the case of Gladys Hill, a widow who wrote to the editors regarding a dream she had, which explained why she spoke so highly of one Elder J. Watt Tuttle. "I dreamed I traveled the darkest, lonesomest valley anyone ever traveled on and went through dark shadows that were still darker than the valley," said Hill. Soon there were great mountains in front and behind, dark and ominous, causing her to fall to her knees in prayer for a way out. A small light on a distant mountain showed itself, and she started toward it. At its peak, there was a strange brightness. Looking for its source, the dreamer noticed a group of "Primitive Baptist people" and a man sitting on a white rock with a crown around his head, from which the light was emanating. He reached for the dreamer's hand, and she fell at his feet. Before the dream ended, he seemed to travel to some heavenly garden filled with angels. "I was received in the Primitive Baptist Church at Clear Spring in 1943," she writes, "and was baptized by this dear brother, the one I saw in the dream, Elder J. Watt Tuttle of Danbury, N. C."[48]

When anomalous events are attributed to a particular god or other religious or spiritual source, it is especially easy to widely dismiss them as primarily related *to* those beliefs; especially, perhaps for the materialist. These experiences, however, seem to come as much to the religious as the nonreligious. Cultural window dressing aside, these are fundamentally similar experiences. They inspire conversion to religion as much as they inspire the religious or nonreligious in other ways—magical, mundane, or otherwise. Speaking broadly, they may greatly alter an individual's life, whatever their religious persuasion. Some are contrived, some are "real." This is inevitable. The importance is to understand their reality, at least insofar as they have been and continue to be experienced, and have been and indeed, will continue to be greatly influential. Historians of religion and others are often aware of phenomena of this kind; however, they are rarely linked specifically to the déjà rêvé phenomenon or to their ongoing visionary relatives. For various reasons, this is a balance that it may be helpful to redress.

8
I Knew That Person Would Come
Mysterious Knowledge of Unknown Arrivals

> *Certain it is—whether the views suggested above be correct or not—there is a prophetic element in human nature, and in some way future experiences are often mirrored with a remarkable degree of fulness and of detail upon the mind.*
>
> Benjamin Fish Austin

In the accounts so far, the individual has primarily been the one to find or come across the stranger out in the world after meeting them first in the vision or dream. At other times, however, while the dreamer certainly still dreams, the object of that dream sometimes comes directly *to* the dreamer or is otherwise come upon without the dreamer's specific input or action. In my book *Telepathic Tales*, a great variety of similar visions were presented from cross-cultural and historical sources for the first time. In the present work, however, *only* accounts in which the person coming is unknown to the visionary are included, and hence they meet the criteria of having been people who were "dreamed of before being seen." That is to say, they are a clear variant of the déjà rêvé phenomenon. Of all our accounts so far, in fact, they might most obviously fall under this category.

WHO CAME TO WHOM?

These accounts are rather important in this area, as often it can be somewhat unclear as to which of the two categories an experience actually fits under. Consider the individual who meets someone they dreamed of in the street, for example; can we always determine who "went to who," as it were? A perfect example comes according to a mythological record of the African country, Rwanda. King Ryangombe, or "Buffalo Horn," was planning to hunt with his son when his wife, Queen Nyavirezi, warned them against it. "I had a dream in which I saw what will happen today," she told them. She warned, among other things, that they would "see a girl with hair all over her body." The king, however, was unmoved and set off regardless. Later, separate events that had been predicted began to unfold, culminating in their meeting a girl all covered in lion-colored hair. The king was soon killed by a buffalo, but not before he ordered the girl to be taken to his wife and make it known her predictions came true. "When the hunters arrived," as the tale goes, "she recognized the lion-girl from her dream."[1]

According to the historical records of the Grande Ligne mission of Québec, one of the *colporteurs* (peddlars of religious books) of that mission, Zéphirin Patenaude, was once going house to house in the parish of St. Dominic in Canada. The day eventually became a cold and bleak February night, and Patenaude looked for shelter. After many refusals, he came to a lonely little house in the fields off the main road where four men were smoking around a stove. Having joined them by the stove and after some conversation, Patenaude worked up the courage to ask for shelter, and one of the men offered to let him lodge in his home. "Well," the man said, "I must tell you why I have treated you so; it is a strange thing, but two weeks ago I was suddenly awaked at two o'clock in the night by a striking dream. I dreamed that a man knocked at my door, and on it being opened to him, he came in, drew a small book from a pocket, and as he opened that book the house was filled with light; it struck me so much that I could not sleep the rest of the night. When I saw you come in the other house I recognized you as the man I had seen in my dream, and of course I felt like befriending you, whilst I wish to know more about you." This fact had apparently been confirmed by "several trustworthy sources."[2]

American television producer, screenwriter, novelist, and director Charles Edward Sellier Jr. gave a dream from a Spanish girl named Teresa in which she saw a tall man in a red tie walking up to her father. Both men seemed cordial. The stranger had a ring and a large Valentine's Day box. Later at a water fountain, Teresa dropped her wallet to the floor when a man went to pick it up—a man wearing red on the same finger as the dreamed man. "Don't lose this," the man told her. "I'm sure it's very important." "Papa," Teresa exclaimed while pointing to the man's tie, "look, it's the man from my dream."[3]

American Buddhist monks Heng Sure and Heng Chauhave another pertinent example. They decided to undertake an ancient ascetic practice that involved bowing every three steps on a two-and-a-half-year pilgrimage along the Californian coast. This was documented in their work, *Silence Echoes*. One of those entries tells of a dream Heng Sure had that prompted him to tell Heng Chau, "We have to be really careful. Double-check all the locks and windows. I just dreamed that some more thieves came to rip us off." Later that evening, Heng Sure wrote a note to Heng that reads as follows.

> You know the dream I had of the thieves? This afternoon I saw you speed up and I followed you about ten minutes later I came up and out of the corner of my eye I saw two men jump the freeway fence and head for the car. I walked ahead and sure enough they were trying to break in, tugging on the doors and windows. I walked

towards them, thinking to talk them out of it perhaps and they saw me coming and split back across the fence and the highway. They were the same guys I saw in the dream, wearing the same clothes and everything. Isn't that funny?[4]

Noteworthy here is that unlike many of the other religious types we have seen, both men were "dumbfounded" by these circumstances, unable to ascribe the dream to any particular source. More importantly, though, who bumped into who, as it were? As we can see from these few accounts, the delineation isn't always entirely clear, if it is there to be made at all. In fact, these accounts could fall under either category. In many ways these accounts echo those of the Scandinavian *vardöger*. The vardöger refers to a strange phenomenon, variously known in northern Europe, by which certain individuals become mysteriously aware of the coming of another. These instances often involve apparitions, or more commonly sounds; however, they are ultimately indistinguishable from these dreams and visions in important ways. We will see that while such things have been assigned to men and women of renown, ordinary people and our own contemporaries have and continue to record the same experiences.

STRANGERS INCOMING

Burmese writer and editor Ma Thanegi served time at Insein Jail near the Burmese capital between 1989 and 1992 following the *8888 Uprising*.* In her biographical work, *Nor Iron Bars a Cage*, Thanegi recounts a dream she had during this period in which she saw a stranger's face in a cell window: "a slender, pale lady with a thin, oval face, wearing a pink-beige homespun jacket." The following evening, a number of new prisoners were brought to the prison, and, as Thanegi writes, "one of them was the person of my dream, although I had never seen her before

*A series of protests and civil unrest in Burma that originated in student uprisings and peaked in 1988.

in real life. Her face was exactly the one that I saw in my dream and she wore the same pink-beige jacket."[5]

Socio-cultural anthropologist and associate professor Amira Mittermaier, while meeting a friend of hers in Cairo, visited that friend's great-aunt Mona, who was about eighty at the time of the encounter. While Mona spoke into Mittermaier's digital recorder of a dream vision in which she experienced being visited by the prophet, it is more interesting for us here to note that Mona told the author her aunt had recognized her immediately. Although her daughter was disbelieving, this was apparently, as Mittermaier writes, "because she had dreamed of me the previous night."[6]

Welsh American explorer, journalist, soldier, and politician Henry Morton Stanley famously recorded his explorations of central Africa. In 1880, in relation to the customs of Uganda, Morton Stanley told of a certain king who one night was troubled in his sleep having seen a man come to him with seemingly ominous tidings. The next morning, in the middle of telling his mother of the dream, his chief consul entered and told him that some man had arrived and was waiting at the gates with news for his ears only. When this man entered the king's chamber, the king said, "This is he whom I saw in my dream."[7] Respected explorers, ethnologists, and anthropologists, in fact, often write of these very instances in which they seemed to have been inexplicably expected by the people they were visiting, despite there often being no conventional way they could have known they were coming. Award-winning folklorist Barre Toelken was especially impressed with these strange encounters, having experienced them himself among the Navajo. He had "no doubt" that these things actually happened, although he made the difficulty in explaining them clear.[8] Alexander Henry, an American-born explorer, writer, and merchant, lived and hunted with the Ojibwe Indians of the Great Lakes between 1763 and 1764. Writing of his time as a fur trader at Michilimackinac, an Ojibwe named Wawatam visited him often at his house and seemed to hold Henry in unusually high regard. According to Wawatam, some years before—having entered the wilderness in order to fast and encounter the Great Spirit—he had a "dream" in which he adopted an Englishman as his own son and friend. As Henry writes, "From the moment he first beheld me, he recognized me as the person that the Great Spirit had pointed out to him as a brother."[9] These experiences are recorded on all continents. According to professor of Christian religious studies Samson Adetunji Fatokun, Chief Sodeke of the West African Yoruba had once warmly welcomed a group of Anglican and Anglo-African missionaries to his land in 1842, as he "had seen the two men in a dream before their arrival."[10]

The late Dan Wooding, formerly a top London journalist, describes in his work *Twenty-Six Lead Soldiers* an incident that occurred while visiting Havana, Cuba. Entering the Havana church, a man he didn't recognize but who reminded him of his father came rushing to meet him. "You're the one," he said. "I knew you would come and pray for me!" The man elaborated further, saying, "Yes, I had a dream that some visitors would come from abroad and that one of them—you—would pray for me so that I would receive a special blessing." The man then makes it very clear to Wooding, "It was your face I saw in the dream."[11]

In his 1908 biography, English actor Richard Mansfield, known for his performances in Shakespeare's plays and *Dr. Jekyll and Mr. Hyde*, experienced what he called a rather "strange happening." Coming toward the end of what was a troubled sleep, Mansfield in a dream hears a cab driving up to the door, a knock, and then he finds D'Oyly Carte's yellow-haired secretary waiting for him (Carte was a talent agent). Mansfield was asked if he could pack up and catch the train in ten minutes, so he left in the cab with the intention to do so. "This was all a dream," he writes, "but here is the inexplicable denouement." Mansfield goes on to note that something about the dream felt uncanny immediately, and later a cab rattled up, the door knocked, and there was D'Oyly Carte's secretary, "just as I saw him in my dreams." Even the same words were spoken at the door, and Mansfield told him, to the man's great surprise, "I was expecting you." Mansfield had no idea how to account for the experience and claimed to have no superstitions. "All I know," he writes, "is that everything happened in the exact order that I have stated it."[12]

In 1774, Newton and Cunningham, two friends of English Romantic poet Anna Seward (1742–1809), were invited to one of her salons to meet John Andre, a newly appointed officer who would be saying his farewells to Seward before leaving for Canada. Cunningham dreamed the night before that he was in a strange forest when he saw three men jump from the bushes and set upon a horseman who had been riding toward them and take him away as a prisoner. Not long after, Cunningham dreamed he was in front of a gallows, surrounded by a crowd, where a man was to be hanged. It was the very same man from the previous dream. Cunningham called this "extraordinary," but more was yet to come. When Andre arrived, Cunningham stood staring at him. Speaking to Newton, he said, "Andre is the very man I saw in my dream that I was telling you about before they came in—the man whom I saw captured in the first dream and then hanged in the second. He was unmistakable."[13]

Simlar to some of the previous examples from his work, Joseph Heinerman relayed the case of a "believing lady," a Presbyterian who was apparently visited by someone from the spirit world who told her that her religion wasn't true. This woman, traveling around Monte Vista, Colorado, recorded on Friday, August 27, 1897, that she had recently visited a certain Brother Cotton. Sister Cotton, however, as the Presbyterian woman writes, "testified that she saw us three different nights in a dream before we came and had described us to her husband, even to the parosol carried under my arm; and that she knew us as soon as we came to the door although we had neither of us ever met her before."[14]

Writing in *The Two Worlds* magazine, a spiritualist monthly founded in 1887 in Manchester, England, a man named A. L. Wareham recounts an experience he had with his mother. When she herself was a child, she dreamed of a strange gentleman coming to her house whom she had "never seen before." He was standing at the door of the room. She was with the other members of her family before he took a seat. The following day, her uncle arived "unexpectedly," and the "picture she had seen in her dream was re-enacted in waking life. He was the same man she had seen in her dream, and did the same things."[15]

Given by Madame Macario in her *Du sommeil, des rêves et du somnambulisme dans l'état de santé et de maladie* was a French account from 1854 in which the woman named had set out for Bourbon-l'Archambault for rheumatic treatment. On the preceding night, one of her cousins dreamed that he saw Madame Macario with her daughter taking the railroad to reach the watering place at Bourbon. When he woke up, he specifically requested of his wife that they prepare to receive "two cousins whom she did not yet know." "They will arrive this very day at Moulins," he said. They both came on the day expected, the only difference being that the weather meant they had to go to a friend's house closer to where they arrived.[16]

A correspondent sent a brace of dreams to *The Path* (a theosophical periodical) in 1890 and requested an explanation from its editors. In one of those, the husband of her friend's sister was to visit in three days, and she stipulated that they had never met, although she assumed him to be "tall and fine looking." That night, as she described it in the correspondence, "I dreamed that I saw a man,—a short man, not handsome, but with a pleasant, intelligent face." He told her he was Dr. C. and that he would be leaving two days earlier than expected. His beard also happened to drop off, leaving him with a mustache in the dream. The following day, her sister came in, saying, "Are you a witch? I have just had a telegram and the Doctor will be here to-night!" "Now comes the funny part," writes the woman in the correspondence, going on to say that the following day they met and "he *was* a short man, looked *just* as he did in the dream, and wore no beard, only a moustache," which apparently had been uncharacteristically shaved off the previous morning.[17]

Another informant of Flammarion gave an account involving his father from 1868. The man, a long-established wine merchant in Paris, told his son of a dream in which while standing on his doorstep, he saw a bus turn into a certain street and pull up at his shop door. His mother got out, but he also saw another traveler, someone "who had been sitting beside my grandmother," as he told it. "This was a lady dressed in black with a large basket on her knees." Both were amused at the apparent improbability that such a dream could have anything to do with reality. That afternoon, however, standing on the doorstep, his uncle's eyes "chanced to turn in the direction" of that very street, and he saw a bus turn up to his shop door. "In this omnibus," the man's son explained in his letter, "there were two ladies, one of whom, my grandmother, got out, and the omnibus went on carrying the other lady just as he had seen in his dream, dressed in black, and with a basket on her lap." They were apparently astonished at the entire thing.[18] Recorded much earlier in the carefully republished diary of William Dyer—a man born in Bristol, England in 1730—was a related account from eight years earlier on July 7, 1762. Dyer writes, "James the waggoner [a business rival of Dyer's] came up to the off: this morn & the sight of the latter made me somewhat shudder as I saw the same man in my dream some nights ago & he looked with exceeding great bitterness upon me & no doubt bitterness was in his heart today tho' it did not appear in his countenancy." Dyer, an everyman whose journal was unlike many of those collected at the time from people of nobler birth, later gives the impression that such things had occurred to him before when he writes, "May I be thankful that God has suffer'd several times (of late months especially) kind hints to be given me in my sleep of any thing particular [which] was soon approaching."[19]

French opera singer Regine Crespin recounts in the epilogue of her memoir that in 1953 she had a strange dream. While coming from Nimes to stay overnight in Paris, she dreamed she was walking along a street with a man on the opposite side who came toward her, stepped on her dress, and tore it. The dream was repeated the following night. After her performance the following evening, a man entered her dressing room, seemingly blushing with embarrassment and asking for her pardon for a remark he had made during the show. "And," Crespin explains in shock, "it was exactly the man from my dream." She asked him if they had ever met, to which he replied in the negative and posed the question as to what explanation could account for such a thing, concluding simply with the word "mystery."[20]

In his book about his own harrowing experiences with locked-in syndrome, Richard Marsh, during a rather severe episode in which he was choking on a buildup of phlegm in the ICU, casually referenced something similar. Marsh found himself at one moment on his hospital bed and at the next, seemingly in a McDonald's waiting in line to be served. A cheerful Hispanic girl takes his order, although when he speaks, she doesn't understand him, and he notices in the back the staff partying and ignoring the customers. "I wake up," writes Marsh, "and see the face from my dream peering around the corner." This, as it turned out, was a "new nurse" who hadn't attended to him before.[21]

There are many more accounts in which the specifics are less forthcoming, and they are therefore less important here; however, they are often suggestive of something beyond the details given. For example, in an analysis of survival experiences published in 1953 by the United States Department of Defense, we read of a radio operator who, after a serious crash over Africa and a long and treacherous number of days in the desert, "had a premonition they would meet someone that day." Although the pilot with him was entirely disbelieving, soon they saw a squadron in the distance, were given water, and were taken back to base in an ambulance.[22]

LEGEND AND LORE

This idea of meeting first in a dream, as a number of others recorded later as psychical or even psychopathological phenomena seem to be, is an ancient and widespread one, and such visions and dreams turn up as long ago, and as far apart as ancient China and Greece. In Ovid's eighth-century CE Latin narrative poem, *Metamorphoses*, and directly related to the origins of Myrmidon, an ancient Greek tribe in Greek mythology, was a tale in which the goddess Juno sent a plague to destroy the people living under the rule of Aeacus, son of Zeus. Aeacus sees a column of ants bringing food up and down an oak tree and considers it a good omen. That night, he dreams as follows:

> *Before my eyes the same oak-tree seemed*
> *to stand, with just as many branches and*
> *with just as many creatures on its branches,*
> *to shake with the same motion, and to*
> *scatter the grain-bearing column on the ground*
> *below. These seemed suddenly to grow*
> *larger and ever larger, to raise them-*
> *selves from the ground and stand with*
> *form erect, to throw off their lean-*
> *ness, their many feet, their black*
> *colour, and to take on human limbs and*
> *a human form. Then sleep departed.*

After waking, Aeacus describes the rest:

> *I went without, and there just*
> *such men as I had seen in my dream I*
> *now saw and recognized with my waking*
> *eyes. They approached and greeted me*

as a king. I gave thanks to Jove, and to my
new subjects I portioned out
my city and my fields, forsaken by their
former occupants; and I called them
Myrmidons, nor did I cheat the name of
its origin.[23]

There is an interesting account told of Ahmad Shah I Wali, ruler of the Muslim Bahmani Sultanate (1422–1436). He was said to have held great reverence for learned men and once sent two men from his court in Inida to Kirman in Persia in order to solicit just such a person, Sham Neamut Oola. He himself could not return with them, and in his place he sent his best disciple, Moola Kootb-ood-Deen, bearing a gift—a box containing a green crown with twelve points for Ahmad. Upon his men's arrival with the person and the gift, Ahmad exclaimed, "Behold, this is the self-same dervish I saw in a dream before I ascended the throne, and who presented me with a green crown, having twelve points! If the box he bears should contain the green crown I saw in my sleep, then, indeed, will my dream be miraculously fulfilled." The king, seeing the details match, was "overcome with astonishment," noting that the crown and the man were identical to those he saw in his dream.[24]

Related to the birth of Rashi, a renowned medieval French rabbi, is the tale in which the prophet Elijah is said to have appeared to his father, Rabbi Yitzchak, telling him to name his son "Shlomo" (his Hebrew title). He was also to wait for the appearance of the man he didn't yet know, Elijah, on the day of the boy's circumcision. Later that evening, a poor man in tattered clothes appears at the door, and Rabbi Yitzchak "immediately recognized him as the man in his dream."[25]

Gregory the Great, in his influential seventh-century *Dialogues*, similarly wrote of Paulinus, bishop of Nola, whom he admired greatly. A widow once came to him and asked for ransom money for her captured son. Paulinus, having checked the coffers, had nothing to offer but himself, and he did in fact offer himself as a slave in the boy's place. Both set out for Africa, and when the woman met with her son's captors, she made the offer. Paulinus, having been asked his trade, told them that he could cultivate a fine garden, and the offer was duly accepted. After some time, the king's son-in-law became fascinated by his new gardener, Paulinus, who would bring fresh herbs to his master's table each day. Paulinus once predicted the king's death to his master, and he was soon summoned by the regent. When the king sat down to his meal, Paulinus arrived as summoned, and the king "began to tremble as soon as he caught sight of him." "Last night in a dream," he exclaimed, "I saw judges sitting opposite me in a courtroom and this man was one of them."[26]

At times, even in these cases, the incumbent stranger is sometimes represented in a symbolic manner to the visionary. In a seventeenth-century Chinese short story, *Wine and Dumplings*, Madam Wang dreams of a white horse coming into her shop and eating her dumpling. That same day, a stranger came to her shop with the surname Ma, which means horse.[27] It was still the case hundreds of years later that these dreams might present symbolically. In another work, historian and author Robert Moss (mentioned previously), gave the case of Eva, who dreamed of a "plump woman with frizzy hair" who came into her office with dogs and became rather angry with her. One of her dogs shrank to the size of a toy and was carried out in a box. Eva, trying to figure out some elaborate meaning behind this dream, went to work and a couple of hours later, "the frizzy-haired woman she had seen in her dream entered the room" and went on a similar tirade with another person.[28] In yet another work, Moss writes that the night before giving a workshop, he dreamed that he threw a woman over a cliff in order to teach her how to fly. On the following day, someone came clumsily into the lodge upon the mountain where the workshop was being held and shook off her rain clothes. Moss says he recognized her as the "woman from my dream."[29]

Returning to China, where many of these visions and dreams may be found, a tale from the ninth century has the daughter of governor

Jao-chu dreaming of a man in impressive clothing and headgear giving her a stern and menacing look. With one hand on his sword, he said, "You shall not contaminate this room with your fetid filth! Move away quickly, or suffer the consequences." Some days later, while the girl was giving birth, "she suddenly saw the man from her dream, who approached the bed curtain and beat her savagely."[30]

From Buddhist sources relating to the Yuan Dynasty period (1271–1368), we read of a master Chung-ho who dreamed that a certain monk entered his monastery, made for the great hall, and sat upon the lion throne that was there. Upon the authority of this dream, the monk told the brother in charge of handling visitors that he should pray, that someone might be arriving, and if they did, they should be brought to him. When someone did arrive, namely a geat Buddhist master named Hai-yun, Chung-ho thought to himself, "This is the monk whom I saw in my dream."[31] The Japanese folktale *Misokai Bridge* has a charcoal maker, Chokichi, dreaming of an old man resembling a hermit who told him to "stand at Misokai Bridge in Takayama, you will hear something good." Chokichi himself, in this case, was the object of someone else's dream. Chokichi met a tofu maker on the bridge and told him his dream, but the man just laughed, saying that he shouldn't believe such things. "I had a dream myself, a while ago," the tofu maker said. "An old man appeared and said something about a man called Chokichi who lived in a village called Sawakami or something like that at the foot of Mt. Norikura." While he wasn't given a face, the other details matched. This was further confirmed later when the tofu maker told Chokichi he had dreamed of a treasure in Chokichi's garden, which was later found.[32]

NATIVE AMERICA AND BEYOND

These very visions are well known and found by the dozens among North and South American Indigenous peoples. They may come spontaneously, or they may specifically be initiated in order to ascertain the identities of incoming parties and have particular bearing as it relates to inter-tribal clashes and related threats. A perfect example of this kind comes from among a band of Nez Perce, the Indigenous people of the Columbia River Plateau, and involved a group dream. Several made the following prophecy based upon their corroborated dreams: "Some day strange people will come over the mountains from the rising sun. They will wear something on their heads with feathers on it. They will eat dogs. They will eat horses. They will mark out lands. They will plant things. They will come to the Clearwater River. Some day they will cause us lots of trouble." Although the majority of the others didn't believe it, it soon came to pass that "strange men really were coming down the river," and the details were a match.[33]

Among the Menominee Indians of Wisconsin, one night a certain warrior dreamed that a "war party of strange Indians was to pass at a certain point." In the dream, he saw the exact location, at a distance of four days, where they were to pass. The following morning, on the basis of this dream, he set out with friends with a party that soon grew to fifty men strong and started in the direction shown in his dream, following the specific directions of the dream to navigate the geography. Later, after preparing for battle, some of the Menominee scouts returned with news that the approaching war party had been spotted. This "file of strange Indians" came just as the dream had indicated.[34] A legend relating to the sacred Hee-Hee stone was known to tribes in Washington such as Okanogan and Colville, and has a beautiful girl, Blue Flower, starting out west toward Okanogan country. She knew of a handsome warrior who lived there named Scrakan, one of three warrior brothers, and she hoped he would like her and they would marry. After making herself beautiful, she noticed the three brothers coming to meet her. As it happened, "in a dream they had learned of her coming, and at daybreak had started out."[35] With less of a legendary bent, it was recorded that a year before his coming among the Chippewa

Indians, American-born explorer and merchant furmaker Alexander Henry was dreamed of. A Chippewa named Wawatam had a dream in which he adopted an English man as a son, a brother, and a friend. When Henry, who was later to settle in Québec following the conquest of New France, arrived, Newton relays that "upon first seeing Henry he had recognized him as the white man of his vision, and regarded him as one of the family henceforth."[36]

Examples relating to war and conflict may also be found far distant and among greatly disparate sources. As far away as Australia, the Aboriginal Ngarigo believed that they could attain various veridical information through their dreams, including "information about approaching enemies." Another example comes from the history of a battle that had been "moulded into a miraculous narrative."[37] According to writings revolving around the twelfth century *Battle of Ourique* in Portugal, King Afonso I of Portugal retires to his tent, falls asleep, and dreams of a "venerable man" who promised him victory. "At this very moment," as the tale goes, "he was aroused by his chamberlain, who alone could enter his tent, and told him there was an old man without who desired to see him." It was the very same man from his dream.[38]

Returning to Africa, a catechist from Lake Victoria district dreamed of a "solid-looking European missionary" who told him, "Lo, this man is to rule over you, from Kantale to Buyango." The dreamer didn't know the man but was convinced from the dream that they would meet. A year later, German missionary Ernst Johanssen came, and the dreamer told him he had seen him before. "Perhaps," replied the missionary, after some initial puzzlement, "you have been dreaming," suggesting the unreality of the situation. The dreamer, however, remembered the dream then and there. "I was astounded for I thought nothing would come of it, and yet, here he was."[39]

An account was given by the highly skeptical English missionary William Holman Bentley (1855–1905) from his time in the Congo. He met a woman who had been charmed by a medicine man. She now apparently had a spirit with her "which would bring her luck, would protect her from evil influences, and which, should a witch approach her to do her harm, would arouse her to a sense of her danger." More specifically, on a certain night, this woman, according to Bentley, had a bad dream. After waking with a sense of horror, she believed that her good fetish spirit had made known to her the approach of a witch. So, rushing out in wild excitement, she screamed and shouted to the fetish and tried to frighten the witch who had indeed come.[40] While the seer, the medicine man, the wizard, or the witch might in some tales be capable of such a thing, certain people—as we had seen with the likes of Stilwell—still claim it as a capacity rather than a one-off. Author Robbie Lunt, for example, writes that "On several occasions, I would dream of people who lived some distance away. These were unusual dreams, being very vivid and very clear. The next day the very people I had dreamed about would appear for an unexpected visit."[41]

AHEAD OF TIME

Like UFOs, a number of these cases might have "mundane" explanations. Like those incorrigible saucers, however, there are always monkey wrenches that might point to something more. Those cases, for example, in which the dream is written down and commented upon before its fruition are of particular interest in this regard. In a dream given by botanical expert and author Chad Mercree, he also noted that during the dream itself—a dream in which a strange woman came to speak with him at work—"it seemed really important to remember her face." The author wrote the dream down and later forgot the whole incident; however, one summer break, the girl from his dream arrived where he worked. "She had the same clothes, hair, look in her eyes, everything."[42]

Elizabeth-Charlotte of Bavaria was a German princess whose collection of letters she had written in her life gives reference to an experience of this kind. One old letter titled *Death of Princess Ragotzi*—dated

February 21, 1722, and written to the noble Raugravine Louisa—gave reference to a strange dream she had heard through her servants that the princess had. She dreamed that a stranger she had never seen before came to her room and offered her a glass of water, which she refused as she wasn't hungry. He told her she should drink as it would be the last dream she'd ever have, at which point she woke up. When she later fell ill, one of the king's doctors, Helvetius, came to see her and she immediately showed signs of distress. When asked, "she replied that Doctor Helvetius reproduced feature for feature before her eyes the man she had seen in her dream."[43] Recalling an earlier chapter involving a doctor from an older issue of the *Post-Dispatch* newspaper of St. Louis, Missouri, we read of a certain Mrs. W. She dreamed in 1883 that after her daughter had just given birth, a doctor arrived, but not their usual family doctor. He was a young "country-looking fellow" with black hair and eyes, wearing gray pants, a black vest, and a blue satin necktie with a coral patten. She told the dream to her daughter and son-in-law the next morning, and four days later, after her daughter had given birth, "her son-in-law brought in a young doctor exactly resembling the man she had seen in her dream, face, dress, and everything."[44]

Writer of poetry and prose Esther Bradley-DeTally, documenting her experiences as an American in Russia in the early nineties with her husband, recorded a vivid dream she had in Kiev in 1991. Vibrant colors swirled around her while she sat between two colored houses. After a strange voice tells her that her father is still alive and that she should open his grave, a man appears dressed in a shirt and bright trousers. "His face is clear," Bradley-DeTally describes. "This isn't my father." The next day, after awakening from dozing off in the afternoon heat, according to the author, "I feel someone's presence and look up to see the man from my dream standing in front of me."[45]

Bonnie Johansson, a travel writer then based in Sydney, Australia, was asked to participate in an experiment by a physicist in which she was to keep a dream journal for a year. During one of these experiences, Johansson dreamed that two men broke into her house and took some unexpected rather than valuable items. Later in the dream, an "exceptionally charming and good-looking police captain arrived." She was particularly struck by this man, and the following Friday, after her house was actually broken into, and after they realized they hadn't taken or damaged anything of value, they called the police. As Bonnie explains, "Lo and behold, guess who turned up—the charming dark-haired police captain from my dream. It was a strange feeling; I kept thinking he must know me because I felt as if I knew him from my dream."[46]

By no means are only typical dreams the origin of these kinds of experiences, something to consider in later cataloging. Relayed in an 1883 issue of *The Spiritual Record* journal was an example of second sight, the first vision of the kind that had ever occurred in the individual's life. Very much in the tradition of a vardøger, Daniel Steward, an inhabitant of the windy Isle of Skye off Scotland, saw five men on horseback riding north one afternoon. Coming to the road having run to meet them, they were gone, which much surprised him, something he would express to his neighbors later when telling them of the strange event. The next day, he saw the same number of men and horses coming down the road, and he "found them to be those that he had seen the day before in a vision." According to the report, those men would have been forty miles distant at the time of the original vision.[47]

A HOLY PERSON COMES

While for the medicine man or shaman in training, the individual's helper spirit or a dead ancestor might offer the information regarding an incoming stranger, in the lives of the saints, communication at a distance is often referred to as being facilitated by God, the Holy Spirit, or some other mediary. The accounts, however, are commonly indistinguishable. After Paul the Hermit—the first hermit—repairs to the wilderness during the third-century Decian persecution, others follow. One of those is Saint Anthony. Anthony thought that he himself was the first hermit, but he learns in a dream that another anchorite, "better than himself," had that claim. Anthony, on the power of this dream, sets out to find Paul, eventually coming close to his dwelling with the help of certain animals and other mythical creatures. Paul, however, was consciously aware of the man's approach and eventually allowed him in, having initially closed the door.[48]

Something similar involved Marguerite Bourgeoys (1620–1700), who was a French religious sister and founder of the Congregation of Notre Dame of Montreal in the colony of New France (now part of Québec, Canada). In 1652, Paul de Chomedey de Maisonneuve, founder of the city of Montreal (then Ville-Marie), visited Troyes where she was staying. Just a few days prior to his arrival, Bourgeouys had a dream that left a great impact on her. "It seemed to her," writes historian Abbé Charles de Glandelet, "that she saw St. Francis of Assisi with two men, one beautiful as an angel, the other bald and wearing a clerical garb like that sometimes worn by a priest going to the country and who was not very learned." After unexpectedly coming face-to-face with de Maisonneuve in the parlor of her convent, she was "struck with astonishment" and exclaimed, "Here is my priest, the one I saw in my dream."[49]

In the lives of the British, Irish, and other saints, these messages are most commonly interpreted as coming from God, an angel, the Holy Spirit, or the Virgin Mary. These are very well represented there and many dozens may be found. In the life of Welsh Saint David (500–589), one account contains two of our visionary types. An angel once came to him and told him that the following day he should travel to Jerusalem, where he would meet two very specific individuals, Eliud and Padarn, before giving further details as to their backgrounds. David set out to where he was told they would be, and he "there found his promised brethren." Furthermore, on the night of their coming, an angel appeared to the patriarch in a dream, saying, "Three catholic men are come from the borders of the West, whom receive with joy, and the grace of hospitality, and thou shalt consecrate them for me into the episcopal order." Acting upon this vision, as people still do, the patriarch made arrangements for their arrival, which occurred the following day.[50]

This same idea comes in an old and fanciful legend pertaining to the much-adored Irish saint Brigid, or Bride. Brigid and her father, having been shipwrecked on the shore of Iona in the Inner Hebrides, were welcomed by the Druids there, who saw in her the fulfillment of some prophecy. She grew up in that place, and one day at the Fountain of Youth on Dun-I, Iona's largest hill, she saw a vision of a beautiful woman. Some time later, Brigid was apparently spirited away over the desert to Bethlehem by a white dove, where her father had been keeping an inn. One time during her father's absence, an elderly man arived at the inn. His wife asked for shelter. As the legend goes, "Brighid [Brigid] recognized her as the lovely woman who had appeared in the vision on Iona.[51] Also attached to her life, according to the ancient Irish *Book of Lismore*—a late fifteenth-century Gaelic manuscript—an old nun asked Saint Brigid to go and commune with the twenty-seven bishops and the saints of Leinster. There, a certain Bishop Ibor told of a vision he'd had the night before her arrival. "Meseems," he said, "that I beheld at night Mary the Virgin in my sleep, and a certain venerable cleric said to me, 'This is the Mary who dwells among you.'" When Ibor saw Brigid entering the assembly, he said, "This is the Mary whom I saw in my dream."[52]

Clearly, like the déjà rêvé experiences we have seen related to healers, doctors, and other men and women of renown, these variants are also made use of in this way. It is fascinating to consider the possibility that such things were known to the saints' biographers, perhaps culled from local legends, beliefs and, of course, the actual dream experiences of certain individuals. Such things still occur with enough frequency that the idea that they might have been "in the air" and implemented in this way is not an unreasonable one.

Preachers, Pastors, and Pioneers

Whatever their meaning, as we have seen with the likes of Crespin, Tubman, and others, these experiences actually occur; they are a real phenomenon, and they turn up in some of history's most prominent and renowned romances and saints' lives. Something similar was true in the life of Patrul Rinpoche, a teacher and author from the Nyingma school of Tibetan Buddhism. One night, at the Trago Monastery, a monk dreamed that he saw a lama who he felt but couldn't know for sure was Shantidiva, an eighth-century Indian philosopher, Buddhist monk, and polymath whom he had never met. The morning after, a wandering lama arrived at the monastery, and as author Matthieu Ricard relays, "the monk recognized him. He looked just like the figure who had appeared in his dream the night before." The monk approached the lama and found him to be Patrul Rinpoche before successfully requesting his company and teachings.[53] Of a similarity that may imply a connection, Rev. Mother Dorothy Paston Bedingfield (c. 1657–1734), foundress among a group of Catholic sisters at Saint Mary's Convent, New York, dreamed in the early eighteenth century of their house falling to the ground, only to be propped up by a little old woman. Just a few days later, "she was not a little astonished to find that her visitor was identical in dress and appearance with the little crooked woman she had seen in her dream."[54]

According to a record of the family history of pioneer and Utah settler John Henry Cooper and his wife, that man's grandfather George Prince—who was an English settler in South Africa—received a "remarkable heavenly manifestation." A strange man in white robes appeared behind him while he was journeying with his son William and told him that an important message related to the gospel would be "brought to him by two men" and that "he would know the men immediately upon seeing them." One day, two elders came to the Prince's home, and George "recognized them as the men from his dream." The happening was apparently related to the Prince family "accepting the gospel."[55]

Chinese Christian preacher and hymnist Witness Lee was told by an informant, Brother Nee from Foochow southeast China, of a dream he had in 1923. He dreamed that a certain Sister Lee, already known to be coming, was arriving to their welcome. In the distance he saw another young lady walking from the boat, and according to Lee, a voice that he ascribed to the Lord said, "This is the co-worker I have prepared for you." Immediately thinking this to be a dream of importance, he ran to where the boat would be arriving in the hope of welcoming Lee. "He had no idea what she looked like before that time," explains the author, "but she was the exact person he had seen in his dream." When she came to him, he said, "I saw her already." He didn't tell Lee of this dream for four years.[56]

During an otherworldly and beautiful dream sequence, Susan Fawcett found herself among the sweet perfume of orchids, making her way through a glowing world of green and light. She found herself in a grassy field when, "all at once," as she describes it, "I saw her. A petite woman with flowing dark hair. Her face tilted toward the sun. Lips moving soundlessly. She turns and greets me with a lopsided grin. A sense of calm enwraps me. Like a hug. She stretches her arms wide. We sit on the soft grass and talk, words I cannot hear. I only know one thing for sure: I'm at peace." Fawcett soon awoke to the rather more harsh reality that her daughter had recently been diagnosed with diabetes, and she had been sleeping in an armchair away from home for the last two nights. After recounting the pain of her own family history of diabetes, she closed her eyes exhausted, and heard the footsteps of someone coming along. She wondered if it was a nurse with more needles, but no; it was a nun, Sister Elizabeth, the hospital chaplain. This strange woman offered words that greatly comforted Fawcett, telling her that everything would be okay, her dark eyes and hair seeming familiar and comforting. "She was the very same woman I'd met in my dreams," Fawcett explains, "identical in every way."[57]

Spiritualist, medium, and near-death experiencer Trudy Lucas set up a Spiritualist church in Perth, Australia, in 1954. Often the members would gather in a small living area in the back of the sanctuary where they would discuss the latest strange events in their lives. According to a snippet of one of those conversations, something of a déjà rêvé had seemingly occurred. "I keep getting this feeling. Something or somebody isn't right here. I don't know whether it's me or someone else. Ahhh . . . you know, I can see a man building up in the corner behind you, Jim. He's the person I saw in my dream the other night. You know what I told you. Here it is, just as I told you." No other details were offered.[58] Much longer ago, Jesuit missionary Bento de Goes (1562–1607), while mortally ill in China, dreamed that a member of the Society of Jesus would arrive from Peking the following day. This turned out to be true when the novitiate Giovanni Fernandes arrived, and he had even ordered certain supplies to be bought from the market based upon this experience. After the arrival of Giovanni, once de Goes "realized what happened," he broke into a hymn with tears in his eyes.[59] That food or other things are specifically prepared upon the authority of these kinds of visions is a feature still found commonly throughout the folklore.

LOVE COMES KNOCKING

Finally here, we return to the realms of romance. According to her great-great-granddaughter, Mennonite Veronica Peachey Schmucker (1791–1884) once dreamed of a "ruddy-bearded stranger come riding through the creek and up the hill." The dream repeated itself two more times between wakings, and each time the same man on the same bay horse with the same white spot on its forehead came up the hill. Later, as her great-great-granddaughter Christina remembers it, "a stranger did come riding through the creek bed and up the hill." When he came to the door, Veronica "recognized him as the man she had seen in her dream." Later, Veronica slipped into the barn specifically to see if the man's horse matched that of her dream, and it did in every detail. They later married.[60]

Author and spiritual teacher Sonia Choquette recorded a dream in which she was making complex calculations on a sheet of paper by a window. A man wearing gold and green robes stood with his back to her, looking at the sky. After her window disappeared, Choquette went over to the man to look out the one he was near, soon after which his hand came down on her shoulder. "His face was very beautiful," the author says. "I started to greet him, but he put his finger up to his lips to silence me." After he motioned for her to come with him, she woke up. A few days later, a roommate of a friend of hers came into her house with the friend while she was preparing to go out with them. When she went to greet them, "there with Jim stood the guy from my dream." They would also eventually marry.[61] Something rather similar to some of the folklore and fables occurred in another anecdote given by French astronomer Camille Flammarion of his old friend Émile de La Bédollière in their early days in journalism together. His future wife then lived at La Charite-sur-Loire and was apparently a woman who had many suitors. She refused them all, however. One day, apparently tired of her family's insistence that she choose, she prayed for the Holy Virgin to come to her aid, and the following night, "she saw, in a dream, a young man in the dress of a traveler, wearing a large straw hat and spectacles." When she woke, she told them this was the man and that she would wait for him. The following summer, Émile de la Bédollière, on a journey through France, stopped at La Charite and went to a subscription ball. "On their arrival the young girl's heart beat tumultuously, her cheeks colored a deep red; the young traveler observed her, admired her, loved her, and some months afterwards they were married." He had never visited there before. Flammarion teased that he could have given numerous such accounts.[62]

During his life, Lee Lipsenthal, MD, was an internationally recognized teacher and author in integrative medicine and physical wellness. In the first few weeks before beginning medical school, Lipsenthal dreamed repeatedly that he was standing at an altar next to an Asian woman with long, dark hair. He knew this was a wedding, although he knew no Asian women and apparently "had no context for the image of this woman." The dream set itself apart from his other dreams even before its fulfillment, so much so that he felt it to be "so real" that he could "reach out and touch it." Soon after, during the very first day of medical school, Lipsenthal noticed a five-foot-tall Asian woman walk through the door with a blue blazer, black hair, and top siders. "I knew," the author wrote, "at that very moment, this was the woman I had dreamed about." They would later agree to marry.[63]

Finally, Laura, an informant of author Judy Wolf—two nights before heading to a weekend festival related to her Wiccan interests—dreamed of herself joining together with a certain man she never met "in the most loving, intimate embrace." During the festival itself, a man named Peter offered to help her gather firewood, at which point the informant was aghast. "I recognized his dark blond hair, trimmed beard and intense blue eyes immediately. He was the man from my dream."[64]

Although it hasn't been extensively documented, one of the more widespread kinds of seemingly extrasensory experiences are those in which some incoming party or individual are discovered or identfied by the dreamer or visionary before their arrival. The saint arriving may be foretold in this way; the shaman in trance might witness animals or other tribes encroaching; one of two or both lovers-to-be may be acquainted in this way before meeting in life; while those as far apart as the Navajo and the Ancient Chinese might prepare food for the arrival of a stranger that had been seen in this way. These accounts are found on all continents and constitute a particularly powerful kind of déjà rêvé, in that the individual seems to play no part in the meeting. The sense of serendipity is particularly palpable in these accounts for that reason, and they, like the other mysterious visions and dreams we have seen up to this point, deserve much further notice.

9
Picture Perfect
Visions Confirmed Through Photography and Art

> *I have observed with amazement—and, I suppose, ill-concealed disdain—how academics are able to proclaim confidently that the evidence of parapsychology is insubstantial, and then display that they don't even know what the evidence is–a lacuna about which they could hardly have been unaware.*
>
> Stephen Braude

While there are numerous other variations of these visions and dreams that could still be explored, our final and especially fascinating subcategory of accounts that fit nicely here and happen to encompass many of the types we have seen to this point, are of a truly unique kind. These are experiences in which the visionary later recognizes the person from a vision or dream, although *not* in life as such. They are not visited by the mysterious object of the vision or dream, nor for the most part do they search them out in the waking world, as have the majority of our experiencers so far. They later identified them, rather, by means of a picture, painting, statue, or some other depiction. Furthermore, this is an old and particularly widespread idea and recorded experience, an idea found in widely separated literature and genres and ultimately tied together nicely by a number of more recent anecdotes. These experiences, too, are often profound, commonly turn up in the religious narratives of mystics and ordinary people alike, and often speak to some great conversion or change within the individual.

A PICTURE OF LOVE

At eighteen years of age, Yelena Razduyeva dreamed of being at the river near her small Russian village when a handsome and tall young man appeared, took her by the hand, and told her, "You will be my bride. My bride before God." Razduyeva awoke with the strong feeling to remember this dream, this man, and remember she did, for years in fact. Another man, Lyosha, had been courting her in the meantime, and despite her lack of love for him, they married. This didn't last, however, and Razduyeva later married again. Even all those years later, this dream stayed with her. A custom of her time and place was that young women would write letters to prisoners, and when one came back to her in reply, something about the handwriting struck her. She felt connected even to that and sent another letter in reply asking for a photo. "I want to see your face," she wrote. When it arrived, she looked at it and said, "He really was the one, the man from my dream—my true love! I'd waited almost twenty years. I can't explain any of this to anyone, it's like a fairy tale." Razduyeva even told her husband at the time. "My love has arrived," she explained, and while he tried to talk her out of it, there was no convincing her. And although there is no indication they met in person, she wrote to him every day from then on.[1]

Author and PhD Philip Rushamenza wished for intervention in his life, going to bed "pleading with God" for a wife. One night soon after, he dreamed of a girl who apparently had all of his preferred qualities. "As I looked at her," Rushamenza wrote, "I shouted, 'praise to the Lord because she is the girl I am looking for.'" Rushamenza later notes that he had never met anyone who resembled her. Some time later, he received a postcard from Ethiopia (Rushamenza kept penpals) that he said made him believe God was involved. "As I opened the post card," the author wrote, "a picture fell into my hands. When I looked at it, my mind flashed back to the dream that I had long ago. This picture reminded me of that girl I had seen in my dream. Everything in the dream was the same. In my dream I had not known where she came from or where I would ever find her, but now I knew where she was from, and I even had her address." Of interest, Rushamenza had initially referred to Ecclesiastes 5:7* as a reason for him not to put much weight behind the initial dream; however, he concluded that "I knew God had answered my prayer, and I knelt to thank Him for helping me find this girl of my dream." Three months later, they set a wedding date.[2]

From a compilation of accounts collected by *Today's Groom Magazine*, we read of Elizabeth Bechtel of Eden Prairie, Minnesota. Her story, worthy of any old romance, was given by Fred Cuellar, an author and diamond expert. When she was very young, Elizabeth dreamed of a strange country filled with ancient walls and children flying kites, one of which drifted over to her. Having spent some time with them, a young boy guided her on a long journey until she recognized the park near her home. The boy, however, had to leave despite her pleading. He promised that someday he would be reunited with her. Years later, Elizabeth meets someone named Jay online. "When he sent me his pictures," she writes, "I recognized his face from my dream. I know that sounds crazy, but it's true. I still had the drawing from before, and

*According to the New International Version of the Bible, Ecclesiastes 5:7 reads, "Much dreaming and many words are meaningless. Therefore fear God." This serves as a warning against casually believing in all dreams. The Bible nevertheless offers the very real possibility that dreams may also be truth telling.

knew it was him." Again here, we see the reluctance in sharing such an experience; the same was true when they met, as she didn't want to "sound too strange." On their wedding night, Jay tells Elizabeth, "I didn't want to tell you this until after the wedding because you might think I'm weird, but when I was a kid, I dreamed about flying a kite with a little girl, and she looked just like you!"[3]

Amy Newmark and Kelly Sullivan Walden had an account from an informant, Heidi Gaul, who had a dream that "felt so real" in which a man with curly salt and pepper hair, brown eyes, and wire-rimmed glasses stood in the kitchen door. She had an impulse to speak to this man, from whom she felt powerfully positive feelings emanating, but he soon vanished. The man's face, as Heidi tells it, was "burned into my mind like a brand, forever committed to memory, whether welcome or not." Then going on to question, "But why? What was so special about this dream figure? Questions riddled my rest until morning." Heidi had been hopeful that her daughter would find love and a man of their faith. This had been what brought them both to sign her up for a related dating site, and while it didn't last long, she and her daughter scanned a few profiles that day after the dream. As she told it, "She opened another and there he was, the man from my dream! His smiling face seemed much younger and his hair darker than the fellow in my vision, but he was unmistakably, undeniably the individual who'd stood in my kitchen's entry, as if waiting for something . . . or someone." It was, in fact, based on the dream itself that they had both collectively decided he was the one for her, and they later married.[4]

Darlene Montgomery, in a chapter fittingly entitled *Man of My Dreams*, writes of an evening when her informant Barbara O'Connell was reading from a book of dream experiences when, after reading a particular story, she saw a picture of the author. "I was stunned," writes O'Connell, "to realize I recognized the man named Patrick; at least he looked very familiar." She thought maybe she had met him through her work, but quickly realized this was not an option logistically. One night, as she looked over her dream journal, she began to recall a man she had seen in her dreams, which she had been recording for some time now. "I especially remembered his eyes. A kind of shiver went up my spine as I realized it was Patrick. I was stunned as I realized I had met him in my dreams many times, but not ever here in the physical life," she wrote. Montgomery even later writes a letter to Patrick explaining that, while she thought he wouldn't think her crazy, she knew him from her dreams and that the letter was a test to see if he knew her also. Alas, he did not. A month later, however, after their correspondence continued, Patrick invited her to Ireland, where he lived. She decided to take the risk, seemingly on the authority of the dreams and their power. Of when they first met, Montgomery writes, "A few moments later, a tall rather gaunt-looking man approached with huge piercing green eyes. As I stood up and looked into his eyes, I felt that I was meeting a loved one I'd been apart from for a very long time. My heart opened immediately and I knew this man had walked right out of my dreams. Later I learned Patrick had recently suffered a gallbladder attack and had spent the last three weeks in hospital on intravenous. Over that time he'd lost thirty pounds, which explained the disparity between the picture I'd seen in the book, and his appearance now." In a twist worthy of any of the old Greek romances or French troubadour tales with their double dreams, Patrick, later reviewing his dream journals, concluded he had in fact been dreaming of her for years; just without a face, everything else was the same. He offered details as specific as the color of her couch before it had been renovated and details of her town. He later admitted to that, and he too knew when they first met in the airport that he had dreamed of her before. They were later to be married, and fascinatingly, as Montgomery writes, "Our beliefs included reincarnation, and based on our dream experiences and other confirmations, we knew beyond a doubt that our upcoming marriage was meant to be."[5]

DRAWING COMPARISONS

The idea that the object of one's dream might be accurately identified as the subject of some image has a truly ancient pedigree and takes various fascinating forms. The Hui people are a predominantly Chinese-speaking ethnoreligious group, mainly from northwestern China, and they follow Islam. The Han are an East Asian ethnic group native to the Chinese Central Plain. A tale related to both the origins of the Hui and the relations between both groups was given to Dong Yi by a Hui man in 1983. During the Tang Dynasty, under the reign of Emperor Li Shimin (626–649), the people became unsettled after numerous bad omens, including hens cackling and ducks laying eggs at the wrong times. One day soon, the emperor dreamed of a burly and strong man wearing a green gown and a turban on his head. He carried a water kettle and Emperor Li's entire golden hall in the other. Li woke up in a cold sweat. Having consulted numerous of his wise men, Xu Maogang, one of his most powerful, told him, "Your Majesty, the man you saw in your dream is a wise and able man in the west. If you could invite him to come to our land, I assure you that this land would be safe." Soon after the order was made, and an envoy traveled west along the Silk Road until they finally arrived in Mecca. They came to the court of a Muslim King who saw their sincerity, and after some negotiation he agreed to send a picture of Muhammad back with them, with the instruction that it was to be looked at only and not worshipped. Li Shimin, when he saw the portrait, was greatly pleased. "This is the very person I saw in my dream, and this is the capable man who can protect my reign and the state. He is worthy of worship." Later, a mosque was built, and it is said the fortunes of the Dynasty, with all its recent bad omens, prospered again.[6]

From the *Upanishads*, composed orally between around 700 BCE and 300 BCE, we can read of Usha, daughter of the powerful king Banasura, who dreams of Aniruddha, grandson of Krishna. Despite the two having never met, she falls in love with Aniruddha and tells her magical friend Chitralekha. Recalling the accounts we have seen in which criminals are described and found based upon a dream, Chitralekha begins to draw portraits of every prince known to her from distant lands, none of which Usha recognized, until finally she draws a portrait of Aniruddha. This was the prince from her dream. Chitralekha, using her magical powers, "transported Aniruddha by magic into the arms of Usha."[7] Likewise, according to Abu'l-Fath—a fourteenth-century Samaritan chronicler—King Darius took the daughter of the Levite Amram, father of the biblical Moses, Aaron, and Miriam, for his son on the authority of just such an experience. Darius's daughter had "seen in her sleep a lad, a goodly youth, standing before her, while someone kept saying to her, 'This shall be your husband.'" Anguished and pining after this man of her dreams, she went to her father, Darius, who would summon many painters who painted many different visages—presumably of known individuals—to show her. Eventually, looking at one in particular, she said, "He resembles this picture," after which her father sent men to search the lands for the man of this likeness. Arriving at Nablus, the son of Amram there was found to resemble the image. When he was brought to Darius's daughter, she said, "This is the very person whom I saw in my dream." Their marriage came soon after.[8] Similarly, Chinese historical records tell us that in the fourteenth century BCE, the emperor dreamed that a highly competent new minister had been sent to him. When he woke up, he described the man in such detail to his court artist (who, in turn, executed the instructions so perfectly) that "no sooner had the portrait been painted and circulated over the empire than the original [person from the dream] was discovered and brought to court."[9] The extent to which it was taken for granted that such a dream might literally reveal truth is again particularly apparent in the Chinese examples.

So seriously was the idea that one could be literally found in a dream or by the knowledge of a dream, it seems that just as in the romances, the lands are often searched far and wide until the truth of the vision is found. Something like these previous accounts was recorded in 1986, over a millenia and a half later. Pandurang Shastri Athavale, otherwise known as Dadaji, was an Indian activist, philosopher, and spiritual leader who devised a set of tenets related to introspection that were based upon the Bhagavad Gita. A variant of this kind of story relates to his life. Shireen, a Bombay-based friend of author and pioneering research psychologist Barbara Brown, told her of David, a young man who having become greatly attracted to Jewish mysticism traveled to Israel to study with the Hasidic rabbis. During the course of his meditations, a face kept appearing in his mind. With each passing hour of meditation, the face would become increasingly clear, to the point that he was able to draw it in "remarkable detail." Some time later, one of his friends visited from Delhi and saw one of these pictures on David's wall. After examining it, he realized it was the same face as the teacher of another friend he knew back in Delhi. He took the picture back to India, confirmed the man's identity with his friend, and invited David to come. A year later this came to pass, and he was now a student of Dadaji. The author later visited Dadaji on the authority of this anecdote. "I could not resist," she wrote, "visiting a guru who had appeared in the vision of someone Shireen knew personally."[10]

A Japanese tale from the *Otogiboko* has its own unique twist and gave rise to art in its own right. During the Bunki Era (1501–1504), a traveling merchant stays overnight in a shrine hall as it had gotten dark and he heard wolves howling menacingly in the distance. He dreams of a man dressed in blue telling him that a noble woman is on the way. This beautiful woman soon arrives with a maidservant as a carpet was spread out over straw for her. Considering her beauty, the merchant wonders if this could be Lady Yokihi, consort of Emperor Genso of the Tang Dynasty (618–907), and wonders whether or not he might be dreaming. The merchant catches her attention, and she offers that he come and drink sake with her. A rather detailed description of the young maid's unique beauty follows. While he drinks of the noblewoman's sake, the maid begins to play the harp while the noblewoman begins to sing. Enchanted, the merchant offers her a gift—a box with a white flower design—while he gives a set of *koto tsume* picks meant for a string instrument to the maid before holding her hand and smiling. The lady becomes jealous and writes a poem.

Wind in the pines,
Don't blow So strongly over
The chrysanthenum hedge
That I have made myself.

She then throws her cup at the maid's face, which begins to bleed. This awakens the merchant from his dream. Now, in the shrine where he had been staying was an *ema*, a kind of woodblock painting depicting the entire scene of his dream: the maid, the man dressed in blue, the wounds to her face, everything. Everything was just as it had been in his dream. No one, it is said, knew who painted the ema.[11]

In Ink and In Stone

Recorded by Latin author Pompeius Trogus in the first century BCE was the related dream of Catumandus, chieftan of the Saluvii, an Iron Age Celto-Ligurian group who lived between the Durance River and the Greek colony of Massalia. He saw a woman wearing a "stern and fiery" expression, claiming to be a goddess. Catumandus awoke, sure that she was the divine protector of the Massaliot Greeks, so he sent ambassadors to Massalia, attempting to broker peace. Later, when Catumandus entered the temple of the goddess Athena in Massalia, he froze. "There before him was her cult statue—the very woman who had appeared in his dream."[12] Whatever the historical reality of this vision, Freeman makes the point—in relation to just how literally the idea was taken that dreams were real links between gods and humans in Celtic religions—that "If Catumandus had a dream of a female goddess like his own Sulevia or Minerva standing between him and Massalia, he would have taken the vision very seriously."[13]

The extent to which such similar variants of these visions are found so disparately is impressive. Also involving a statue, Joan Bennet, originally from Gettysburgh, was "haunted" by a recurring dream. Over and over, starting in the 1970s and spanning more than a decade, she would dream she was standing outside a farmhouse with a very weathered top floor. Through the gaps in the wall, she would see a painting rendering a man and a woman in Civil War dress. Later, having heard of a Pennsylvania West Pointer, John Fulton Reynolds, she became greatly interested in his life. Joan visits Gettysburg, and a number of markers are dedicated to his memory. In the Soldier's National Cemetery, she was shocked when she looked up at a bronze statue of the man himself. There was an indescribable sense that he was the man from her dream. Later, exploring the souvenir shops of Gettysburg, "a chill passed through her body, for she could not believe what she was staring at through the shop window. There, in a gallery, hung the painting that had haunted her imagination for so many years." Aside from the dress being slightly different, "everything else about that painting was almost identical to what I'd seen in my dream," Joan explained. Perhaps most intriguingly, she also found that the painting had been created in 1997, twenty years after she had first seen it in her dream.[14]

After spending some much needed and greatly beneficial time at a spiritual workshop in Maryland, author Mhogani Pearl was having recurring dreams that she was back there. She was a part of the staff in the dream and held a high position. "A woman kept appearing in my dreams, and often leading me to replace someone." The dream returned often enough to disturb Pearl. Some time later, during the last day of a New York sabbatical, she had a woman approach her and say, "I have someone who I want you to meet." She was shown a photo of a woman she recognized. "I couldn't believe this was real," she wrote, "but the photo was her! It was the woman from my dreams." The dream had a powerful impact on the author, who began "crying uncontrollably."[15]

MASTERS, SAINTS, SALVATION

Something that becomes increasingly clear in examination of these unique variants is that visions and dreams of this kind are often specifically attached to the lives of mystics, saints, and others of special renown. The veridical nature of the image, which is later found to correlate with the visionary figure, is seen as instilling zeal or something alike in the individual. More than one of those is to be found in the life of the nineteenth- to twentieth-century Indian saint, Sai Baba of Shirdi. One has Lakhmichand of Delhi, who dreamed in 1910 of a bearded *sadhu* (a religious ascetic, mendicant, or any holy person in Hinduism and Jainism) surrounded by devotees and bowed respectfully to him. Later, Lakhmichand was visiting the house of Das Ganu for kirtan, a kind of ritualistic narration ritual. Ganu kept a photograph of Sai Baba before him during the practice, and "as soon as Lakhmichand saw the photograph he identified it as that of the sadhu whom he had seen in his dream."[16]

A number of accounts are also attached to the life of nineteenth-century Indian mystic and preacher Ramakrishna Paramahansa. In one of those, an Austrian artist, Frank Dvorak, saw a saint in a dream whom he assumed to be an Indian man. Later, reading Max Mueller's booklet, *A Real Mahatman* on the life and sayings of Ramakrishna "quite by accident," he realized it was this man he had dreamed of after looking at his photograph.[17] Another of those accounts that had a life-changing effect involved a woman named Laura Franklin Glenn. While sitting alone one afternoon in Boston, as she tells it, "suddenly two figures stood beside me. The face of one shone with a super-earthly smile." Both figures soon vanished. In the spring of 1902, after becoming a member of the Vedanta Society, her eyes "fell upon a photograph" hanging over the mantel. "I stood there transfixed," Laura remarks. "It was the figure I had seen in Boston."[18]

Award-winning writer, filmmaker, and speaker Phil Cousineau had an informant, Susan Foster, who told him that in 1994 she began dreaming repeatedly of an Indian woman. "She always gave me sound advice to come and see her," Foster wrote. Later that summer, while attending a dream seminar with Stephen Aizenstat, PhD, Foster writes that she was "walking with a friend when a picture fell out of a book. It was the woman from my dreams."[19]

Coming again to the work of Robert Thurber who collected a number of these accounts, he himself while traveling in India met a Japanese man at an ashram. This man told how, while living in Los Angeles as a businessman, he had been initiated into a kind of meditation originating in the Far East and used meditation techniques a lot. For seven years, a certain "radiant and noble figure" whom he didn't recognize would appear to him at important times in his life. He eventually hears the man's voice telling him to go to Delhi, where he should be initiated specifically by the master living in Sawan Ashram. As Thurber explains, "The Japanese man didn't even know the name of the Master at the ashram. When the Master showed the man a picture of Baba Sawan Singh, the man was filled with joy, for he recognized the noble Saint who had been helping him for the past seven years."[20] At thirteen years old, another informant of Robert Thurber "fell into a trance" after his teacher put on a record of Indian classical music. A master spoke to him and said, "You are mine and I will come back to you during your lifetime." "From that very moment," the man tells us, "my search for the Master began and I waited for His words to come true." In his thirties, and after a terrible automobile accident from which he had "miraculously regained" his health, he saw a picture in a spiritual newspaper of Sant Thakar Singh, formerly a spiritual teacher in the contemporary Sant Mat lineage of Sikh religious leaders. "I recognized him at once," he told the author. "It was He Who had appeared to me inside when I was listening to the music in the classroom." He received the relevant initiation soon after.[21]

Author Diane Allen had an anecdote in which her informant told of a "very vivid dream" in which he "saw a man with a dark robe on and a beard." The man asked him some questions regarding what he was planning to do for God in the moment and in the near future. "Shortly after that dream," the informant writes, "I went to confession to Father Solcia at Our Lady of the Rosary parish. At the end of the confession, Father Solcia handed me a prayer card and said, 'Padre Pio is praying for you.' On the prayer card was a picture of the same man I had seen in my dream. Below the picture was his name, Padre Pio."[22]

Many dozens of accounts of such pictorial recognition could be found among the lives of the saints and stretching back hundreds of years. Fourth-century theologian and pope Athanasius of Alexandria had a number attached to his life. Dreams and visions were often, if not more than often, involved in his followers eventually finding him. In one particularly relevant example, it is written that Emperor Basil I "had a vision of St. Irene" who announced her name three times. In the morning, Basil immediately sent a retinue to the nunnery of Chrysobalanton in Byzantium, along with an artist tasked with painting her face. It is said that the envoys held her in conversation long enough that she could be accurately depicted, and when the portrait was returned to Basil, "he was frightened by the resemblance of the icon to the woman of his vision."[23]

Ordinary People and Extraordinary Saints

Saints Peter and Paul are said to have appeared to the fourth-century emperor Constantine, who was suffering from leprosy at the time. They told him that Saint Sylvester could show him a pool in which he could bathe to be cured. When Sylvester was sent for, he "showed the emperor a picture of the two saints, whom Constantine immediately recognized as the persons in his dream."[24] One of the more unique examples of this type is the story of the tenth-century Byzantine monk, preacher, and Christian Orthodox saint Nikon Metanoeite. After his death, an artist hired to paint his likeness was having trouble producing an image of a man he had never seen when a monk entered his house and claimed to have the likeness of Nikon. The image is said to have become imprinted automatically on the board when the artist goes to finish. The monk, the "apparition," then disappeared, and the painting was confirmed to have "striking similarity" to Nikon.[25]

Numerous examples can be found especially among the lives of the Byzantine saints. After the death of Maria the Younger in the mid-tenth-century, she appeared in a vision to a recluse painter who had never seen her before and asked him to paint her icon "as you see me now." After the old man produced her image "as he has seen her in his dream" and sent it to the Turkish town of Vize, the inhabitants who had known her while alive were "amazed by the likeness to the woman they had known."[26] Without wishing to draw too heavily on their excellent paper, the reader is directed to the work of Kazhdan and Maguire, who also referenced the case of a young Jewish woman to whom the Virgin and St. Demetrios appeared at night in the mid-ninth century. Later, she saw various images in a baptistery and was "immediately able to pick out from the others the icons of the two saints."[27]

While in hagiographical analysis it is assumed narratively that the saint "has to appear in a vision to the artist so that the icon can be made,"[28] we note that the very same kinds of things are still recorded. While this may or may not be relevant on a case by case basis, it seems that the fact should certainly be kept in mind during any analysis. As opposed to their often patently didactic counterparts, after all, there is no requirement for such things to happen to the average person, and yet they continue to do so. One of those came from Schemanun Seraphima, who gave a case from 1952 in which "P," a Croatian man doing military service along Bulgaria's southern border during a particularly snowy and cold winter, suddenly collapsed and fell into a deep sleep. Due to a series of unfortunate events in which after a raid he was found sleeping and assumed to have deserted, he was later sentenced to death by firing squad. His mother dozed off one night when a "majestic elder" appeared to her and said, "Much-suffering mother, come to me in the Russian Church, and I will help you!" Thinking she had seen a man in some holy icon, she looked but couldn't find this in the church. The next night, she is told by the man in a dream that she was in the right place but did not come down to him. She now realized "that this was no hallucination" and went again to the Russian Church and inquired about the location of the icons. Directed to the basement, she saw a portrait of Archbishop Seraphim, whom she had never seen before, and recognized him "as being the very Elder who, in her dream, had promised to help her." Her prayers immediately began. Upon leaving, she met a lawyer who helped her save her son's life. It is said the woman became a believer in God as opposed to the atheist she was before due to this experience.[29]

Another came from Antonina A. Vajin, a Russian woman living in Australia and related to St. Herman (1756–1837) of the Russian Orthodox Church. Her grandson, Andrusha, hadn't been enthusiastic about attending school, having been crying and scared to go in, threatening to run away. "One day," Vajin writes, "I saw a dream: Some monk came into our house, went to the corner where the icons are, and sang the Paschal canon, and then turning to me said loudly: 'Christ is risen!' I answered him: 'In truth He is risen!' and led my grandson by the hand and made him say 'Christ is risen' to the monk. Andrusha said it and the monk answered 'In truth He is risen,' and stroked him on the head." She then woke up wondering who the figure was and what his intentions were. This occupied her mind for some time after.

That same day, taking in the mail, Vajin found a letter from an Abbess Ariadna with a little icon printed on it of St. Herman. "I received the answer to the question that had been troubling me," she writes. "It was St. Herman I had seen in my dream, just as on the icon I received from Abbess Ariadna." With great joy, she and Andrusha kissed the little icon, and apparently he had gone to school without issue from that time on, the icon and its ties to his grandmother's dream apparently comforting him greatly.[30]

Greatly shifting scenes, from among a collection of stories recorded by students, alumni, faculty, and friends of Loma Linda University School of Medicine, there was an account in which a young Buddhist girl claimed, "I have seen your God before," before recounting the relevant dream. Two demons chased her to the edge of a large drop. She knew she could either let them catch her or take a leap into the unknown space beyond the edge. She chose to jump and landed with a weightlessness that felt like pillows. She landed on a giant hand. Looking up, a robed figure towered over her, "the most kind and loving face," she writes, that she had "never seen before." Some weeks later, while walking past a Christian bookstore, the girl tells us, "I was impressed to look inside. On the wall was a picture of the same person I saw in my dream. I had to go in and see who it was. It was your God! Now I know your God is a loving God."[31] Much more recently in California, a Peruvian UPS driver was delivering goods to an ashram. While dropping off pallets, psychologist Tedd Zeff happened to be passing by and told the driver a little about Amma—the Hindu spiritual teacher, guru, and humanitarian whose work was there—and handed him a brochure. According to Zeff, the Peruvian man "suddenly became very serious as he stared at the photo of Mother." "That lady," he said, while pointing at her picture, "came to me last night in a dream." According to Zeff, he has met "several people over the years" who also told him that "Amma had come to them in a dream before they met her in person."[32]

David Bunn Martine writes about a spirituality church he would go to during the sixties, a time after which he "had dreams" that he was "going to different places and would see this man who was always the same certain man from my dreams. He would have different guises like a policeman, or someone just walking along. I always saw this same man and wondered who it was." Later, the author finds out that he was the head of this spiritualist church. His friends wanted him to attempt to recognize the man based on his dream without them pointing him out. Martine accurately identifies the man in a large picture at the entrance of that church.[33]

Author Harry Bound recorded in his diary the experience of a woman he was taking an evangelistic course with. She had been troubled by a recurring nightmare where a man would be beckoning her toward. Some weeks later she was watching a video presentation, and *The Light of the World*, a famous painting of Jesus standing at a door with no handle was shown. The woman, according to Bound, gasped and said, "That is the man from my dreams!" Echoing a previous chapter, Bound's interpretation was that the "Holy Spirit" had "prepared her heart with those dreams."[34] Humanitarian, world peace leader, and author Maya Tiwari claims that around the time after the devastating death of her father, she dreamed of him wearing white robes and facing away from her. After some time he turns around, the robe turns orange, and the dreamer realizes this is not her father after all, but someone she had "never seen before," a stoic man who looked her straight in the eyes. Two weeks later, her friend offered a tape of Vedic chantings. "When I looked at the photograph on the box," Tiwari writes, "I was astonished to see the face from my dream! The person chanting was Swami Dayananda Saraswati, who would become my beloved guru."[35]

English anthropologist Henry Savage Landor recorded a related dream in his own personal journal. In 1844, his father dreamed he was sitting weaving at his loom when a knock came on the door. A tall, fair, blue-eyed man, apparently of "noble, majestic bearing," entered. This stranger proceeded to instruct his father through the night, still in the dream, until the "plan of salvation" was made clear to him. The man then made his departure, and Henry awoke. His father, also named Henry, pondering the identity of this man, was sure no elder knew. Later, another elder brought a portrait of the prophet Joseph Smith, and according to Henry Savage, "my father instantly recognized the face as the man of his dream."[36]

MEDIA AND MURDER IN MOTION

As with so many seeming psychical occurrences, large numbers of these experiences seem to gather, or at least be most remembered around tragedy, murder, and death. American television writer, producer, and director Alan Landsburg printed a case from 1969 related to the Sharon Tate murders in which Mrs. Elaine F. from Pennsylviania dreamed she was looking out from the trees at an ongoing party. They seemed to be celebrating something when suddenly, people dressed in black with bushy hair came out of nowhere and killed the partygoers. Ten days later, Mrs. F. recognized Charles Manson in the papers as the man she had seen in her dream.[37] A fascinating and obscure account recorded in the *Spastics News* magazine, which ran between 1984 and 2012, comes bookended with a very similar caveat. Two weeks before a murder in Atlanta, Liz Calcutt-Jones—a poetry prize winner—claimed to have seen "one of the men involved and the location of a dry river bed with a body in it." "Everyone thinks you're a lunatic," Calcutt-Jones lamented. "Well-I know I'm weird but I saw this man so clearly I could give an identikit picture of him." Later, Calcutt-Jones was watching the news when the murder broke when she, in her own words, "saw the man from my dream."[38]

Given to the psychical and spiritualist *Light* publication in 1891 was an account from one M.A. Oxon that occurred in 1854 while she was living in New Brunswick. Oxon dreamed that a tall Indian man jumped out and seized the reigns of her horse as she was coming down the main street. After she struck the man, he fled. Oxon followed, but soon lost sight of him after he dipped into an alley and into a doorway above which was written "Inquest room." The floor of the room inside seemed to be covered in grass. After inquiring after the Indian man and being told he could be found at Little River Bridge and that his canoe would be covered in blood, Oxon awoke. Going into town to do some shopping in order to take her mind off the dream, Oxon was accosted by a woman who told her, "Oh, madam, if you had been here a few minutes ago you would have seen a terrible sight; a body has floated in just under us here, with the face and the palms of the hands cut away," at which point Oxon fainted, later coming to in the hospital. Two years after what had been a murder, the man was caught in Canada, and as Oxon tells it, "he answered in every particular to the man I had seen in my dream." Interestingly, too, she had initially been asked to identify an Indian suspect while in hospital as her husband had informed the police of her dream; however, based upon the experience, she told them he was not the one and he was subsequently released.[39]

Claimed psychic Norm Pratt recorded multiple such experiences, including one related dream involving a missing twenty-three-year-old girl, Susan Hult. Being interested in the case, Doug, a close friend of Pratt's rang him and told him that in a dream Susan had sat on the side of his bed and spoke to him. Doug wished to know what she looked like, so Pratt sent him a picture. "Moments later," according to Pratt, "Doug phoned back. She was the girl—from his dream."[40] American novelist CG Fewston, in a *Letter from the Author* section of his fictional *A Time to Love in Tehran*, writes of a related vision that, according to his own hand, helped inspire and guide the work itself. Living in Ho Chi Minh City, Vietnan, Fewston dreamed vividly of a beautiful Iranian woman and awoke very sure of her name, Leila. Months of research later, Fewston discovered this was a real woman. Having seen her online, he said she "was this same woman from my dream." She was Princess Leila Pahlavi. Certainly, one can argue that somewhere in the author's mind such a figure may have been known. What comes into fascinating clarity, however, is that—as we had earlier speculated regarding the old stories—literary works may be directly inspired by such experiences. Experiences in which one might dream, or at least *think* they have dreamed of a stranger whom they later discover to be a real person.[41]

In 2003, author Michelle Bankson dreamed she was at church with some other women when four beautifully dressed others walked in. Turning to her friend in the dream, Bankson asked her if she knew the identity of one of these women. "That's Kay Arthur," she told Bankson. The dream ended soon after she had heard the name. The following day, turning on the TV, Bankson writes that her "heart began to beat a little faster." "Then I thought it was going to explode when the TV camera panned to Mrs. Arthur! The lady who was on my TV screen was exactly the same lady who had been in my dream." She had heard of Kay just once before, very near the time of the dream, but had never seen her. The entire experience, like many of those we have already seen, was attributed to God.[42]

William Oliver Stevens gave a case from 1936 in which his own son didn't appear at the breakfast table, and so his mother went to check on him. He told her he had had a "terrible dream," in which he found himself floating above the ground behind a car in which there was a young man and a girl. A tall, thin, foreign man got out, lay on the grass with a cigarette, and strangely said, "I feel a terribe miasma." He was soon fatally injured. "It was all so clear," Stevens' son said, before noting, "that I am sure it really happened somewhere." There will be something about it in the paper today. Let's watch for it." Sure enough, when the paper arrived that afternoon, Stevens' son jumped up from his chair and said, "There! that is the very man I saw in my dream! It was a photograph of a dark young man, the Count of Covadonga." Stevens notes that the dream was described eight hours before the paper arrived.[43]

DEATH, GHOSTS, AND NEAR DEATH

Recorded in her autobiography, *Time Out of Mind*, the English author of historical novels Joan Grant (1907–1989), in what she called one of the "most important" dreams of her life, found herself staring at a distant mountain through a window. A young and beautiful woman with her dark hair in two plaits entered the room with two children whom Joan sensed were to be her responsibility. She woke up soon after they ran toward her, and these words stayed with her: "Go to Leslie. [Grant's partner] Tell him his mother sent you. Tell him you know what to do." Later, while visiting La Carolina in Argentina to meet Leslie's family, Grant entered her father-in-law's living room. She describes it as being lit by a skylight, not particularly comfortable, and with a red and cracked wallpaper over which were dozens of framed photographs. "One was of Leslie's mother," Grant wrote, "instantly recognisable as the woman I had seen in my dream; and the other of Leslie and Malcolm taken the month before she died, with golden ringlets and white kid button boots, with lace collars on their velvet suits . . . the clothes in which she had brought them to me"[44] (The previous being a reference to the clothes the children wore in the dream).

Swiss psychoanalyst Aniela Jaffe (who worked with Carl Jung), in her often underappreciated *Apparitions and Precognition*, offered an interesting example from Switzerland. Presumably quite some time before the book's publication in 1963, a man recalls a clear and moonlit night in his youth in which a tall male figure emerged from behind the curtains in his room and moved toward the bed. He and his brother both noticed the figure was headless but carrying its own head, which stared at them. Around fourteen years after that, according to the informant, his father was looking through old photographs and papers when his brother cried out. He pointed out a photo to the informant, and as the informant explains, "I was equally frightened—we recognized head and features of our night visitor." They later discovered the man had hanged himself in that room.[45]

Pioneering botanist and parapsychologist Louisa Rhine gave the case of an Illinois man who, during World War II dreamed that Jim, the marine son of his next-door neighbor, came through his parents' backyard and into the house alongside another boy in uniform he didn't recognize. Three days later came news that Jim had been killed at the "very time" of the dream. When the man was shown a photograph of Jim's closest pal, who was also killed at that very time, "he recognized him as the person he had seen in his dream."[46]

Darrah Perez, Native American spiritual author of the Blackfeet, Northern Arapaho, and Eastern Shoshone, dreamed in 2016 of a young girl she didn't recognize running toward her husband before they embraced. The face of this girl was "imprinted" in Perez's mind. Within the week, the community lost a young girl that her family knew, but she did not personally know and clearly did not recognize in the dream. Later, however, as the author explains, "I saw her picture and became broken with saddened tears. What I saw was the exact same girl from my dream." Of special interest here, and as we have seen a number of times previous, the author composed a piece of poetry in the wake of this affecting experience.[47]

One March night in 1973, Floridian Kris Kelly dreamed of a beautiful woman with red hair sitting at an organ in a church. Doris, a friend of Kelly's, had been urging her to begin dating, and this stranger in the dream told Kelly to write an ad in a certain way and send it to a particular newspaper. Upon waking, she wrote it down but did not send it. Three days later, she dreamed of the woman again, who told her, "Respond only to the typewritten letter." It turned out that Doris sent the ad. Two weeks later, a large envelope came in the mail. To Kelly's astonishment, only one was typewritten. After reading just a little, she contacted this man, Jim Kelly, right away. They hit it off in a whirlwind romance. One night, going through some of Jim's old picture albums, Kelly describes that "As I turned a page, one of the pictures startled me. It was a photograph of a woman with red hair. She was sitting at an organ, just like the woman who had appeared in my dream. When I asked Jim about the picture, his eyes filled with tears. He said that the woman in the photograph was his late wife, Georgia, who had died of cancer several years earlier." Kelly notes that she had never known the woman or seen her, and that she had played the organ for churches in the community.[48]

From Key West, Florida, Amy, an informant of David Sloan—who is staying at the Eaton Lodge—awoke from a dream that she was in a doctor's office, a patient lying on the table with the doctor standing over them. Hearing footsteps in the hallway, Amy went to investigate but found nothing. That morning at breakfast, some of the guests said they hadn't heard any footsteps; some confirmed they had. That night, she dreamed of the same doctor again and began to wonder if there was some special meaning to the dream. After a shower and some coffee, Amy got talking to the former owner of the lodge while exploring a museum, and he told her that it was a fine home for "Gen and the doctor." "What doctors?" Amy interrupted. It turned out the lodge once served as a doctor's office, and she had been staying in that very room. Though he couldn't tell her what the doctor looked like, he told her he was a Doctor Warren and referred Amy to the library, where she looked through the relevant historical documents. "She requested the album from the historian," Sloan tells us. "As he emerged from the walk-in vault with the open book, Amy nearly fainted. Though the photo only gave a side view, she could tell right away that the man in the picture was the doctor who had appeared in her dreams." When the historian told her she looked like she'd seen a ghost, Amy responded, "I think I have."[49]

In Patrick Mahony's biography of Belgian playwright, poet, and essayist Maurice Maeterlinck (1862–1949), Maeterlinck tells the author an ostensibly true story from his youth that came to him from a close friend. He dreamed he was at the bottom of a fresh water well, surrounded by dark walls and full of "breathless panic." Eventually coming to the surface, this young man saw—shadowed in front of a stormy sky—a woman's face he didn't recognize and making wild gestures of panic. This man, at the time unaware of his past and having grown up in an orphanage, found a letter from his mother—whom he had never met—that described an incident from his childhood in which he was indeed pulled from a well. Setting off to Holland and to an address given in the letter, this young man arrived and toured the house. Wandering from room to room, he entered a high-ceilinged antechamber, at the far end of which was a portrait. "Above all," he told Maeterlinck, "I knew I had seen the face somewhere before. In a flash, it was all made clear to me. Here was the woman's face I had seen in my dream at the mouth of the well." This was his mother, a woman he had never seen a likeness of. The powerful effects of this experience are soon made clear. "In a way," the man told Maeterlinck, "it transformed the pattern of my life, proving to me that the subconscious mind, so subtle and powerful, is able to penetrate the veil of the unknown past."[50]

Author Stephen Redding similarly writes that dreams "may allow the unseen to look briefly through a window into our day." One experience that contributed to his sense of things in this regard was a recurring dream he had as a young farm boy in which a certain face and voice often told him, "Get up! Stay up! Look up!" For some time, the dream frustrated Redding with its seemingly cryptic yet meaningful details, until one day when he visited his maternal grandmother, Mona, who asked him to walk the wooden staircase with her so she could show him pictures of his other family and ancestors. Looking upon many of them, most being long dead, Redding writes of that moment: "And then, there she was, the face from my dreams. She looked almost regal, but locked in time as she stared at me." "That's her, that's her. There she is," Redding exclaimed to his grandmother, to whom he then related the dreams. She had been a long-dead teacher named Gertrude. Of great interest, too, Redding's experiences with this ghostly Gertrude character and discovering that she had really lived contributed directly to his afterlife beliefs. "How did it become part of my conviction that no one and nothing that truly lives completely dies?" he writes, before noting, "Certainly the visitations of Gertrude were part of this knowing."[51]

American sculptor and author Malvina Hoffman wrote in her 1965 autobiography an incident "that occurred," although regarding which she notes she makes "no effort to explain, but these are the facts." Hoffman awoke from a dream in which the figure of a man with a clearly defined face came near her and asked, "What are you going to do about this?" That morning, having told her unimpressed mother of the dream, Hoffman picked up the newspaper and found that a terrible accident had occurred in Boston Back Bay Station and that Gervase Elwes, the English tenor, had taken a misstep and died. "Mother," Hoffman remembers crying, "I feel sure this is the man who spoke to me in my dream!" Serendipitously, Elwes's wife would later come to Hoffman for her services, and when they spoke about Hoffman's dream, Elwes showed her a photograph of her husband. "I was dumbfounded," Hoffman wrote. "I feel sure this is the man who spoke to me in my dream!" The sculptor concluded this even in her own words: "There are mysterious moments in life that we cannot explain, but the sequence of unpredictable events relating to this portrait was certainly more than coincidental."[52]

Recalling earlier examples, such as the dream that encouraged the dreamer to move to Hawaii, author and minister David Oh once dreamed of a young woman praying for him and apparently seeing luggage while doing so. A man standing on a stage suddenly exclaimed that the luggage was symbolic of the fact that he, David, would be moving, living somewhere else. Oh had a sense, which he ascribed to God, that he should move his family to Redding, and this dream seemed to bolster that notion, so he looked on the website to research a particular ministry school. "I saw a picture of a man and immediately recognized him. He was the man from my dream who had interpreted the meaning of the luggage." The man turned out to be the founder of that school, and after explaining that he and his family then moved to Redding, he notes, "This is the power of dreams," and ascribes the experience to his god.[53]

Author and professor emerita Gloria Feman Orenstein writes of describing a dream to her shaman teacher, who was Sami (Finno-Ugric peoples of Norway, Sweden, Finland, and of the Kola Peninsula in Russia). In this dream, Orenstein would be taken to the house of the "Great Shaman of Samiland" and "shown a photo of the very person who had appeared in my dream as my spirit guide." In this case, Orenstein learned this was the "exact image" of her Sami shaman teacher's grandfather and concluded the dream was therefore an actual visit from the spirit of the deceased.[54] Fascinatingly, and once more, we see that these experiences seem to bolster, and may even foster afterlife beliefs in the first place. This is something seemingly less attended to in the literature and a fascinating future avenue of inquiry for those so inclined.

In returning to the work of Theresa Francis-Cheung, we find the same. Francis-Cheung had the case of Natasha, who at fifteen was suddenly awoken from her sleep by the form of a slim man with a face that was seemingly somewhat familiar. She woke her mother and asked if she could see the same thing, to which the answer came that no, she must have been dreaming. Ten minutes later, Natasha awoke again to the man kneeling down beside her. Around one month later, as she tells Francis-Cheung, "my mother and I were looking through some old photographs that were stored away and I came across a photo of a young man. I recognised him straight away as the man who had visited me." Asking her mother who this was and speaking to how these experiences might be differently interpreted, the answer came that it was her father when he was in his early thirties, a time when she had never seen him. While her mother was convinced she must have seen the photograph before, the informant's response was, "I knew that I had never seen that picture before. I know now that it was my father visiting me to say he was OK and keeping well."[55]

British astrologer and occult author Sybil Leek, once called Britain's most famous witch, was on her way to St. Louis, Missouri, to be a guest speaker for the Theosophical Society. She was to speak on psychic phenomena, but upon reaching the platform, a vision came upon her. Looking out at the crowd, a shining light rising like a flame moved from the center of the hall toward her. "Within the light," Leek writes, "I could distinguish the face of an elderly woman, a face I did not recognize." Leek felt that she had been somewhat possessive during the lecture and spoke on a subject other than what was intended. Leek was escorted to the main lobby by author Charles Luntz who said, "Look, we put your photograph side by side with the one of Madame Blavatsky." While Leek knew her by name as the deceased founder of the Theosophical Society, she had never seen her. "I recognized the face instantly," Leek writes, after turning her attention to the painting, "It was the one I had seen within the light, the woman whose spirit I felt had merged with mine."[56]

Bill and Judy Guggenheim, in their seminal 1995 work *Hello from Heaven*, had numerous cases of this kind. One of those had Ann Marie, a secretary and bookkeeper in California, who had been dealing with the heartbreak of a stillbirth. Three months later, she dreamed of a woman holding her child, who appeared to be six to nine months old. "I didn't recognize the woman who was holding her," Ann Marie told it. "She was an older lady, pretty good sized, and her hair was braided up." The woman told her she was her grandmother Robinson, who she later found out died when she was one or two. "I never knew her and I had never seen a picture of her," the informant wrote, and yet when her aunt came to visit, she brought some family photos. "I picked Grandmother Robinson out right away! She looked exactly the way I had seen her a couple of weeks earlier—same dress, same size, same hair. I had never seen that picture before."[57] One more account from that work has a hotel housekeeper, Lucille, woken by the form of a man at the end of her bed, who tells her that her mother is looking for her and that she should reciprocate. The experience actually prompted Lucille to search for her biological mother, whom she apparently found in just one phone call. After describing the man at the foot of her bed to her mother, the reply came, "That's your grandfather!" "When we met," Lucille tells it, "she showed me a picture of my grandfather, and that was the man who had been standing at the foot of my bed."[58] Something related comes from author Phyllis Hobe, who writes that "Once, when I was around seventeen, my real mother came to me in a dream. And this was strange, since I didn't even know what she looked like. Because of the war, we had no pictures of her. Yet when I told my grandmother what she looked like in my dream, she sobbed and said I described her perfectly."[59]

Near-Death Visions

Something of interest to be brought into the conversation as regards the déjà rêvé experience would be the near-death experience. Why? There are a number of examples in which the individual, during their episode, meets someone they have never met before and recognizes them later in a photograph. Assuming that the NDE occurs at a time when little to no normal cognitive functions can be occurring—an interpretation that fits with the research—it would be challenging to explain how the individual in the photograph could be remembered and added to the experience post hoc, indeed, post-dream or vision. A dream or vision, of course, seemingly requires a brain. There could be alternative explanations, of course; however, less ordinary interpretations should not be left aside. Future research may want to consider the near-death literature and the extent to which it may hold relevance in approaching the déjà rêvé phenomenon, or at least importantly analagous visions, for if it can be established that one does not need a brain as such to have one, it could be hypothetically extended to those undergoing déjà rêvé that the source, therefore, might not be as clear as it has been speculated.

American cardiologist Maurice Rawlings describes the case of a forty-eight-year-old man who had a related experience after a cardiac arrest. During his near-death experience, he visited another world full of light and lush, beautiful flora. He went on to meet both his stepmother and his biological mother, who had died when he was just fifteen months old. A few weeks into his recovery after the event, his aunt visited and brought a picture of his mother posing with a number of other people. Rawlings's informant had no difficulty picking his mother out of the group, of whom he had never seen a picture, much to the great astonishment of his father.[60] Humanistic psychologist and founder of the International Association for Near-Death Studies Margot Grey—in her often overlooked and excellent British study, *Return From Death*—offered a case from England in which a near-death experiencer found themselves in a similarly bright and beautiful garden, this time filled with pomegranate trees. There, the informant met not only her grandfather but also a stranger, a woman with whom she was unfamiliar. Grey writes that sometime after the near-death experience, when visiting a relative's house, the informant's parents were amazed when she recognized her great-grandmother in a photograph. She pointed it out and said, "That's the lady I saw, and that's my grandfather." Both had died long before she was born, and she had never seen either of them.[61]

Author Marisa St. Clair reports on the case of Durdanda Khan, a Pakistani woman who, at just two years of age, died for approximately fifteen minutes. After being revived, she said that she had been to the stars and that she had met her dead grandfather and his mother in a beautiful tree-filled garden. Several months later, when Khan and her family were visiting some other relatives, she correctly identified a person in a photo as her grandpa's mother. Khan would later paint a picture of the garden she was in during her near-death experience.[62] During a near-death experience given by Dr. Jeffrey Long, his informant, Missy, after suffering head trauma during an automobile accident, found herself traveling up a tunnel and meeting her deceased sister. "I saw a child that I recognized as a sister of mine who had died in a fire," she recalled.

"I was only a year or so when she died, but I knew it was her. She had a strong family resemblance. Much later, when I was older, I confirmed it was my sister when I saw pictures of her in the family photo album."[63]

Neurosurgeon Eben Alexander, during his own rather elaborate and idiosyncratic NDE, met a very particular woman riding beside him on the wing of a butterfly while he was in a coma. Later, seeing a picture of his biological sister, whom he'd never met, Alexander claims this was the same woman.[64] While there can be doubt as to the impact these experiences might have upon the individual and how commonly they are ascribed to supernatural causes, this is not always the case. Neuroscientist, philosopher, and popular author Sam Harris was rather skeptical of Alexander's particular case, criticizing his methods of verification and apparent unfamiliarity with the relevant science and literature. Harris himself, however, had a similar experience. He once made a trip to meet the renowned Tibetan Lama, Dilgo Khyentse Rinpoche in Nepal, but before leaving, something strange occurred. "I had a dream in which he seemed to give me teachings about the nature of the mind," Harris wrote. Harris found the dream fascinating for the reasons that the teachings themselves were "novel, useful, and convergent with what I later understood to be true," further noting, "and I had never met Khyentse Rinpoche, nor was I aware of having seen a photograph of him." Harris, later arriving in Nepal, writes that "I was struck by the sense that he really did resemble the man in my dream." Harris was impressed with the experience but unwilling to suggest what he arbitrarily calls a "magical" explanation. Harris writes that perhaps it would have been "more fun" to believe it was, and although there is a certain flippancy in the language that might belie the impact of the experience on others (rarely has *fun* been a term used in the present work so far by the experiencers, for example), this was nevertheless his conclusion. "I did not believe that Khyentse Rinpoche had *really* appeared in my dream. And I certainly would never have been tempted to use this experience as conclusive proof of the supernatural."[65]

During a shared death experience, one or more people seem to share in the transition and experiences of another who is dying at the time. Raymond Moody and Paul Perry gave an account in 2010 in which the informant, Dana, seemed to co-experience her husband's life review at his end. She experienced a light as he was on his deathbed and says that "everything we ever did was in that light." She saw her husband, Joey, doing things before they ever met and saw him with girls he had been with before her. "Later," the informant notes, "I searched for them in his high school yearbook and was able to find them, just based on what I saw during the life review during his death." One can only imagine the profundity of sensing the verifiable truth in this vision with such confirmation in the waking world.[66]

During a near-death experience that occurred in the process of an unsuccessful surgery, one young woman met a soldier who introduced himself as her grandfather, Samuel, whom she had never met. He had a message for her father regarding issues with their relationship when he was alive. After recovering, she asked her father about Samuel, someone he had never even met in conversation before. Later, in her drawer, she found a picture of a soldier, a young man who "looked just like the Grandfather Samuel that she met in her NDE."[67]

Death and the End in Sight

From 1927 was the case of a Scandinavian woman who, one afternoon after finishing the dishes, lay down to rest. Soon after closing the blinds and falling asleep, this woman perceived another woman coming toward her—a woman who, to the dreamer's surprise, seemed to be floating. With a pleading expression on her face, this woman said, "My name is in the papers but not within the book," before disappearing. When she related the incident to her husband and described the woman, he "recognized her as his uncle's wife who had died and was buried in their native village." After much tedious genealogical research, the identity was confirmed.[68]

Joel Martin gave a case from 1995 in which the informant Donna, two weeks prior to the death of her son Rory, had dreamed that someone was strangling him while she screamed at the mother of whoever it was that did it. Rory had apparently died by riding into a steel cable strung across a wooded path. Around a month after his death, Donna dreamed "no ordinary dream," in which the sounds and colors seemed "more real than real." She apparently realized immediately that this was a visit from Rory. He emerged from a car alongside another boy she didn't recognize. They told Donna they were "going to the horses." When she asked Rory who the boy was, he told her, "Oh, that? That's Time Russ," although she couldn't place the name. This experience was so convincing that Donna was now assured of Rory's survival. Donna later came into possession of a book in which she read the story of a deceased Long Island boy called Tim Wresch, who had been born with two chambers in his heart rather than the normal four. Donna became curious enough to reach out to the boy's parents. She discovered he loved horses, and according to Martin, Tim's mother, Helena, "confirmed that Tim fit the description of the boy in Donna's dream and sent her a photograph of Tim. Donna had no doubt that Rory and Tim were friends on the other side."[69]

In what was a rather elaborate account, Matuauto Sipau dreamed in 1976 of his deceased mother appearing (looking a little different than life) alongside Catherine the Great, Nicholas II, and some others, and he was told that they were his mother's relatives. At the time of the dream, however, Matuauto, a Samoan, was entirely unaware of these historical personages. Based on the dream—and one other that followed involving speaking Russian with a Russian man—Matuauto set about finding information by traveling to the university's Utah library with a Polish friend and checking out Russian history books. He came across a chapter dealing with the Romanov czars and inexplicably found himself feeling great love for Peter the Great. This led him to Peter III, who married Catherine. "As I looked through the pages for the name of Catherine II," Matuauto wrote, "I came to a picture of the woman who came to me in my first dream as my mother." He continued to stare at the picture for half an hour. The next day borrowing a World Encyclopedia, Matuauto writes, "I turned to volume N to look up Nicholas I and II [son of Catherine]. Across the page from the entry for Nicholas I was [saw] a picture. When I looked at it, I was amazed! There in this picture were the same girls, woman, man, and boy whom I had seen in my first dream, the people who came to me as my mother's relatives." The man began to cry, feeling sadness and love upon reading of their deaths and how they were executed.[70]

Finally here in our explorations of déjà rêvé, and coming full circle to our accounts related to love, Jenny Smedley had an experience from her informant Sarah, who told her that when she first met her husband at an event, he had given her his number, but she had thrown it away as she was rather down at the time. A few days later, Sarah dreamed that a teenage boy came to her and told her to "find the man again." Powerfully, Sarah noted, "I've never been so sure of the truth of anything in my life," before setting out to find the number. When she was unsuccessful, she went to a similar event the following month, and sure enough, he was there. Surprisingly, in a twist worthy of the ancient shared dreams we have seen, this man told her, "I knew you'd be here, and I'm going to marry you." Of most interest here, however, as Sarah explains, "We got together and when I first visited his house I was stunned and surprised to find a picture in his room of the boy who had visited me in my dream." Sarah later finds this was his son, who had died some years previous in a car accident. Speaking once more to the dynamic regarding afterlife beliefs, she was then convinced his son's actual spirit had guided her to him.[71]

Near-death literature is replete with examples in which unknown deceased loved ones are met with and later recognized in photographs.

The same is true of the literature pertaining to ghosts generally; the haunter may later be recognized in the same way. Such things are commonly discarded as glitches of memory and perception; however, little is presented in favor of these conclusions. Furthermore, while such explanations may cover a number of cases, we cannot therefore suggest we know they would cover all cases. Where these experiences occur during a dream or vision, they respectively may be considered cousins of the déjà rêvé phenomenon or something importantly similar. Less often have the old accounts been connected to these, and that—whatever its ultimate meaning—is hopefully the contribution here. The idea and reported experience that one may dream or otherwise envision another and later recognize them by various means such as a painting, a graven image, or a statue is a truly old one. The effects of these experiences upon the individual are often similar to the experiences confirmed by the actual meeting in life of the vision's object. They have been well known across various religious traditions and implemented toward various and similar ends by the hagiographer, the historian, and others. Like the rest of the accounts in this book, they too deserve much further notice from this perspective.

Epilogue

The phenomenon of dreaming of a person, place, or thing before encountering them in life is a culturally and historically persistent human experience. In various places and times, these experiences have been specifically sought, sometimes being predicated upon the belief that dreams may truthfully reveal the location of people and things generally. This, in turn, speaks to just how widely it has been believed that the soul may literally visit distant places while the individual sleeps. Often, these are spontaneous and at times, strikingly profound. This comes out in the annals and the memorates alike. The general idea that the dream might reveal truthfully fundamentally stems from experiences in which the dream profoundly coincided with the external world. These are dreams so great in number that they seem, in their sheer volume, to give lie to the notion that our capacity to perceive is confined to the recognized channels of perception. This work, however, may simply constitute a history of errors in memory and perception, or a combination of both. This alone, I hope, would make for an interesting clinically related curiosity.

Regarding déjà rêvé specifically, this work suggests a variety of further areas to explore and elaborate upon. More granular analysis may better categorize such things. The tales could be analyzed in an attempt to draw comparisons between the kinds of people who have had these experiences, both then and now. While an upcoming work will deal in more detail with dreaming of places before they are come upon in life, rather than people, this is another area ripe for inquiry. Further work could illuminate the relationship between these kinds of experiences and the NDE. Much work remains to be done in finding many more early modern accounts of this kind rather than the usual flurry of allusions to the general beliefs or related divination. Very little literature exists on experiences of this kind despite much interest in certain corners during the mid- to late nineteenth century and early to mid-twentieth century. Despite the many questions that arise, one thing is abundantly clear: these experiences have impacted individuals, communities, and indeed, the historical record to a far larger extent than has been recognized to this point. We have seen how—both in their general and specific details—our contemporaries have experienced largely similar and often indistinguishable dreams, visions, and later encounters as occur in the oldest tales, the romances, and the folklore. The aftereffects too are often similar between these sources, connecting them in important ways. The kinds of beliefs that emerge in their wake are also strikingly similar. Knowledge of those traditions and tales is clearly not a necessity in whether or not one might undergo what is nevertheless an experience indistinguishable from those traditions. This, of course, would always have been the case, and the spontaneous déjà rêvé may therefore have been the specific impetus for some of the great romances, dream visions, legends, and tales that we have seen. This is manifestly not an unreasonable possibility. We have seen the truth of this, after all, with the likes of Shaw's *Pygmalion*, among others. There is much further work to be done here too.

It may be, in the final analysis, that there is some mundane explanation in a high percentage of the cases presented here. Mundanity, of course, is a relative term, and there could still be said to have been much magic in the making of these strange occurences in that case. These experiences, in their ubuiqity, in the earnestness of their often discerning subjects, and in their strange capacity to impell movement and change, however, may also be suggestive of something much more. They take their place alongside the many other still inexplicable and non-ordinary human experiences that, in a moment, may change our very sense of things. In the life of the individual, a certain divine imbalance may be brought to bear upon the predictable monotony that daily life may sometimes become, thus turning our thoughts to higher things. We have seen this in the individuals turning to love, to religion, to belief in spirits and otherworldly guidance on the authority of these visions and dreams. These are experiences that, while often less dramatic, compare in this way to some of the most well known of this kind, such as encounters with the psychedelic, apparitions at the moment of a loved one's death, or journeys to other realms during the near-death experience. Whatever else comes of the consideration and study of these and related expriences, they warrant greater attention from all quarters for these reasons alone. Whatever we may think of those reporting these things, and they *will* continue to do so, we should be open, at least, to the idea that they may know something about this strange universe we find ourselves in, something that we ourselves do not.

Acknowledgments

Firstly, a huge thanks to my editors, Albo Sudekum and Karen Gordon, for their much-needed attention to detail and suggestions. Thanks go also to Aaron Davis for the beautiful cover art and to Gary Lachman for his wonderful foreword. Thanks very kindly to you, the reader, for picking up this book, and I hope, at the very least, some sense of the number of strange corners of human experience there are still yet to be explored is imparted, whatever their ultimate origins. These, after all, are shy and delicate specimens (if I may borrow the words of Alister Hardy), hard to pin down, and most often come unbidden to those unsuspecting. For those that have found life, love, and meaning through experiences of this kind, however, there is no doubt as to their importance.

Notes

PREFACE

1. Godbey, "The Influence of Alexander's Conquest Upon Jewish Life," 182.

INTRODUCTION. DÉJÀ RÊVÉ AND PRECOGNITION

1. Funkhouser and Schredl, "Frequency of Déjà Vu," 60.
2. Irwin, "Psychology of Déjà Vu," 197.
3. Sno,"Déjà vu and Jamais vu," 340.
4. *Buchanan's Journal of Man*, "Telepathic Mysteries," 41–42.
5. Funkhouser, "'Dream' Theory of Déjà Vu," 107.
6. Funkhouser, "'Dream' Theory of Déjà Vu," 107–8.
7. Markova and Berrios, "Paramnesias and Delusions of Memory," 315.
8. Markova and Berrios, "Paramnesias and Delusions of Memory," 326.
9. Eranimos and Funkhouser, "Eastern Understanding Déjà Rêvé," 155.
10. Funkhouser and Schredl, "Frequency of Déjà Vu," 62.
11. Ryback and Sweitzer, *Dreams Come True*, 6.
12. Curot et al., "Déjà-rêvé: Prior dreams," 875–85.
13. Brown, *Déjà Vu Experience*, 5–6.
14. Brown, *Déjà Vu Experience*, 113.
15. Sno, "Déjà vu and Jamais vu," 338.
16. Sno and Linszen, "Déjà Vu Experience," 1587.
17. Brown, *Déjà Vu Experience*, 114.
18. Markova and Berrios, "Paramnesias and Delusions of Memory," 327.

19. Thorpe, "Déjà Rêvé Is Déjà Vu."
20. Cartagenova and Smith, "What Does It Mean?"
21. LaMotte, "No, You Haven't Read."
22. Forsythe, "Déjá Rêvè."
23. Perry, *Shelley's Relationship to Plato*, 55–56.
24. Dodd, "Déjà Rêvé."
25. Funkhouser, "'Dream' Theory Déjà Vu," 107.

1. DÉJÀ RÊVÉ, BELIEF, AND THE POWER OF DREAMS

1. Shames, *Amazing Mentors*, 48.
2. Bernice Pauahi Bishop Museum, *Memoirs*, 498.
3. Heppner, *Seeds of Disquiet*, 112–13.
4. Broomfield, *Other Ways of Knowing*, 165.
5. Jenkins, *Balance Point*, 139–41, 150–51.
6. Omarr, *Spirit Guides*, 309–17.
7. Fontana and Fontana, *Bullseye Marriage*, 24.
8. Evans, *Sufferings in Africa*, 68–70.
9. Rismay, *Science Sacred Scripture*, 125–26.
10. Riley, *Sufferings in Africa*, 70.
11. Green, *Sightseeing Undiscovered Country*, 140–42.
12. [boringmom33], "Met someone in real life that I had met in a dream." Reddit, r/HighStrangeness, June 19, 2023.
13. Bridges, *Through Eyes of Innocent*, 18.
14. Radha, *Realities of Dreaming Mind*, 198–200.
15. Goldhammer, "Herzl and Freud," 194.
16. Blosfelds, *Stormtrooper on the Eastern Front*, 59–60.
17. Equiano, *Kidnapped Prince*, 100.
18. Calkhoven, *Harriet Tubman*, 70–71.
19. Bradford, *Harriet Tubman*, 118.
20. Cheung, *Celtic Angels*, 235.
21. Friedenthal, *Goethe*, 475.
22. "Strange Dream Fulfilled," 139–41.
23. Bourne, *Dancing with Witches*, 178.
24. Chauran, *Clairvoyance for Beginners*, 25–26.
25. Minkoff, *Return to Who You Are*, 125–27.

26. Gollnick, *Meanings of Dreams*, 14–16.
27. Hyslop, "Clairvoyant Diagnosis," 188–89.
28. Piozzi, *Thraliana*, 336–38.
29. Isaacson, *Healing Land*, 277.
30. Deacon, *Australia Down Under*, 187–88.
31. Isaacson, *Healing Land*, 277–78.
32. Mewborn, "Life of Sarah Hamilton," 1–5.
33. Gurney et al., *Phantasms of Living*, 267–68.
34. Williams, *Memories*, 16–17.
35. Borret, "English Solicitor's Note Book," 245–48.
36. Bartlett, *Psi Trek*, 76–77.
37. Abercrombie, *Inquiries Intellectual Powers*, 285–87.
38. Hare, *Story of My Life*, 52–54.
39. *The National Police Gazette*, "A Wonderful Dream," 6.
40. Glass, *Foresaw the Future*, 192–93.
41. Berlitz, *Charles Berlitz's World*, 93–94.
42. Benn, *China's Golden Age*, 273–74.
43. Rawlins, "Abiah Darby's Dream," 108–9.
44. "Dreaming to Some Purpose," 27–28.
45. Holdich, *History of Crowland Abbey*, 76.
46. Bushkovitch, *Religion and Society in Russia*, 123–25.

2. THE OLD, THE NEW, AND BELIEFS THAT MOVE

1. Marigny, *History of Arabians*, 175–76.
2. Lasker, "Gersonides on Dreams," 47.
3. "A Remarkable Dream."
4. Child, "The Second Sight," 172–73.
5. Elliot, *Apocryphal New Testament*, 281.
6. Morison, *Malachi to Matthew*, 28–29.
7. Burch, *She Who Dreams*, x, 202.
8. Palavestra, *Legends of Old Sarajevo*, 58–59.
9. Neale, *Annals of Virgin Saints*, 376–77.
10. Hassan, *American Catholic Catalog*, 157–59.
11. Coulombe, *History of the Popes*, 260–61.
12. Gurian, *Love's Journey*, 91–92.
13. Curtis, *Persian Myths*, 56.

14. Rabb, *National Epics*, 216–17.
15. Uthaymeen, *Explanation of Riyadus-Saliheen Volume 5*, 520–21.
16. Ure, *Rumanian Folk Tales*, 45–56.
17. Schattschneider, *Through Five Hundred Years*, 23–24.
18. Knappert, *Indian Mythology*, 194.
19. Ramanujan, *Folktales from India*, 305.
20. Ray, *Tribals of Orissa*, 18.
21. Elswit, *East Asian Story Finder*, 74.
22. Yun, *Opening Mind's Eye*, 66–68.
23. Laloy, *Mirror of China*, 61.
24. Shiyuan, *Wandering Spirits*, 107.
25. Shiyuan, *Wandering Spirits*, 140.
26. Ni, *Book of Changes*, 649–50.
27. Ury, *Times Now Past*, 67–69.
28. Inglis, *Power of Dreams*, 126.
29. Mayer, *Ancient Tales Modern Japan*, 307.
30. Lewis, *After Atheism*, 66.
31. Haire, *Be Brave*, 119–135.
32. Adeney, *Unchanging Commission*, 62.
33. Davis, *Native America Twentieth Century*, 476–77.
34. Dorsey, *Pawnee Mythology*, 52–56.
35. Dorsey, *Pawnee Mythology (Part I)*, 414–25.
36. Grant, *Bit of Truth*, 53–60.
37. Landes, *Ojibwa Woman*, 156.
38. Handy, *Marquesan Legends*, 81–82.
39. Bierhorst, *Mythology of South America*, 218.
40. Thomas, *Warrior Herdsmen*, 176.
41. Meurant, *Sixty Years Ago*, 74.
42. Huxley, *The Invisibles*, 121–22.

3. HEALERS AND SAINTS, SUFIS AND SHEIKS

1. Rawlinson, *Book of Enlightened Masters*, 133.
2. Tosun, *Bahauddin Naqshband*, 14–15.
3. Jerrahi, *Irshad*, xxv.
4. Barks, *The Glance*, xiv–xv.
5. Geaves, *Sufis of Britain*, 38.

6. Bloomquist, *God Shall Grow Up*, 315–16.
7. Pinto, "Mystery of Nizamuddin Dargah," 120.
8. Chandrasekhar, *Stopped in Our Tracks*, 39–40.
9. Amritaswarupananda, *Ammachi*, 266.
10. Singh, *Great Sikh Saints*, 47–49.
11. "Conversations of Swami Sivananda," 417–19.
12. Trungpa, *Collected Works Trungpa*, 355.
13. Longkumer, *Narratives of Belonging*, 51.
14. McRae, *In Search of Shangri-La*, 100–101.
15. Namkhai Norbu Rinpoche, *Crystal and Way of Light*, 8–10.
16. "Arthur Schopenhauer," 49.
17. Kearney, *Faces of Goddess*, 110–12.
18. Barasch, *Healing Dreams*, 200–201.
19. Harvey, *Six Korean Women*, 108–109.
20. Steinmetz, *Pipe, Bible, Peyote*, 121–22.
21. Mast, *Caroline's Consent*, 139.
22. Harner, *Cave and Cosmos*, 135.
23. Donnell, *Transcendent Dreaming*, 67–71.
24. Trafzer, *Earth Song, Sky Spirit*, 3.
25. Kwilecki, *Becoming Religious*, 187.
26. Bosworth, *New Studies in Acts*, 50.
27. Deloria, *Singing for Spirit*, 20–22.
28. Muzorewa, *Rise Up & Walk*, 30–32.
29. Cohen, *Honoring Medicine*, 299–300.
30. Morris, *They're Not Gone*, 191–98.
31. Stoia, "Patient Portent," 61.
32. Hodgson, "Psychical Research. Premonitions," 180–83.
33. Crafts, *The Reason Why*, 76–77.
34. Hartglass, "Adele Bloch-Bauer and Me," 32–42.
35. Gould, *Yawning Contagious*, 80–81.
36. Lukara, *Riding Grace*, 141–42.
37. Heinerman, *Spirit World Manifestations*, 21.
38. Cannon, *Gospel Truth*, 4.
39. Ewing, "Dream of Spiritual Initiation," 62–63.
40. Ewing, "Dream of Spiritual Initiation," 61.
41. Vijavargiya, *Swami Ramanand*, 2.
42. Eagle, *Beyond the Lodge*, 104.

43. Eagle, *Beyond the Lodge*, ix–x.
44. Connor, *Shamans*, 21.
45. Randolph, *Ozark Magic and Folklore*, 127–28.
46. Macpherson, "Samoan Medicine," 40.
47. Aldhouse-Green, *World of Druids*, 19.
48. Gaume, *Catechism of Perseverance*, 194.
49. Whelan, *Macbeth*, 14.
50. Hyslop, "Clairvoyant Diagnosis," 47.
51. Matthews, *The Cohongoroota*, 93–95.
52. Thurber, *Believe in Miracles*, 46.
53. Thurber, *Believe in Miracles*, 12.
54. Keeney, "Shakers of St. Vincent," 205–06.
55. Keeney, "Shakers of St. Vincent," 210–11.
56. Chetanananda, *Swami Subodhananda*, 158–59.
57. Schwartz, *Leaves from Garden of Eden*, 130–34.
58. Bowes, *Word Within*, 91–92.
59. Kao, *Classical Tales*, 125–26.
60. Brower, "Holy Man Shinano Province," 218–23.
61. Baring-Gould and Fisher, *British Saints*, 390–91.
62. Russell, *The Pima Indians*, 375–79.
63. Young, *Memoirs of John R. Young*, 47–53.
64. "Memoir," 2–3.

4. DIVINATION AND DREAMS

1. Rouvelas, *Greek Traditions and Customs*, 58.
2. Zampounis, *Watch Your Manners*, 63.
3. O'Hanlon, *Irish Folklore*, 240.
4. Welsch, *Nebraska Pioneer Folklore*, 268–69.
5. MacNeil, *Tales Until Dawn*, 399.
6. MacNeil, *Tales Until Dawn*, 401.
7. Soltow, *Quilting the World Over*, 73.
8. Emrich, *Folklore of Love and Courtship*, 38.
9. Pendel, *Thirty-Six Years*, 74–76.
10. Guthrie, *Old Scottish Customs*, 71–72.
11. Newell, *Games and Songs*, 99.
12. Moore, *Folk-lore of Isle of Man*, 125.

13. Noe, *Witches' Dream Book*, 87.
14. Garber, *Exploring Ethnic Vancouver*, 223.
15. Waugh, "Canadian Folk-Lore," 30.
16. Wintemberg and Wintemberg, "Folklore from Grey County, Ontario," 96.
17. Daniels and Stevens, *Encyclopaedia of Superstitions*, 67.
18. Sikes, *British Goblins*, 304.
19. Schell, *Werner's Readings and Recitations*, 56.
20. Clucas and Clucas, *Pocket Guide to Dreams*, 84.
21. Tally, "Courtship and Marriage," 140.
22. Wilde, *Ancient Legends, Mystic Charms*, 156.
23. Hart, *Flora of County Donegal*, 390–91.
24. Halliwell-Phillipps, *Popular Rhymes and Nursery Tales*, 217–18.
25. Liebman, *From Caravan to Casserole*, 46.
26. Akeroyd, *Vegetables for the Gourmet Gardener*, 17.
27. Day, *The Celtic Calendar*, 237.
28. Halliwell-Phillipps, *Popular Rhymes and Nursery Tales*, 216.
29. Day, *The Celtic Calendar*, 360.
30. Aubrey, *Miscellanies*, 103.
31. Aubrey, *Miscellanies*, 103.
32. Miles, *Christmas in Ritual*, 215.
33. Dragic, "Love Divinations," 620.
34. *The World and Its Peoples*, 101.
35. Daniels and Stevens, *Encyclopaedia of Superstitions*, 67.
36. Coulton, *Life in the Middle Ages Vol I*, 146.
37. *Missouri: WPA Guide*, 455–56.
38. Dragic, "Love Divinations," 625.
39. Daniels and Stevens, *Encyclopaedia of Superstitions*, 68.
40. MacDermott, *Bulgarian Folk Customs*, 219.
41. MacDermott, *Bulgarian Folk Customs*, 193.
42. Bainton, *Mammoth Book of Superstition*, 49.
43. Beam, *Traditions of Christmas*, 217.
44. Villa and Matossian, *Armenian Village Life*, 133.
45. Miyatovich, "Psychic Science," 421.
46. Monger, *Marriage Customs*, 288.
47. Monger, *Marriage Customs*, 99.
48. Westwood, "The Seasonal Round," 88.
49. Stovel, "Tatiana's Letter, A Literary Legacy."

50. *The Agawam Advertiser*, 1976.
51. Hauptmann, "Spanish Folklore from Tampa, Florida," 23.
52. Hand, *Brown Collection North Carolina Folklore*, 588–89.
53. Constantinidou-Partheniadou, *Travelogue in Greece*, 62.
54. Hyatt, *Folk-Lore from Adams County*, 394.
55. Chiasson et al., "Acadian Folklore," 658.
56. Daniels and Stevens, *Encyclopaedia of Superstitions*, 88.
57. Eason, *Complete Guide to Fairies*, 119.
58. Abbott, *Macedonian Folklore*, 50–51.
59. Westwood, "The Seasonal Round," 91.
60. Dunwich, *A Witch's Halloween*, 147.
61. Dunwich, *A Witch's Halloween*, 148.
62. Day, *The Celtic Calendar*, 213.
63. Halliwell-Phillips, *Popular Rhymes and Nursery Tales*, 215.
64. Laws, *The History of Little England*, 409.
65. Thomas and Thomas, *Kentucky Superstitions*, 42.
66. O'Moore, "Kathleen of Mora," 458.
67. Elliot, *Azerbaijan*, 52.
68. MacKenzie, *Dreams and Dreaming*, 76–77.
69. Sweet, *Tell Toqaan*, 204.
70. Faigao, "Filipino Love Oracles," 547.
71. Reed, *Papua New Guinea's Last Place*, 108.
72. Asai, *The Otogiboko*, 269.
73. Gwathmey, *Lots of Luck*, 63.
74. Aschwanden, *Karanga Mythology*, 262.
75. Stanton, *Images of Aboriginal Australia*, 63.
76. Stanton, *Images of Aboriginal Australia*, 339.
77. Hendricks, *Roosters, Rhymes*, 51.
78. Ergil, "Turkish Superstitions and Traditions."
79. Philpot, *The Sacred Tree*, 107–108.
80. MacKenzie, *Dreams & Dreaming*, 75.
81. MacKenzie, *Dreams & Dreaming*, 76.

5. DREAM VISIONS AND REAL DECISIONS

1. O'Neill, *Selected Letters of Eugene O'Neill*, 45.
2. Guest, *The Mabinogion: Lady Charlotte Guest*, 81–89.
3. Murphy, "Aislinge Oengusso—Dream of Oengus."

4. MacKenzie, *Wonder Tales*, 33–49.
5. Rugoff and Low, *Harvest World Folk Tales*, 262–66.
6. Schlauch, *Romance in Iceland*, 13–14.
7. Moore, "Jaufre Rudel," 527.
8. Dronke, *Rise of European Love-Lyric*, 166.
9. Levin, *Dreaming the English Renaissance*, 114–15.
10. Webster, *Sacred Sierra*, 189–91.
11. Singleton, *A Guide to the Opera*, 217.
12. Moore, "Jaufre Rudel," 527.
13. Guerber, *Legends of the Middle Ages*, 163.
14. Brown, *Book of Saints and Friendly Beasts*, 126–30.
15. Marquand, *Flowers of Ten Centuries*, 13.
16. Moore, "Jaufre Rudel," 529.
17. Dronke, *Rise of European Love-Lyric*, 165–66.
18. Blankenagel, *Heinrich von Kleist*, 157, 166.
19. Blankenagel, *Heinrich von Kleist*, 163.
20. Gerould, *Grateful Dead*, 56–57.
21. Boratov, "Epico-Novelistic Narrative," 35.
22. Schwartz, *Invisible Kingdoms*, 12–24.
23. Levy, *Three Dervishes*, 19–32.
24. Moxon, *Peter's Halakhic Nightmare*, 476–77.
25. Reik, *Creation of Woman*, 64–65.
26. Fernandez-Armesto, *1492*, 270.
27. Lyons, *Arabian Epic*, 2.
28. Schlauch, *Romance in Iceland*, 64.
29. Schlauch, *Romance in Iceland*, 65.
30. Walker and Uysal, *Tales Alive in Turkey*, 34–54.
31. Walker and Uysal, *Tales Alive in Turkey*, 265.
32. Tawney, *Katha Sarit Sagara*, 553–54.
33. Lienhard, "Classical Poetry," 240.
34. Lienhard, "Classical Poetry," 244–45.
35. Behl et al., *Manjhan Madhumalatai*, xviii.
36. Husain, *Islamic Garden*, 165–69.
37. Hwang Pae-gang, *Korean Myths*, 2006: 97.
38. Hegel, "Heavens and Hells," 3.
39. Kao, *Classical Tales of the Supernatural*, 130–32.
40. Mackerras, *Chinese Theatre Modern Times*, 18.

41. Hearn, *Kwaidan*, 111–18.
42. Hearn, *Kwaidan*, 35–41.
43. Beckwith, *Romance of Laieikawai*, 371–72.
44. Andersen, *Myths and Legends*, 267–83.
45. Blackwood, *Buka Passage*, 548–49.
46. Gillison, *Culture and Fantasy*, 341.
47. Blackwood, *Buka Passage*, 549.
48. Hungry Wolf, *Ways of Grandmothers*, 142–44.
49. Schwarz, *Windigo*, 28–33.
50. Bierhorst, *Latin American Folktales*, 157–59.
51. Morris, *African Myths*, 28–31.
52. Knappert, *African Mythology*, 169–70.
53. Tortolano, *Samuel Coleridge-Taylor*, 171.
54. Disraeli, *Contarini Fleming*, 211–24.
55. Brown, *Brodie's "Nineteteen Eighty-Four,"* 25.
56. Moss, *Secret History of Dreaming*, 106.

6. LOVE AT SECOND SIGHT

1. Silver, *The Darker Side*, 227.
2. Fors, *Limits of Matter*, 27.
3. Fors, *Limits of Matter*, 30.
4. "Women of the Underground."
5. Biesanz, *Helmi Mavis*, 81.
6. Monroe, *Novel and Society*, 94.
7. Beitman, *Connecting with Coincidence*, 36–38.
8. "Bella Cooke's Life Work," 564.
9. Ament, *Everything That Matters*, 202–203.
10. Harris, *The Adair County News*, 1901.
11. Chapman, *The Golden Ones*, xiii, 19–26.
12. McKelvey, *Gift of Barbed Wire*, 164–65.
13. Ellison, *The First Snow*, 160.
14. Garfitt, *The Horseman's Word*, 324.
15. Bridges and Niuwenhuyse, *A Golden Love*, 39.
16. Kieft, *Innersource*, 50.
17. "Search Is Made for Armada Gold," 19.
18. Abbott, *Macedonian Folklore*, 79–80.

19. Rogers, *Soul Mates*, 34.
20. Inglis, *Power of Dreams*, 159–60.
21. Morris, *Faith in Every Footstep*, 21–23.
22. Livon, *The Happy Medium*, 166–68.
23. Lee, *Virginia Ghosts*, 124.
24. Dickerson, *House of Cards*, 313–14.
25. Feather, *The Gift*, 121.
26. Vissell and Vissell, *Meant to Be*, 56–60.
27. Mbenoun, *More Than a Great Partner*, 29–30.
28. Kieft, *Innersource*, 223.
29. Vissell and Vissell, *Meant to Be*, 9.
30. [Thin-Comfortable-597], commenting on [A5TR0N0T], "Meeting a Soul Mate in Dreams." Reddit, r/AstralProjection, August 18, 2023.
31. Toporowitch, *At Your Command*, 24–25.
32. Lewis and Hamilton, *Tabernacle Stories of Faith*, 203–205.
33. Spangler, *Dreams and Miracles*, 141–42.
34. Burstein, *Lincoln Dreamt He Died*, 65.
35. St. Clair, *The Butterfly Garden*, 78–79, 95.
36. Kearney, *Sundays with TJ*, 216–18, 224–23.
37. Gindikin, *Physicists and Mathematicians*, 23.
38. Giglioni, *Synesian Dreams*, 575.
39. Port Arthur Founder, "Connection to Supernatural," 2016.
40. Leibnitz, *Human Understanding*, 514.
41. Gaddis, "Romantic Dreams," 15.
42. Beatty, *Ferdinand de Lesseps*, 327.
43. Simons, *Networks of Dissolution*, 179–90.
44. Bobrick, *East of the Sun*, 177.
45. Garth, *Tolkien Great War*, 72.
46. Ebon, *Beyond Space and Time*, 69–71.
47. Gaddis, "Romantic Dreams," 14.
48. Quilliam, *Women on Sex*, 167.
49. Prince, *Noted Witnesses*, 272–73.
50. Schnell, *The Initiation*, 13–14.
51. Crowe, *Night Side of Nature*, 51–52.
52. Lennox, *Llewellyn's Book of Dreams*, 53–54.
53. [Wobgyn], commenting on [deleted], "Has anyone dreamt of their twin flame years before meeting them? Is it a cruel joke from the universe or do

we reunite?" Reddit, r/twinflames, November 15, 2021.

54. [suspicious_duck], commenting on [anneschwarzenbach], "I met someone I was shown in a dream 10 years ago." Reddit, r/Thetruthishere, June 28, 2021.
55. Aguirre, *Encounters Other Side*, 69–70.
56. Michaels, *Second Chance Goodbye*, 23–24.
57. Noffke, "The Warriors of Peace," 5.
58. Davis, *The Heart of Healing*, 11.
59. Davis, *The Heart of Healing*, 24–26.
60. Gaddis, "Romantic Dreams," 14.
61. Michael, *Finding Your Soul Mate*, 3–21.
62. Frazer, *Mabel Dodge Luhan*, 59, 70–71.
63. [Interesting-Show-553], commenting on [Adorable_Decision826], "Dreaming about Twin Flame before seeing them." Reddit, r/twinflames, April 17, 2023.
64. Private communication with the author.
65. [rutilated04], "Dreamt of my husband before I ever met him." Reddit, r/Psychonaut, January 11, 2023.
66. [Intelligent_Sir-2796], commenting on [rutilated04], "Dreamt of my husband before I ever met him." Reddit, r/Psychic, January 21, 2023.
67. Randles, "USA and Isle of Man," 9–12.
68. Bliss, "Mysteries of Mediumship," 67.
69. Ebon, *Beyond Space and Time*, 21–25.
70. Hunt, *Natural History of Love*, 51.
71. Stevens, *The Mystery of Dreams*, 232.

7. GOD OF THE GAPS

1. Robinson, *Frank B. Robinson*, 155–56.
2. Porter, *Walls Fall Down*, 152.
3. Bennett, *Daughter of Zion!*, 111–21.
4. Swindall, *Freedom from Depression*, 142.
5. Howell, *Not Through with You*, 81–82.
6. Ferguson, *Countee Cullen*, 8–9.
7. Murphy, *Telepsychics*, 41.
8. Francis and Bridges, *A Golden Love*, 118.
9. Lindenburgh, *Miracles & Messages*, 13.

10. Snow, "Popular Medicine in a Black Neighborhood," 49.
11. "Dream."
12. Madison, *Healing From God*, 90–91.
13. Sutherland, *Transformed by the Light*, 117–18.
14. Kline, *I Could Use a Miracle*, 285.
15. Stibal, *Work with God*, 170–71.
16. Robinson, *Frank B. Robinson*, 32–33.
17. Kunz, *Reminiscences John W. Woolley*, 33–35.
18. Campbell, *Dance with Me Daddy*, 189.
19. Scheller, *Operation Exodus*, 35–36.
20. Van Natta, *A Miraculous Life*, 39–40.
21. Bolz, *God Secrets*, 124.
22. Clarke, *Mother Mary of St. Euphrasia*, 130–31.
23. Jones, *Quietism*, 39–40.
24. Bouix, *Autobiography of Blessed Mother*, 12.
25. Serdans, *I'm Moving Two*, 123.
26. Allen, *Depths of Iniquity*, 42–44.
27. Taylor, *Baptists on American Frontier*, 148.
28. Fuller, *When Teens Pray*, 152–54.
29. Musick, *Life After Heaven*, 160.
30. Heinerman, *Eternal Testimonies*, 153–56.
31. Heinerman, *Spirit World Manifestations*, 151–52.
32. Cox, *Called to Serve*, 183–84.
33. "Woke Up to Gospel," 76.
34. Nelson, "Should an Elder Choose," 10.
35. Ruoff, *Testimonies of Restoration*, 189–92.
36. Shipp, *Champions of Light*, 34.
37. Mansson McGinty, *Becoming Muslim*, 63.
38. Myers, "What Faith Will Do," 12.
39. Taft, *Mrs. Mary Taft*, 68–70.
40. Rea, *Diary Serenus Gardner*, 27.
41. Ricci, *China in Sixteenth Century*, 221.
42. Furutan, *Stories of Baha' u'llah*, 16–19.
43. Madison, *Healing from God*, 82.
44. Lanktree, *Narrative of Matthew Lanktree*, 53.
45. Moulton, *Young Pastor's Wife*, 239–40.
46. Bence, *His Mysterious Ways*, 30.

47. Wickramaratne, *My Adventure in Faith*, 101–3, 177–80.
48. Hill, "Experience," 154–55.

8. I KNEW THAT PERSON WOULD COME

1. Knappert, *African Mythology*, 210–11.
2. Lafleur, *Semi-Centennial Historical Sketch*, 25–26.
3. Sellier, *Miracles and Other Wonders*, 180–90.
4. Sure and Ch'ao, *Silence Echoes*, 242–43.
5. Thanegi, *Nor Iron Bars a Cage*, 79.
6. Mittermaier, *Dreams That Matter*, 164–65.
7. Stanley, *Stanley in Africa*, 323.
8. Toelken, "Moccasin Telegraph," 45–48.
9. Drimmer, *Captured by Indians*, 75.
10. Van Gorder, *Violence in God's Name*, 81.
11. Wooding, *Twenty-Six Lead Soldiers*, 170.
12. Wilstach, *Richard Mansfield*, 71–73.
13. Inglis, *Power of Dreams*, 126–27.
14. Heinerman, *Spirit World Manifestations*, 249–50.
15. Wareham, "Soul Science," 260.
16. Flammarion, *L'inconnu*, 425–26.
17. Julius, "Tea Table Talk," 321–22.
18. Flammarion, *L'inconnu*, 462.
19. Barry, *Diary of William Dyer*, 26.
20. Crespin, *On Stage, Off Stage*, 260–61.
21. Marsh, *Locked In*, 150–51.
22. Howard, *Sun-Sand and Survival*, 38.
23. Ovid, *Ovid Six Volumes III*, 385–89.
24. Briggs, *Rise of Mahomedan Power*, 258–59.
25. Isaacs and Olitzky, *Sacred Moments*, 42–43.
26. Zimmerman, *Saint Gregory*, 112–14.
27. Birch, *Stories from Ming Collection*, 109.
28. Moss, *Conscious Dreaming*, 96.
29. Moss, *Dream Gates*, 164.
30. Kao, *Tales of the Supernatural*, 248.
31. de Rachewiltz et al., *In Service Khan*, 228.
32. Mayer, *Ancient Tales Modern Japan*, 76.

33. Clark, *Indian Legends Northern Rockies*, 70.
34. Hoffman, *Yesterday Is Tomorrow*, 120–21.
35. Clark, *Indian Legends Pacific Northwest*, 114–15.
36. Newton, *Mackinac Island*, 104.
37. Charlesworth et al., *Religion Aboriginal Australia*, 223.
38. "Portuguese History," 152.
39. Sundkler, *Christian Ministry in Africa*, 25–26.
40. Bentley, *Life On The Congo*, 91.
41. Rountree and Lunt, *Exorcising the Demons*, 13.
42. Mercree, *Way of Psychic Heart*, 196–97.
43. Stevenson, *Letters of Madame*, 286–87.
44. Myers, "The Subliminal Self," 521–23.
45. Bradley-DeTally, *Without a Net*, 69–74.
46. Dossey, *Reinventing Medicine*, 131–33.
47. Child, "The Second Sight," 171.
48. de Voragine, *Golden Legend of Jacobus*, 88–89.
49. Charron, *Mother Bourgeoys (1620–1700)*, 31–34.
50. Rees, *Cambro British Saints*, 437–38.
51. Jaffray, "Iona, The Sacred Isle," 256.
52. Stokes, *Lives of Saints*, 319–20.
53. Matthieu, *Enlightened Vagabond*, 24.
54. Coleridge, *St. Mary's Convent*, 127.
55. Carter, *John Henry and Gertrude Cooper*, 270–71.
56. Lee, *History of the Church*, 115–16.
57. E.O.G., *Mysterious Ways*, 117– 20.
58. Locke, "Who am I," 114–15, 122–23.
59. Ricci, *China in the Sixteenth Century*, 518.
60. Rich, *Mennonite Women*, 46.
61. Choquette, *The Psychic Pathway*, 210–12.
62. Flammarion, *L'inconnu*, 427.
63. Lipsenthal, *Enjoy Every Sandwich*, 16–23.
64. Wolf, *Spiritual Life Rafts*, 79–81.

9. PICTURE PERFECT

1. Aleksievich, *Secondhand Time*, 437–39.
2. Rushamenza, *The Rope*, 80–88.

3. *Today's Groom Magazine, The Groom to Be's*, 43–46.
4. Newmark and Walden, *Chicken Soup*, 256–59.
5. Montgomery, *Conscious Women*, 51–54.
6. Li and Luckert, *Mythology and Folklore of Hui*, 245–47.
7. Knappert, *Indian Mythology*, 252.
8. Bowman, *Samaritan Documents*, 120–21.
9. Thomson, *The Land and the People*, 171.
10. Brown, *Through the Mind of India*, 164–65.
11. Dykstra, *The Otogiboko*, 134–37.
12. Freeman, *Philosopher and Druids*, 84–85.
13. Freeman, *Philosopher and Druids*, 85.
14. Asfar and Thay, *Ghost Stories*, 199–206.
15. Pearl, *Dear Yvette*, 157–62.
16. Kamath and Kher, *Sai Baba of Shirdi*, 1991.
17. Deshikatmananda, "He Teaches," 521.
18. Deshikatmananda, "He Teaches," 520–21.
19. Cousineau, *Coincidence or Destiny?*, 67.
20. Thurber, *Believe in Miracles*, 44–45.
21. Thurber, *Believe in Miracles*, 62–63.
22. Allen, *Pray, Hope*, 367.
23. Kazhdan and Maguire, "Byzantine Hagiographical Texts," 6.
24. Metford, *Dictionary of Christian Lore*, 236.
25. Kazhdan and Maguire, "Byzantine Hagiographical Texts," 5.
26. Kazhdan and Maguire, "Byzantine Hagiographical Texts," 5–6.
27. Kazhdan and Maguire, "Byzantine Hagiographical Texts," 7–8.
28. Kazhdan and Maguire, "Byzantine Hagiographical Texts," 5.
29. Seraphima, *Saint Seraphima*, 175–77.
30. Vajin, "Saint Herman Guardian Angel," 237–38.
31. Hadley, *Morning Rounds*, 105.
32. Zeff, *Amma*, 36–37.
33. Martine, *Time and Memories*, 281–82.
34. Bound, *Poppy's Faith*, 101–102.
35. Tiwari, *Path of Practice*, 67.
36. Heinerman, *Spirit World Manifestations*, 134–37.
37. Landsburg, *Strange Phenomena*, 43.
38. "Liz, Atlanta and a 'Vision.'"
39. Oxon, "Notes by the Way," 457.

40. Pratt, *The Spirit Tracker*, 156.
41. Fewston, *Time to Love.*
42. Bankson, *G.I. God Imitator*, xi–xiv.
43. Stevens, *Mystery of Dreams*, 113.
44. Grant, *Time Out of Mind*, 117.
45. Jaffe, *Apparitions and Precognition*, 134–35.
46. Rhine, *The Invisible Picture*, 71–72.
47. Perez, *It's Forever Happening*, 71–74.
48. Miller et al., *Heavenly Miracles*, 14–17.
49. Sloan, *Ghosts of Key West*, 33–36.
50. Mahoney, *Maurice Maeterlinck*, 152–59.
51. Redding, *More or Less*, 46–47.
52. Hoffman, *Yesterday Is Tomorrow*, 193.
53. Oh, *Beginning in the Prophetic*, 76–77.
54. Orenstein, "Toward an Ecofeminist Ethic," 175.
55. Cheung, *Celtic Angels*, 161–62.
56. Leek, *Reincarnation*, 5.
57. Guggenheim and Guggenheim, *Hello From Heaven*, 253–4.
58. Guggenheim and Guggenheim, *Hello From Heaven*, 253–54.
59. Hobe, *Eternal Moments*, 33.
60. Rawlings, *Beyond Death's Door*, 17–22.
61. Grey, *Return From Death*, 89.
62. Punzak, *A Spiritual Hypothesis*, 102.
63. Long, *Evidence of Afterlife*, 130.
64. Harris, *Waking Up*, 183.
65. Harris, *Waking Up*, 183–85.
66. Moody and Perry, *Glimpses of Eternity*, 10–12.
67. Varga, *Call From Heaven*, 165–66.
68. Taylor, "World Of Spirits," 231–32.
69. Martin and Romanowski, *Love Beyond Life*, 389–406.
70. Matuauto, "Samoan with Russian Ancestry," 150–55.
71. Smedley, *Soul Mates*, 115.

Bibliography

Abbott, G. F. *Macedonian Folklore.* Cambridge: The University Press, 1903.

Abercrombie, John. *Inquiries Concerning the Intellectual Powers and the Investigation of Truth.* London: John Murray, 1838.

Adeney, David H. *The Unchanging Commission.* Chicago 10: Inter-Varsity Press, 1955.

Aguirre, Cliff. *Encounters with the Other Side: My Experiences with After Death Visitations.* n.p.: Aguirre Business Group, 2016.

Akeroyd, Simon. *Vegetables for the Gourmet Gardener: A Practical Resource from the Garden to the Table.* Upper Saddle River, NJ: R.R. Donnelley & Sons Company, 2000.

Aldhouse-Green, Miranda. *The World of the Druids.* London: Thames & Hudson, 2005.

Aleksievich, Svetlana. *Secondhand Time: The Last of the Soviets.* New York, NY: Random House, 2017.

Allen, Diane. *Pray, Hope, and Don't Worry: True Stories of Padre Pio.* San Diego, CA: Avantine Press, 2009.

Allen, William. *The Depths of Iniquity Cast Up: And the Sovereignty of God's Grace Displayed in the Life, Experience, and Thirty-Eight Years' Ministry, of William Allen.* London: Hougston & Stoneman, 1851.

Ament, Pat. *Everything That Matters: Remembering Rock Climbing.* Fruita, CO: Two Lights Publishing, 2004.

Amritaswarupananda, Swami. *Ammachi: The Life of the Holy Mother Amritanandamayi.* San Ramon, CA: Mata Amritanandamayi Center, 1995.

Andersen, Johannes Carl. *Myths and Legends of the Polynesians.* Rutland, VT: Charles E. Tuttle Company Publishers, 1969.

Anderson, Allen, and Linda Anderson. *Horses with a Mission: Extraordinary True Stories of Equine Service.* Novato, CA: New World Library, 2009.

Andreasen, Suz. *Dreaming the Future: The Ultimate Dream Guide.* Virginia Beach, VA: A.R.R. Press, 2001.

"A Remarkable Dream." Daily Nevada State Journal, May 30, 1889.

"Arthur Schopenhauer." *The Cornhill Magazine* 58/61 (1888): 31–52.

Asai, Ryoi. *The Otogiboko: A Collection of Ghost Stories of Old Japan.* Translated by Yoshiko Dykstra. Honolulu: Kanji Press, 2014.

Aschwanden, Herbert. *Karanga Mythology: An Analysis of the Consciousness of the Karanga in Zimbabwe.* Gweru, Zimbabwe: Mambo Press, 1989.

Asfar, Dan, and Edrick Thay. *Ghost Stories of the Civil War.* Edmonton: Ghost House Publishing, 2015.

"A Strange Dream Fulfilled." *The Spiritualist* 17/12 (1880): 139–41.

Aubrey, John. *Miscellanies.* London: Printed for Edward Castle, 1696.

"A Wonderful Dream: It Reveals the Mystery of a Foul Murder and Clears Up a Strange Dissapearance." *The National Police Gazette* (New York), February 7, 1880.

Bainton, Roy. *The Mammoth Book of Superstition.* London: Robinson, 2016.

Bankson, Michelle. *Becoming a G.I. God Imitator: Basic Training for the Soul.* n.a. Xulon Press, 2004.

Barasch, Marc. *Healing Dreams: Exploring the Dreams That Can Transform Your Life.* New York: Riverhead Books, 2000.

Baring-Gould, Sabine, and John Fisher. *The Lives of the British Saints Volume IV.* London: The Honorable Society of Cymmrodorion, 1913.

Barks, Coleman. *The Glance: Songs of Soul-Meeting.* New York: Viking/Arkana, 1999.

Barry, Jonathon. *The Diary of William Dyer: Bristol in 1762.* Edited by Madge Dresser, Peter Fleming and Roger Leech. Bristol: Bristol Record Society, 2012.

Bartlett, Laile E. *Psi Trek: A world-wide investigation into the lives of psychic people and the researchers who test such phenomena as healing, prophecy, dowsing, ghosts, and life after death.* New York: McGraw-Hill, 1981.

Beam, Linda, J. *Traditions of Christmas and the Stories Behind Them.* n.a. FaithPoint Press, 2008.

Beatty, Charles. *Ferdinand de Lesseps: A Biographical Study.* London: Eyre & Spottiswoode, 1956.

Beck, Martha. *Steering by Starlight: Find Your Right Life, No Matter What.* New York: Rodale Books, 2008.

Beckwith, Martha, trans. *The Hawaiian Romance of Laieikawai.* Washington: Govt. Print. Off., 1918.

Behl, Aditya, Simon Weightman, and Sham Pandey, trans and eds. *Manjhan Madhumalatai: An Indian Sufi Romance.* Oxford: Oxford University Press, 2000.

Beitman, Bernard. *Connecting with Coincidence: The New Science for Using Synchronicity and Serendipity in Your Life.* Deerfield Beach, FL: Health Communications, Inc., 2016.

"Bella Cooke's Life Work." The Christian Herald and Signs of Our Times. January 1, 1890.

Bence, Evelyn. *His Mysterious Ways: More Than Coincidence.* New York, MJF Books, 2010.

Benn, Charles. *China's Golden Age: Everyday Life in the Tang Dynasty.* Oxford, NY: Oxford University Press, 2004.

Bentley, W. Holman. *Life On The Congo.* London: The Religious Tract Society, 1875.

Berlitz, Charles Frambach. *Charles Berlitz's World of Strange Phenomena Volume 2: Strange People and Amazing Stories.* London: Sphere, 1990.

Bernice Pauahi Bishop Museam. *Memoirs of the Bernice Pauahi Bishop Museum of Polynesian Ethnology and Natural History Volume 4.* Honolulu: The Museum, 1916–1917.

Bierhorst, John. *Latin American Folktales: Stories from Hispanic and Indian Traditions.* New York: Pantheon Books, 2002.

Bierhorst, John. *The Mythology of South America.* New York: Quill/W. Morrow, 1988.

Biesanz, Mavis Hiltunen. *Helmi Mavis: A Finnish-American Girlhood.* Cambridge, MN: North Star Press of St. Cloud, Inc., 1989.

Birch, Cyril, trans. *Stories from a Ming Collection: Translations of Chinese Short Stories Published in the Seventeenth Century.* New York: Grove Press, Inc., 1960.

Blackwood, Beatrice. *Both Sides of Buka Passage: An Ethnographic Study of Social, Sexual, and Economic Questions in the North-Western Solomon Islands.* Oxford: At The Clarendon Press, 1935.

Blanche, E. Ferguson. *Countee Cullen and the Negro Renaissance.* New York: Dodd, Mead & Company, 1966.

Blankenagel, John. *The Dramas of Heinrich von Kleist: A Biographical and Critical Study.* Chapel Hill: University of North Carolina Press, 1931.

Bliss, Vincent. "The Mysteries of Mediumship." *Light* 16/787 (1896): 67–69.

Bloomquist, Wayne. *God Shall Grow Up: Body, Soul & Earth Evolving Together.* Sparks, NV: Pondy Pub., 2001.

Blosfelds, Mintauts. *Stormtrooper on the Eastern Front: Fighting with Hitler's Latvian SS.* Barnsley: Pen & Sword Military, 2008.

Bobrick, Benson. *East of the Sun: The Epic Conquest and Tragic History of Siberia.* New York: Poseidon Press, 1992.

Bogard, Travis, and Jackson R. Bryer, eds. *Selected Letters of Eugene O'Neill.* New Haven: Yale University Press, 1988.

Bolz, Shawn. *God Secrets: A Life Filled with Words of Knowledge.* Studio City, CA: ICreate Productions, 2017.

Boratov, Pertev. "The Tale in the Epico-Novelistic Narrative." Translated by Mona Fikry. In *Studies in East European Folk Narrative,* edited by Leah Degh, 4–47. Indiana: American Folklore Society and the Indiana University Folklore Monograph Series, 1978.

Borret, Baxter. "Leaves From An English Solicitor's Note Book VI. A Sunday Afternoon Nap And Its Consequences." *The Green Bag* 12/5 (1900): 245–48.

Bosworth, Edward Increase. *New Studies in Acts.* New York: Young Men's Christian Association Press, 1908.

Bouix, Marcel. *Autobiography of the Blessed Mother Anne of Saint Bartholomew: Inseparable Companion of Saint Teresa, and Foundress of the Carmels of Pontoise, Tours and Antwerp.* Translated by Sister Mary Anna Michael. St. Louis, MO: Collins Printing Co., 1917.

Bound, Harry H. *Poppy's Faith: A Grandfather's Journal of His Encounters with God.* Bloomington, IN: Authorhouse, 2013.

Bourne, Lois. *Dancing with Witches.* London: Robert Hale, 1988.

Bowes, Peter. *The Word Within.* Milwaukee, WI: Sophia Publishing, 2006.

Bowman, John, trans and ed. *Samaritan Documents: Relating to Their History, Religion, and Life.* Pittsburgh, PA: The Pickwick Press, 1977.

Bradford, Sarah. *Harriet Tubman: The Moses of Her People.* Gloucester, MA: Peter Smith, 1981.

Bradley-DaTally, Esther. *Without A Net: A Sojourn in Russia.* Jamestown, NY: Sorry Gnat Press, 1998.

Bridges, Laura Dawn, and Craig Francis Niuwenhuyse. *A Golden Love: Relationships of Divine Enchantment.* Bloomington, IN: Balboa Press, 2012.

Bridges, Senaria B. *Through the Eyes of the Innocent: A Diary of Child Abuse.* New York: iUniverse, Inc., 2010.

Briggs, John, trans. *History of the Rise of the Mahomedan Power In India Till the year A.D 1612 Vol 2.* Calcutta, India: Editions India, 1829.

Broomfield, John. *Other Ways of Knowing: Recharting Our Future with Ageless Wisdom.* Rochester, VT: Inner Traditions, 1997.

Brower, Robert. "The Holy Man of Shinano Province." In *Anthology of Japanese Literature Volume One: Earliest to Mid-Nineteenth Century,* edited by Donald Keene, 218–23. New York: Grove Press, 1955.

Brown, Abbie. *The Book of Saints and Friendly Beasts.* Boston: Houghton Mifflin, c1900.

Brown, Alan. *The Déjà Vu Experience: Essays in Cognitive Psychology.* New York: Pychology Press, 2004.

Brown, Barbara. *Travels Through the Mind of India.* Dallas, TX: Saybrook Publishing Company, 1986.

Brown, George Eric. *Brodie's Notes on George Orwell's Nineteteen Eighty-Four.* London: Pan Books, 1977.

Burch, Wanda Easter. *She Who Dreams: A Journey Into Healing Through Dreamwork.* Novato, CA: New World Library, 2003.

Burden, Zora. "Excerpts from Women of the Underground: Music: Miss Mercy-The GTOs," *Zora Burden: Writer, Artist, Poet,* accessed February 13, 2024.

Burstein, Andrew. *Lincoln Dreamt He Died: The Midnight Visions of Remarkable Americans from Colonial Times to Freud.* New York: Palgrave Macmillan, 2013.

Bushkovitch, Paul. *Religion and Society in Russia: The Sixteenth and Seventeenth Centuries.* New York: Oxford University Press, 1992.

Calkhoven, Laurie. *Harriet Tubman: Leading the Way to Freedom.* New York: Sterling, 2008.

Campbell, Rob. *Dance with Me Daddy: His Story of Building Healthy Churches Around the World.* Fairfax, VA: Xulon Press, 2002.

Cannon, George Q. *Gospel Truth Volume 1. Discourses and Writings of President George Q. Cannon.* Compiled and Edited by Jerreld L. Newquist. Salt Lake City, UT: Deseret Book Company, 1974.

Card, Harold E., Jr. "Indians of Royal Blood Are Baptized." In *Faith Like the Ancients Vol. 2,* Compiled by N.B. Lundwall, 27–28. Manti, Utah: Mountain Valley Publishers, 1968.

Cartagenova, Mari, and Luke Smith. "What Does It Mean When You Have Déjà Vu with Dreams?" Wikihow, December 13, 2023.

Carter, Kate. *Treasures of Pioneer History Volume Six.* Salt Lake City, UT: Daughters of Utah Pioneers, 1957.

Chandrasekhar, K. *Stopped in Our Tracks: Stories of U.G. in India From the Notebooks of K. Chandrasekhar.* New Delhi, India: Smriti Books, 2010.

Chapman, Carole. *The Golden Ones: From Atlantis to a New World.* Mystic, CT: CPS, 2001.

Charlesworth et al., eds. *Religion in Aboriginal Australia.* St. Lucia, Qld: University of Queensland Press, 1984.

Charron, Yvon. *Mother Bourgeoys (1620–1700).* Translated by Sister Saint Godeliva. Canada: Beauchemin, 1050.

Chauran, Alexandra. *Clairvoyance for Beginners: Easy Techniques to Enhance Your Psychic Visions.* Woodbury: Llewellyn Publications, 2014.

Chetanananda, Swami. *Swami Subodhananda: Life, Teachings, Reminiscences, Letters.* Kolkata: Advaita Ashram, 2016.

Cheung, Theresa. *Celtic Angels: True Stories of Irish Angel Blessings.* London: Simon & Schuster, 2012.

Chiasson, Anselme et al. "Acadian Folklore." In *Acadia of the Maritimes: Thematic Studies from the Beginning to the Present,* edited by Jean Daigle, 625–678. Moncton, NB: Chaire D'etudes Acadiennes, 1995.

Child, Lydia Maria. "The Second Sight." *The Spiritual Record* 1/3 (1883): 166–77.

Choquette, Sonia. *The Psychic Pathway: A Workbook for Reawakening the Voice of Your Soul.* New York: Crown Trade Paperbacks, 1995.

C. J. T. Folklore and Legends: Scotland. W. W. Gibbings, 1899.

Clark, Ella E. *Indian Legends from the Northern Rockies.* Norman, OK: University of Oklahoma Press, 1973.

Clarke, A. M. *Life of Reverend Mother Mary of St. Euphrasia Pelletier: First Superior General of the Congregation of Our Lady of Charity of the Good Shepherd of Angers.* London: Burns and Oates, Limited, 1895.

Clarke, Ella E. *Indian Legends of the Pacific Northwest.* Berkeley, CA: University of California Press, 1966.

Clark, LaVerne Harrell. *They Sang for Horses: The Impact of the Horse on Navajo and Apache Folklore.* Boulder, CO: University Press of Colorado, 2011.

Clements, Jonathon. *An Armchair Traveller's History of Finland.* London: The Armchair Traveller, 2014.

Clucas, Philip; Clucas, Douglas. *A Pocket Guide to Dreams.* Bath, UK: Parragon, 2008.

Cohen, Kenneth. *Honoring the Medicine: The Essential Guide to Native American Healing.* New York: Ballantine Books, 2003.

Coleridge, Henry James, trans. *St. Mary's Convent: Micklegate Bar New York (1686–1887).* London: Burns and Oats, 1887.

Connor, Nancy. *Shamans of the World: Extraordinary First Person Accounts of Healings, Mysteries, and Miracles.* Boulder, CO: Sounds True, 2008.

Constantinidou-Partheniadou, Sofia. *A Travelogue in Greece and a Folklore Calandar.* Translated by Michael Papapetrou. Athens, Greece: Published by Sofia Constantindou-Partheniadou, 1992.

"Conversations of Swami Sivananda." *Prabuddha Bharata* 11/53 (1948): 417–23.

Corkery, Daniel. *The Hidden Ireland.* Dublin: Gill and Son, 1967.

Coulton, George. *Life in the Middle Ages Vol I.* London: Cambridge University Press, 1928.

Coulombe, Charles. *A History of the Popes: Vicars of Christ.* New York: MJF Books, 2003.

Cousineau, Phil. *Coincidence or Destiny?: Stories of Synchronicity that Illuminate Our Lives.* York Beach, ME: Conari Press, 2002.

Cox, Kenneth. *Called to Serve: The Ken Cox Story.* Nampa, ID: Pacific Press Publishing Association, 2010.

Crespine, Regine. *On Stage, Off Stage: A Memoir.* Boston: Northeastern University Press, 1997.

Crookes, William. *Researches in the Phenomena of Spiritualism.* London: J. Burns, 1874.

Crowe, Catherine. *The Night Side of Nature or, Ghosts and Ghost Seers.* London: George Routledge and Sons, 1866.

Curot et al. "Déjà-rêvé: Prior dreams induced by direct electrical brain stimulation." *Brain Stimulation* 11/4 (2018): 875–85.

Curtis, Vesta. *Persian Myths.* London: The British Museum Press, 2009.

Daniels, Cora Linn, Charles Stevens editors. *Encyclopaedia of Superstitions, Folklore, and the Occult Sciences of the World.* Detroit: Gale Research Co., 1971.

Davis, Bruce, and Genny Wright Davis. *The Heart of Healing. An Amazing Journey of Spiritual Initiation. A True Story of Incredible Love.* Toronto: Bantam Books, 1985.

Davis, Mary B., ed. *Native America In The Twentieth Century: An Encyclopedia.* New York: Garland Publishing, Inc., 1994.

Day, Brian. *The Celtic Calendar.* Saffron Walden, UK: C.W. Daniel, 2003.

Deacon, Christine A. *Australia Down Under: Exploring Australia's Underwater World.* Sydney: Doubleday, 1986.

Delanne, Gabriel. *Evidence for a Future Life ("L'ame Est Immortelle").* Translated by H. A. Dallas. London: Philip Wellby, 1904.

de Rachewiltz et al., eds. *In The Service of the Khan: Eminent Personalities of the Early Mongol-Yuan Period (1200–1300).* Wiesbaden: Harrassowitz Verlag, 1993.

Deshikatmananda, Swami. "He Teaches His Own Message." *Prahbuddha Bharata or Awakened India* 95/12 (1896): 518–22.

Desiderio Pinto, S. J. "The Mystery of the Nizamuddin Dargah: The Accounts of Pilgrims." In *Muslim Shrines in India: Their Character, History, and Significance,* 112–24, edited by Christian W. Troll. New Delhi: Oxford University Press, 2003.

de Voragine, Jacobus. *The Golden Legend of Jacobus de Voragine Part One.* Translated by Granger Ryan and Helmut Ripperger. London: Longmans, Green and Co., 1941.

Dickerson, David Ellis. *House of Cards: The True Story of How a 26-year-old Fundamentalist Virgin Learned About Life, Love and Sex by Writing Greeting Cards.* New York: Riverhead Books, 2009.

DiPiazza, Francesca. *Finland in Pictures.* Minneapolis: Twenty-First Century Books, 2011.

Disraeli, Benjamin. *Contarini Fleming: A Psychological Romance & The Rise of Iskander.* London: Longmans, Green, and Co., 1871.

Dodd, Justin. "Déjà Rêvé: Video Explains the Creepier Version of Déjà Vu" Inverse Health, May 13, 2019.

Donnell, Christina. *Transcendent Dreaming: Stepping Into Our Human Potential.* Minneapolis, MN: Winds of Change Books, 2008.

Dorsey, George A. *The Pawnee Mythology.* Lincoln: University of Nebraska Press, 1997.

Dorsey, George A. *The Pawnee Mythology (Part I).* Washington, DC: Carnegie Institution of Washington, 1906.

Dossey, Larry. *Reinventing Medicine: Beyond Mind-Body to a New Era of Healing.* New York: HarperSanFrancisco, 1999.

Dragic, Marko. "Love Divinations of the Croats in the Context of the European Cultural Heritage." *European Scientific Journal* 10/14 (2014): 618–35.

"Dream: Fifty Years Wed, Golden Anniversary for Mr. and Mrs. Thomas Brace." *Chicago Daily Tribune* (Chicago), June 18, 1903.

"Dreaming to Some Purpose," *The Spiritualist* (London), January 19, 1877.

Drimmer, Frederick, ed. *Captured by the Indians: 15 Firsthand Accounts 1750–1870.* New York: Dover, 1985.

Dronke, Peter. *Medieval Latin and the Rise of European Love-Lyric Volume 1: Problems and Interpretations.* Oxford: Clarendon Press, 1965.

Dunwich, Gerina. *A Witch's Halloween: A Complete Guide to the Magick, Incantations, Recipes, Spells, and Lore.* Avon, MA: Provenance Press/Adams Media, 2007.

Eagle, Chokecherry Gall. *Beyond the Lodge of the Sun: Inner Mysteries of the Native American Way.* Rockport, MA: Element, 1997.

Eason, Cassandra. *A Complete Guide to Fairies and Magical Beings.* London Piatkus, 2001.

Ebon, Martin, ed. *Beyond Space and Time: An ESP Casebook.* New York: The New American Library, 1967.

Editors of *Guideposts* (E.O.G.). *Mysterious Ways: More Than Coincidence.* New York: Guideposts, 2016.

Elliot, J. K. *The Apocryphal New Testament: A Collection of Apocryphal Literature in an English Translation.* Oxford, Clarendon Press, 1993.

Elliot, Mark. *Azerbaijan: With Excursions to Georgia.* Hindhead: Trailblazer, 2001.

Ellison, Bob. *The First Snow: A Journal About a Man's Faith-Based Journey Through Grief.* Bloomington, IN: Westbow Press, 2014.

Elswit, Sharon Barcan. *The East Asian Story Finder: A Guide to 468 Tales from China, Japan and Korea, Listing Subjects and Sources.* Jefferson, NC: McFarland & Company, Inc., Publishers, 2009.

Elwin, Verrier. *The Muria and Their Ghotul.* Calcutta: Oxford University Press, Bombay 1947.

Emrich, Duncan. *The Folklore of Love and Courtship: The Charms and Divinations, Superstitions and Beliefs, Signs and Prospects of Love, Sweet Love.* New York: American Heritage Press, 1970.

Equiano, Olaudah. *The Kidnapped Prince: The Life of Olaudah Equiano.* Adapted by Ann Cameron. New York: Alfred A. Knopf, 1995.

Eranimos, Boban; Funkhouser, Art. "An Exploratory Study of the Eastern Understanding of Déjà rêvé Reve (Already Dreamed) Experiences in Kerala-Indian Culture." *Dreaming* 33/2 (2022): 153–63.

Ergil, Leyla Yvonne. "Turkish Superstitions and Traditions to Find Your Soul Mate." Daily Saba. May 06, 2021.

Ewing, Katherine P. "The Dream of Spiritual Initiation and the Organization of Self Representations among Pakistani Sufis." *American Ethnologist* 16 (1989): 56–74.

Faigao, Vicente. "Filipino Love Oracles." *Philippine Magazine* 33/1 (1904): 546–48, 557.

Feather, Sally. *The Gift: ESP, the Extraordinary Experiences of Ordinary People.* New York: St. Martin's Press, 2005.

Fernandez-Armesto, Felipe. *1492: The Year Our World Began.* London: Bloomsbury, 2011.

Fewston, CG. *A Time to Love in Tehran.* Castroville, TX: Black Rose Writing, 2015.

Flammarion, Camille. *L'inconnu: The Unknown.* New York: Harper & Brothers, 1900.

Fontana, Francis, and Sarah Fontana. *Bullseye Marriage: Intentionally Targeting a Great Relationship.* n.a., 2010.

Fors, Hjalmar. *The Limits of Matter: Chemistry, Mining, and Enlightenment.* Chicago: The University of Chicago Press, 2015.

Forsythe, Francesca. "Déjá Rêvè: An Intriguing Phenomenon of the Mind." Learning Mind, November 8, 2019.

Frazer, Winifred. *Mabel Dodge Luhan.* Boston: Twayne, 1984.

Freeman, Philip. *The Philosopher and the Druids: A Journey Among the Ancient Celts.* New York: Simon & Schuster, 2006.

Freud, Sigmund. "Dreams and the Occult." In *Psychoanalysis and the Occult,* edited by George Devereux, 91–109. New York: International University Press, Inc., 1970.

Friedenthal, Richard. *Goethe: His Life and Times.* New York: World, 1963.

Fuller, Cheri. *When Teens Pray.* Sisters, OR: Multinomah, 2002.

Funkhouser, Arthur, and Michael Schredl. "The Frequency of Déjà Vu (Déjà Rêve) and the Effects of Age, Dream Recall Frequency and Personality Factors." *International Journal of Dream Research* 3/1 (2010): 60–64.

Funkhouser, Arthur. "The 'Dream' Theory of Déjà Vu." *Parapsychological Journal of South Africa* 4/2 (1983:) 107–23.

Furutan, Ali-Akbar, comp and ed. *Stories of Baha' u'llah.* Translated by Katayoon and Robert Crerar with the help of friends. Oxford: George Ronald, 1986.

Gaddis, Vincent H. "Romantic Dreams-Do They Ever Come True?" Sedalia Democrat (Sedalia), March 1, 1970.

Garber, Anne. *Exploring Ethnic Vancouver.* Burnaby, BC: Serious Publishing, 1995.

Garfitt, Roger. *The Horseman's Word: A Memoir.* London: Jonathon Cape, 2011.

Garth, John. *Tolkien and the Great War: The Threshold of Middle Earth.* Boston: Houghton Mifflin Company, 2003.

Gaume, Monsignor, trans. *The Catechism of Perseverance Vol III.* New York: Benziger Brothers, 1882.

Geaves, Ron. *The Sufis of Britain: An Exploration of Muslim Identity.* Cardiff: Cardiff Academic Press, 2000.

Gerould, Gordon Hall. *The Grateful Dead: The History of a Folk Story.* London: Published for the Folk-Lore Society by David Nutt, 1908.

Giglioni, Guido. "Review of Synesian Dreams: Girolamo Cardano on Dreams of Prophetic Communication, by Girolamo Cardano and Jean-Yves Boriaud." *Bruniana & Campanelliana* 16/2 (2010): 575–84.

Gigot, Francis, E. *Special Introduction to the Study of the Old Testament.* New York: Benziger Brothers, 1901.

Giles, Herbert. *Strange Stories from a Chinese Studio.* Shanghai: Kelly & Walsh, Limited, 1916.

Gillison, Gillian. *Between Culture and Fantasy: A New Guinea Highlands Mythology.* Chicago: University of Chicago Press, 1993.

Gindikin, Semyon Grigorevich. *Tales of Physicists and Mathematicians.* Boston: Birkhauser, 1988.

Glass, Justine. *They Foresaw the Future: The Story of Fulfilled Prophecy.* New York: G.P. Putnam's Sons, 1969.

Godbey, A. H. "The Influence of Alexander's Conquest Upon Jewish Life." *The Biblical World* 38/3 (1911): 171–84.

Goldhammer, Leo. "Herzl and Freud." In *Herzl Year Book Volume I,* edited by Emanuel Neumann, 194–196. New York: Herzl Press, 1958.

Gollnick, James. *The Spiritual, Social, and Scientific Meanings of Dreams: What Do Our Dreams Teach Us?* Lewiston: The Edwin Mellen Press, 2013.

Gould, Francesca. *Why Is Yawning Contagious?: Everything You Ever Wanted to Know About the Human Body—and Some Things You'd Rather NOT Know.* London: Portrait, 2007.

Grant, Agnes, ed. *Our Bit of Truth: An Anthology of Canadian Native Literature.* Winnipeg, MB: Pemmican Publications Inc., 1990.

Grant, Joan. *Time Out of Mind: The Past in Your Astrological Birth Chart & Reincarnation.* London: Morrison and Gibb Limited, 1972.

Guerber, Hélène. *Legends of the Middle Ages.* American Book Company, 1896.

Guest, Charlotte. *The Mabinogion Translated by Lady Charlotte Guest.* London: Published by J.M. Dent & Sons Ltd., 1910.

Gurian, Michael. *Love's Journey: The Seasons and Stages of Relationship.* Boston: Shambala, 1995.

Gurney, Edmund et al., *Phantasms of the Living Volume I.* London: Trübner and Co., 1886.

Guthrie, E. J. *Old Scottish Customs: Local and General.* London: Hamilton, 1885.

Green, Louisa Oakley. *Sightseeing in the Undiscovered Country: Tales Retold by a Psychic Bystander.* Bloomington, IN: iUniverse, 2015.

Grey, Margot. *Return from Death: An Exploration of the Near-Death Experience.* London: Arkana, 1985.

Guggenheim, Bill, and Judy Guggenheim. *Hello from Heaven: A New Field of Research ~ After-Death Communication ~ confirms that life and love are eternal.* New York: Bantam Books, 1996.

Gwathmey, Emily. *Lots of Luck: Legend & Lore of Good Fortune.* Santa Monica, CA: Angel City Press, 1994.

Hadley, Donna R. *Morning Rounds: Daily Devotional Stories.* Loma Linda, CA: Loma Linda University Press, 2008.

Haire, D. B. *Be Brave: Believing That One Person Can Change the World.* Las, Vegas, NV: Next Century Publishing, 2016.

Handy, Craighill. *Marquesan Legends.* Honolulu, Hawaii: The Museum, 1930.

Hand, Wayland, editor. *The Frank C. Brown Collection of North Carolina Folklore Volume 6.* Durham, NC: Duke University Press, 1952.

Hare, Augustus J. C. *The Story of My Life Volume II.* New York: Dodd, Mead and Company, 1896.

Harner, Michael. *Cave and Cosmos: Shamanic Encounters with Another Reality.* Berkeley, CA: North Atlantic Books, 2013.

Harnisch-Lacey. *People Like Us: My Life with Rob Lacey.* Grand Rapids, MI: Zondervan, 2011.

Harris, Charles, founder. *The Adair County News* 4/38 Wednesday, July 31, 1901.

Hartglass, Caryn. "Adele Bloch-Bauer and Me." In *25 Women Who Survived Cancer: Notable Women Share Inspiring Stories of Hope,* 32–42, edited by Mark Evan Chimsky. South Portland, ME: Sellers Publishing, 2016.

Hart, Henry. *Flora of the County Donegal.* Dublin: Sealy, Bryers & Walker, 1898.

Harvey, Youngsook Kim. *Six Korean Women: The Socialization of Shamans.* St. Paul: West Pub. Co., 1979.

Hauptmann, O. H. "Spanish Folklore from Tampa, Florida: (No. IV) Superstitions." *Southern Folklore Quarterly* 2/1 (1938): 11–30.

Hearn, Lafcadio. *Kwaidan: Stories and Studies of Strange Things.* Boston: Houghton Mifflin Company, 1904.

Heinerman, Joseph. *Eternal Testimonies: Inspired Testimonies of Latter-Day Saints.* Manti, UT: Mountain Valley Publishers, 1974.

Heinerman, Joseph. *Spirit World Manifestations.* Salt Lake City, UT: Magazine Printing and Publishing, 1978.

Hendricks, George. *Roosters, Rhymes, and Railroad Tracks: A Second Sampling of Superstitions & Popular Beliefs in Texas.* Dallas: Southern Methodist University Press, 1980.

Heppner, Cheryl. *Seeds of Disquiet: One Deaf Woman's Experience.* Washington, DC: Gallaudet University Press, 1992.

Hertzberg, Brenda Haws. *John Henry and Gertrude Cooper Family History.* Placentia, CA: Creative Continuum, 2001.

Halliwell-Phillipps, James. *Popular Rhymes and Nursery Tales: A Sequel to the Nursery Rhymes of England.* London: John Russell Smith, 1849.

Harris, Sam. *Waking Up: Searching for Spirituality Without Religion.* London: Black Swan, 2015.

Hassan, Bernard. *The American Catholic Catalog.* San Francisco: Harper & Row, 1980.

Hegel, Robert. "Heavens and Hells in Chinese Fictional Dreams." In *Psycho-Sinology: The Universe of Dreams in Chinese Culture,* edited by Carolyn Brown, 1–11. Washington, DC: Distributed by Arrangement with University Press of America, 1988.

Hill, Gladys. "Experience." *Zions Landmark* 78/1 (1867): 154–55.

Hobe, Phyllis. *Eternal Moments: Stories of Divine Miracles.* New York: Guideposts Book, 2004.

Hodgson, Richard. "Psychical Research. Premonitions." *The Arena* 5/29 (1892): 175–86.

Hoffman, Malvina. *Yesterday Is Tomorrow: A Personal History.* New York: Crown Publishers, 1965.

Hoffman, Walter James. *The Menomini Indians.* Washington: Government Printing Office, 1896.

Holdich, Benjamin. *The History of Crowland Abbey.* Stamford: Printed and Published by J. Drakard, 1816.

Homer. *Pope's Translation of Homer's Iliad: Books I, VI, XXII, XIV.* Edited by William Cranston Lawton. New York: Globe School Book Company, 1900.

Howard, Richard. *Sun-Sand and Survival: An Analysis of Survival Experiences in Desert Areas.* Alabama: Arctic, Desert, Tropic Information Centre, Air University, 1953.

Howell, Chevaneeze. *Be Inspired . . . God Is Not Through With You Yet.* n.a. Xlibris, 2016.

Hungry Wolf, Beverly. *The Ways of My Grandmothers.* New York: Quill, 1982.

Hunt, Morton. *The Natural History of Love.* New York: Grove Press, 1959.

Husain, Ali Akbar. *Scent in the Islamic Garden: A Study of Deccani Urdu Literary Sources.* Karachi: Oxford University Press, 2000.

Huxley, Francis. *The Invisibles: Voodoo Gods in Haiti.* New York: McGraw-Hill Book Company, 1966.

Hwang Pae-gang. *Korean Myths and Folk Legends.* Translated by Young-Hie Han, Se-Joong Kim and Seung-Pyong Chwae. Fremont, CA: Jain Publishing Company, 2006.

Hyatt, Harry. *Folk-Lore from Adams County, Illinois.* New York: Alma Egan Hyatt Foundation, 1935.

Hyslop, James. "Clairvoyant Diagnosis and other Experiments." *Proceedings of the American Society for Pyschical Research* 2/2 (1908): 139–206.

Hyslop, James H. *Enigmas of Psychical Research.* Boston: Herbert B. Turner & Co., 1906.

Iddings Bell, Bernard. *The Church in Disrepute.* New York: Harper & Brothers Publishers, 1943.

Imbrogno, Phillip. *Files from the Edge: A Paranormal Investigator's Explorations Into High Strangeness.* Woodbury, MN: Llewellyn Publications, 2010.

Inglis, Brian. *The Power of Dreams.* London: Grafton Books, 1987.

Irwin, Harvey. "The Psychology of Déjà Vu: Have I Been Here Before?" *Psi Research* (1984): 196–97.

Isaacs, Ronald H., and Kerry M. Olitzky, eds. *Sacred Moments: Tales from the Jewish Life Cycle.* Northvale, NJ: Jason Aronson Inc., 1995.

Isaacson, Rupert. *The Healing Land: A Kalahari Journey.* London: Fourth Estate, 2001.

"I Woke Up To The Gospel." *Ensign* 43/8 (2013): 76.

Jaffe, Aniela. *Apparitions and Precognition: A Study from the Point of view of C.G. Jung's Analytical Psychology.* New Hyde Park, NY: Univ. Books, 1963.

Jaffer, Mehru. *The Book of Muhammad.* New Delhi: Viking, 2003.

Jaffray, Robert. "Iona, The Sacred Isle," *The Caledonian* (April 5), 1912.

Jenkins, Joseph. *Balance Point: Searching for a Spiritual Missing Link.* Grove City, PA: Jenkins Pub., 2000.

Jerrahi, Sheikh Muzaffer Ozak al-. *Irshad: Wisdom of a Sufi Master.* Translated with an Introduction by Muhtar Holland. Amity, NY: Amity House, 1988.

Jones, Rufus M. "Quietism." *The Harvard Theological Review* 10/1 (1980): 1–51.

Julius. "Tea Table Talk." *The Path* 4/10 (1890): 321–24.

Kamath, M. V., and V. B. Kher. *Sai Baba of Shirdi: a Unique Saint.* Bombay: Jaico Publishing House, 1991.

Kao, Karl, ed. *Classical Tales of the Supernatural and the Fantastic: Selections from the Third to the Tenth Century.* Hong Kong: Joing Publishing Co., 1985.

Kazhdan, Alexander, and Henry Maguire. "Byzantine Hagiographical Texts as Sources on Art." *Dumberton Oaks Papers* 45 (1991): 1–22.

Kearney, Celine. *Faces of the Goddess: New Zealand Women Talk About Their Spirituality.* North Shore City, N.Z.: Tandem Press, 1997.

Kearney, Janis Faye. *Sundays with TJ: 100 Years of Memories on Varner Road.* Little Rock, AR: Writing Our World Press, 2014.

Keeney, Bradford. "Shakers of St. Vincent." In *Shamans of the World: Extraordinary First Person Accounts of Healings, Mysteries, and Miracles,* 189–212, edited by Nancy Connor. Boulder, CO: Sounds True, 2008.

Kline, John Webb. *I Could Use a Mircale Right Now: Miraculous Intervention for Difficult Times.* Victoria, BC: Trafford, 2004.

Knappert, Jan. *African Mythology: An Encyclopedia of Myth and Legend.* Hammersmith, London: Diamond Books, 1995.

Knappert, Jan. *Indian Mythology: An Encyclopedia of Myth and Legend.* Hammersmith, London: The Antiquarian Press, 1991.

Kroeber, Alfred. *Handbook of the Indians of California.* Berkeley: California Book Company, 1967.

Kunz, Rhea. *Reminiscences Of John W. Woolley And Lorin C. Woolley - Volume 2.*

Kwilecki, Susan. *Becoming Religious: Understanding Devotion to the Unseen.* Lewisburg, PA: Associated University Presses, 1999.

Lafleur, Theodore. *A Semi-Centennial Historical Sketch of the Grand Ligne Mission: Read at the Jubilee Gathering, Grande-Ligne, Oct. 18th, 1885.* Montreal: Printed by D. Bentley & Co., 1885

Lacey, Sandra, and Steve Stickley. *People Like Us: Life with Rob Lacey.* Grand Rapids, MI: Zondervan, 2011.

Laloy, Louis. *Mirror of China.* New York: Knopf, 1936.

LaMotte, Sandee. "No, You Haven't Read This Déjà vu Story Before." CNN Health. January 8, 2016.

Landes, Ruth. *The Ojibwa Woman: Male and Female Life Cycles Among the Ojibwa Indians of Western Ontario.* New York: Norton, 1971.

Landsburg, Alan. *In Search of Strange Phenomena.* New York: Bantam, 1977.

Lanktree, Matthew. *A Biographical Narrative of Matthew Lanktree.* Belfast: James Wilson, 1836.

Lasker, Daniel J. "Gersonides on Dreams, Divination, and Astrology." In *Proceedings of the Eighth World Congress of Jewish Studies: Division C; Talmud and Midrash, Philosophy and Mysticism, Hebrew and Yiddish Literature,* edited by David Krone, 47–52. Jerusalem: World Union of Jewish Studies, 1982.

Laws, Edward. *The History of Little England Beyond Wales and the non-Kymric Colony Settled in Pembrokeshire.* London: George Bell, 1888.

Leek, Sybil. *Reincarnation: The Second Chance.* New York: Bantam, 1975.

Lee, Marguerite du Pont. *Virginia Ghosts.* Revised Edition. Verryville, VA: Virginia Book Company, 1966.

Lee, Witness. *The History of the Church and the Local Churches.* Anaheim, CA: Living Stream Ministry, 1993.

Leibnitz, Gottfried Wilhelm. *New Essays Concerning Human Understanding.* Translated by Alfred Gideon Langley. New York: The Macmillan Company, 1896.

Lennox, Michael. *Llewellyn's Little Book of Dreams.* Woodbury MN: Llewellyn Publications, 2017.

Levin, Carole. *Dreaming the English Renaissance: Politics and Desire in Court and Culture.* New York, NY: Palgrave Macmillan, 2008.

Levy, Reuben, trans. *The Three Dervishes: And Other Persian Tales and Legends.* London: Humphrey Milford, 1923.

Lewis, David C. *After Atheism: Religion and Ethnicity in Russia and Central Asia.* New York, NY: St. Martin's Press, 2000.

Lewis, Kim, and Denise Hamilton, compilers. *Tabernacle Stories of Faith: Snapshots of God's Faithfulness to His People at Tabernacle Baptist Church. Cartersville, Georgia.* n.p.: Xulon Press, 2007.

Liebman, Malvina. *From Caravan to Casserole: Herbs and Spices in Legend, History, and Recipes.* Miami, FL: E. A. Seemann Pub., 1977.

Lienhard, Siegfried. "A History of Classical Poetry: Sanskrit - Pali - Prakrit." In *A History of Indian Literature Volume III,* 1–307, edited by Jan Gonda. Wiesbaden: Otto Harrassowitz, 1984.

Lindenburgh, Marlene. *Miracles & Messages: Wondrous True Stories of God's Intimate Encounters.* Phoenix, AZ: Life Branch Publishing, 2003.

Lipsenthal, Lee. *Enjoy Every Sandwich: Living Each Day as if It Were Your Last.* New York: Crown Archetype, 2011.

Li, Shujiang, and Karl W. Luckert. *Mythology and Folklore of the Hui, A Muslim Chinese People.* Translations by Fenglan Yu, Zhilin Hou, and Gangui Wang. Albany, NY: State of New York University Press, 1994.

Livon, Jodi. *The Happy Medium: Awakening to Your Natural Intuition.* Llewellyn Publications, 2009.

Locke, Ralph G. "Who am I in the city of Mammon? The self, doubt and certainty in a Spiritualist Cult." In *Practice and Belief: Studies in the Sociology of Australian Religion,* edited by Alan W. Black and Peter E. Glasner, 108–133. Sydney: George Allen & Unwin, 1983.

Long, Jeffrey. *Evidence of the Afterlife: The Science of Near-Death Experiences.* New York, NY: HarperOne, 2010.

Longkumer, Arkotong. *Reform, Identity and Narratives of Belonging: The Heraka Movement in Northeast India.* London: Continuum, 2010.

Lukara, Alissa. *Riding Grace: A Triumph of the Soul.* Ahsland, OR: Silver Light Publications, 2007.

Lyons, M. C. *The Arabian Epic: Heroic and Oral Story-Telling Volume 3, Texts.* Cambridge: University Press, Cambridge, 1995.

MacDermott, Mercia. *Bulgarian Folk Customs.* Philadelphia: Jessica Kingsley, 1998.

MacDonald, Margaret Read, ed. *The Folklore of World Holidays.* Detroit: Gale Research, 1992.

MacKenzie, Donald. *Wonder Tales from Scottish Myth & Legend.* London: Blackie and Son, 1917.

MacKenzie, Norman. *Dreams & Dreaming: The Symbolic Language of the Night World of the Mind.* London: Bloomsbury Books, 1989.

Mackerras, Colin. *The Chinese Theatre in Modern Times, from 1840 to the Present Day.* Amherst: University of Massachusetts Press, 1975.

MacNeil, Joe Neil. *Tales Until Dawn: The World of a Cape Breton Gaelic Story-Teller.* Kingston and Montreal: McGill-Queen's University Press, 1987.

Macpherson, Cluny. "Samoan Medicine." In *Healing Practices in the South Pacific,* 1–50, edited by Calire D. F. Parsons. Laie, Hawaii: University of Hawaii Press, 1985.

Madison, Richard. *Healing from God.* New Kensington, PA: Whitaker House, 1998.

Mahony, Patrick. *Maurice Maeterlinck, Mystic and Dramatist: A Reminiscent Biography of the Man and His Ideas.* Washington, DC: The Institute For The Study of Man, 1984.

Mansson McGinty, Anna. *Becoming Muslim: Western Women's Conversion to Islam.* New York: Palgrave Macmillan, 2006.

Marcia Minkoff, Miriam. *Return to Who You Are: One Woman's Journey to Her True Self.* Buffalo, NY: Miriams Drum Publications, 2009.

Marigny, Francois Augier de. *The History of the Arabians, Under the Government of the Caliphs Vol III.* London: Printed for T. Payne, D. Wilson, and T. Durham, 1758.

Markova, Ivana S., and German E. Barrios. "Paramensia and Delusions of Memory." In *Memory Disorders in Psychiatric Practice,* edited by German E. Berrios and John R. Hodges, 313–37. Cambridge, UK: Cambridge University Press, 2000.

Marquand, Eleanor C. *Flowers of Ten Centuries: Catalogue of an Exhibition.* New York: The Pierpoint Morgan Library, 1947.

Marsh, Richard. *Locked In: One Man's Miraculous Escape from the Terrifying Confines of Locked-In Syndrome.* London: Piatkus, 2014.

Martine, David Bunn, ed. *Time and Memories: Oral Histories and Stories of a Shinnecock-Apache-Hungarian Family.* n.p.: Lulu Com, 2013.

Martin, Joel, and Patricia Romanowski. *Love Beyond Life: The Healing Power of After-Death Communications.* New York, NY: HarperCollinsPublishers, 1997.

Mast, Dolorita. *Through Caroline's Consent: Life of Mother Teresa of Jesus Gerhardinger Foundress of the School Sisters of Notre Dame 1797–1879.* Baltimore, MD: School Sisters of Notre Dame, 1958.

Matthews, Theodore D. *The Cohongoroota.* Edited by The Junior Class Shepherd College State Normal School. Shepherdstown, WV: Shepherd College State Normal School, 1928.

Matthieu, Ricard. *Enlightened Vagabond: The Life and Teachings of Patrul Rinpoche.* Boulder, CO: Shambhala, 2017.

Matuauto, Sipuao J. "A Samoan with Russian Ancestry." In *Links of Forever: Inspirational Stories of Lineage and Love.* Compiled by Connie Rector and Diane Deputy. Salt Lake City, UT: Bookcraft, 1977.

Mayer, Fanny Hagin, trans. *Ancient Tales in Modern Japan: An Anthology of Japanese Folk Tales.* Bloomington, IN: Indiana University Press, 1985.

Mbenoun, Kleber. *More Than a Great Partner: How to Find and Keep the Right Mate.* Bladensburg, MD: Dove Christian Publishers, 2016.

McGill, Cindy. *What Your Dreams Are Telling You: Unlocking Solutions While You Sleep.* Minneapolis, MN: Chosen, 2013.

McKelvey, Robert. *A Gift of Barbed Wife: America's Allies Abandoned in South Vietnam.* Seattle, WA: University of Washington Press, 2002.

McRae, Michael. *In Search of Shangri-La: The Extraordinary True Story of the Quest for the Lost Horizon.* London: Penguin, 2004.

"Memoir: A Letter." *The Telescope.* New York, June 5, 1824.

Mercree, Chad. *The Way of the Psychic Heart: Developing Your Spiritual Gifts in the Everyday World.* Woodbury, MN: Llewellyn Publications, 2014.

Metford, J. C. J. *Dictionary of Christian Lore and Legend.* London: Thames & Hudson, 1983.

Meurant, Louis Henri. *Sixty Years Ago; or, Reminiscences of the Struggle for the Freedome of the Press of South Africa and the Establishment of the First Newspaper in the Eastern Province.* Cape Town: Saul Solomon & Co., 1885.

Mewborn, J. M. "The Life and True Experience of Sarah Hamilton, A Natural and Spiritual Vagabond in the Earth." *Zion's Landmark* 14/6 (2008): 1–5.

Michaels, Marianne. *A Second Chance to Say Goodbye.* Haverford, PA: Infinity Publishing, 2002.

Miles, Clement. *Christmas in Ritual and Tradition, Christian and Pagan.* Adelphi Terrace, London. T. Fisher Unwin, 1912.

Miller, Jamie C., et al., *Heavenly Miracles: Magical True Stories of Guardian Angels and Answered Prayers.* New York: HarperCollins Publishers, 2000.

Missouri: The WPA Guide to the "Show Me" State. St. Louis, MO: Missouri Historical Society Press, 1998.

Mittermaier, Amira. *Dreams That Matter: Egyptian Landscapes of the Imagination.* Berkeley, CA: University of California Press, 2011.

Miyatovich, Chedo. "Psychic Science in Serbia." *Light* 36 (1916): 421–22.

Monroe, Elizabeth N. *The Novel and Society: A Critical Study of the Modern Novel.* Port Washington, NY: Kennikat Press, Inc., 1965.

Monger, George. *Marriage Customs of the World: From Henna to Honeymoons.* Santa Barbara, CA: ABC-CLIO, 2004.

Montgomery, Darlene. *Conscious Women—Conscious Lives.* Toronto, ON: White Knight Publications, 2004.

Moody, Raymond, and Paul Perry. *Glimpses of Eternity: Sharing a Loved One's Passage from This Life to the Next.* New York, NY: Guideposts, 2010.

Moore, Arthur. *The Folk-lore of the Isle of Man: Being an Account of its Myths, Legends, Superstitions, Customs and Proverbs.* London: D. Nutt, 1891.

Moore, Olin H. "Jaufre Rudel and the Lady of Dreams." *Publications of the Modern Language Association* 29/4 (1914): 517–36.

Morison, Walter. *From Malachi to Matthew: Three Lectures on the Period Between the Old and New Testaments.* London: James Nisbet & Co., 1879.

Morris, A. P. *They're Not Gone: A Collection of True Stories from People Reunited with Their Loved Ones Who've Passed Away.* n.p.: Outskirts Press, Inc., 2009.

Morris, Neil. *African Myths.* London: Franklin Watts, 2008.

Morris, Nina L, ed. *Faith in Every Footstep: A Collection of Pioneer Histories of Members of Hibbard 2nd Ward.* n.a. Church of Jesus Christ Latter-Day Saints, 1997.

Moss, Robert. *Conscious Dreaming: A Spiritual Path for Everyday Life.* New York: Crown Trade Paperbacks, 1996.

Moss, Robert. *Dream Gates: An Explorers Guide to the Worlds of Souls, Imaginations and Life Beyond Death.* New York: Three Rivers Press, 2006.

Moss, Robert. *The Secret History of Dreaming.* Novata, CA: New World Library, 2009.

Moulton, Horace. *The Young Pastor's Wife. Memoir of Elizabeth Ann Moulton: Containing Her Biography, Diary, Letters, Etc.* Boston: Waite, Peirce and Company, 1845.

Moxon, John. Peter's *Halakhic Nightmare: The "Animal" Vision of Acts 10:9–16 in Jewish and Graeco-Roman Perpsective.* Tubingen, Germany: Mohr Siebeck, 2017.

Murphy, Anthony. "Aislinge Oengusso - The Dream of Oengus," Mythical Ireland, September 14, 2022.

Murphy, Joseph. *Telepsychics: Tapping Your Hidden Subconscious Powers.* Marina del Ray, CA: DeVorss Publications, 1987.

Musick, Steven R. *Life After Heaven: How My Time in Heaven Can Transform Your Life on Earth.* Colorado Springs, CO: Waterbrook, 2017.

Muzorewa, Abel Tendekai. *Rise Up & Walk: The Autobiography of Bishop Abel Tendekai Muzorewa.* Edited by Norman E. Thomas. Nashville, TN: Abingdon, 1978.

Myers, Frederic. "The Subliminal Self." *Proceedings of the Incorporated Society for Psychical Research* 11/27–29 (1895): 334–593.

Myers, J. "What Faith Will Do." *The War Cry* (Toronto), September 29, 1962.

Neale, John. *Annals of Virgin Saints.* London: Masters, 1846.

Nelson, Taylor. "Should an Elder Choose His Mission?" *Improvement Era* 28/1 (1927): 9–10.

Newell, William Wells. *Games and Songs of American Children.* New York: Harper & Brothers Publishers, 1884.

Newmark, Amy, and Kelly Sullivan Walden. *Chicken Soup for the Soul: Dreams and Premonitions—101 Amazing Stories of Miracles, Divine Intervention, and Insight.* Cos Cob, CT: Chicken Soup for the Soul Publishing, 2015.

Newton, Stan. *Mackinac Island and Sault Ste Marie Picturesque and Legendary.* Grand Rapids: Black Letter Press, 1976.

Ni, Hua-Ching. *The Book of Changes and the Unchanging Truth.* Malibu, CA: Shrine of the Eternal Breath of Tao, 1990.

Noe, A. H. *The Witches' Dream Book and Fortune Teller.* New York: Henry J. Wehman, 1885.

Noffke, Will. "The Warriors of Peace." *KFPA FM94 Folio: Celebrating Berkeley,* May 1984.

Norbu, Namkhai. *The Crystal and the Way of Light: Sutra, Tantra and Dzogchen. The Teachings of Namkhai Norbu.* Compiled and Edited by John Shane. New York: Routledge & Kegan Paul, 1988.

Oh, David. *Beginning in the Prophetic: Learning How to Say What the Father Is Saying.* Haymarket, VA: Burning Lamp Media & Publishing, 2012.

O'Hanlon, John. *Irish Folklore: Traditions and Superstitions of the Country, with Humorous Tales.* Glasgow: Cameron & Ferguson, 1870.

Omarr, Sydney. *Sydney Omarr's Spirit Guides. With Trish MacGregor.* New York: Signet Book, 2003.

O'Moore, Sidney. "Kathleen of Mora." *The Christian Lady's Magazine X* (1834): 450–60.

Orenstein, Gloria Feman. "Toward an Ecofeminist Ethic of Shamanism and the Sacred." In *Ecofeminism and the Sacred,* edited by Carol J. Adams, 172–190. New York: Continuum, 1993.

Ovid. *Ovid In Six Volumes III: Metamorphoses (In Two Volumes, I, Books I–VIII).* Translated by Frank Justus Miller. Cambridge, MA, Harvard University Press, 1916.

Oxon, M. A. "Notes By The Way." *Light* 11/560 (1891): 457.

Palavestra, Vlajko. *Legends of Old Sarajevo.* Translated by Mario Susko and William Tribe. Zemun: Most Art, 2003.

Pearl, Mhogani. *Dear Yvette: Shattered Fairytales.* Atlanta: MhoganiPearl Press, 2015.

Pendel, Thomas Franses. *Thirty-Six Years in the White House.* Washington: The Neale Pubishing Company, 1902.

Perez, Darrah J. *It's Forever Happening.* n.a. Lulu Press, Inc., 2016.

Philpot, J. H. *The Sacred Tree, or, The Tree in Religion and Myth.* London: Macmillan and Co., 1897.

Perry, Winifred Almina. "Shelley's Relationship to Plato." Master's Thesis. University of Illinois, 1914.

Piozzi, Hester Lynch. *Thraliana: The Diary of Mrs. Hester Lynch Thrale (Later Mrs. Piozzi) 1776–1809 Volume I 1776–1784.* Edited by Katharine C. Balderston. Oxford: At the Clarendon Press, 1942.

Port Arthur Founder. "Claimed Connection to the Supernatural." Beumont Enterprise (Beaumont), September 28, 2016.

Porter, Phillip. *Let the Walls Fall Down: A Call for Men to Bridge the Barriers That Prevent Them from Finding Success in Life, with W. Terry Whalin.* Orlando, FL: Creation House, 1996.

"Portuguese History." *Dublin University Magazine* 170/29 (1847):143–160.

Pratt, Norm. *The Spirit Tracker: A True Story of How Awakening Psychic-Intuitive Ability Led to Finding a Missing Girl.* Ymir, BC: Intuitive Publishing, 2007.

Prince, Walter. *Noted Witnesses for Psychic Occurrences.* Boston, MA: Boston Society for Psychic Research, 1928.

Punzak, Daniel. *A Spiritual Hypothesis: An Inquiry into Abnormal and Paranormal Behavior.* Bloomington, IN: AuthorHouse. Kindle

Pu Songling, *Strange Tales from a Chinese Studio.* Translated and Annotated by Herbert A. Giles. Third Edition Revised. Shangai: Kelly & Walsh Limited, 1916. Edition, 2017.

Quilliam, Susan. *Women on Sex: Women of All Ages Talk Intimately About Every Aspect of Their Sexual Experiences.* New York, NY: Barricade Books, 1994.

Rabb, Kate. *National Epics.* Chicago, AC: McClurg, 1896.

Radha, Swami Sivananda. *Realities of the Dreaming Mind.* Spokane, WA: Timeless Books, 1994.

Ramanujan, A. K., ed. *Folktales from India: A Selection of Oral Tales from Twenty-Two Languages.* New York: Pantheon Books, 1991.

Randles, Jenny, ed. "Cases from the USA and Isle of Man, Greater Manchester, Lancashire, Merseyside, Staffordshire." *Northern UFO News* 132 (1988): 9–12.

Randolph, Vance. *Ozark Magic and Folklore.* New York, NY: Dover Publications, 1964.

Rawlings, Maurice. *Beyond Death's Door.* Nashville: T. Nelson, 1978.

Rawlins, F. L. "Abiah Darby's Dream." *The Journal of the Friends Historical Society* 11 (1914): 108–9.

Rawlinson, Andrew. *The Book of Enlightened Masters: Western Teachers in Eastern Traditions.* Chicago: Open Court, 1997.

Ray, B.C., ed. *Tribals of Orissa: The Changing Socio-Economic Profile.* New Delhi: Gian Publishing House, 1989.

Rea, Serenus G. *Missionary Diary of Serenus "Rea" Gardner: November 8, 1910 to October 5, 1912.*

Redding, Stephen. *More or Less.* New York: iUniverse, Inc., 2009.

Reed, Adam. *Papua New Guinea's Last Place: Experiences of Constraint in a Postcolonial Prison.* New York: Berghahn, 2004.

Rees, William Jenkins, trans and ed. *Lives of the Cambro British Saints.* Llandovery: William Rees, 1853.

Reik, Theodor. *The Creation of Woman: A Psychoanalytic Enquiry into the Myth of Eve.* New York: George Braziler, Inc., 1960.

Rhine, Louisa E. *The Invisible Picture: A Study of Psychic Experiences.* Jefferson, NC: McFarland, 1981.

Ricci, Matteo. *China in the Sixteenth Century: The Journals of Matthew Ricci 1538–1610.* New York, NY: Random House, 1953.

Rich, Elaine Sommers. *Mennonite Women: A Story of God's Faithfulness, 1683–1983.* Scottdale, PA: Herald Press, 1983.

Riley, James. *Sufferings in Africa: Captain Riley's Narrative.* Edited by Gordon H. Evans. New York: Clarkson N. Potter, Inc., 1965.

Robinson, Frank B. *Life Story of Frank B. Robinson.* Moscow: Printed on the Presses of the Review Publishing Company, 1934.

Rogers, Rita. *Soul Mates: A Practical Spiritual Guide to Finding True Love.* London: Pan, 2000.

Rougemont, Claire. *The National Dream Book.* Philadelphia: David McKay, 1901.

Rountree, David M., and Robbie Lunt. *Exorcising the Demons: Combatting Evil in a Very Haunted House.* New York: Rosen Publishing, 2016.

Rouvelas, Marilyn. *A Guide to Greek Traditions and Customs in America.* Bethesda: Nea Attiki Press, 2002.

Rugoff, Milton, ed. *A Harvest of World Folk Tales.* New York: The Viking Press, 1949.

Ruoff, Norman, compiler. *Testimonies of the Restoration: A Second Volume of Testimonies from the Pages of the Restoration Witness.* Independence, MO: Herald Publishing House, 1971.

Rushamenza, Philip J. *The Rope That Saves Me.* Brushton, NY: Teach Services, 2002.

Russ, Michael. *Finding Your Soul Mate.* York Beach, Maine: L Samuel Weiser, Inc., 1992.

Russell, Frank. *The Pima Indians.* Tucson: University of Arizona Press, 1975.

Ruud, Jay. *Encyclopedia of Medieval Literature.* New York: Facts on File, 2006.

Ryback, David, and Letitia Sweitzer. *Dreams That Come True: Their Psychic and Transforming Powers.* New York: Doubleday, 1988.

Schattschneider, Allen W. *Through Five Hundred Years: A Popular History of the Morvaian Church.* Bethlehem, PA: Moravian Church in America, 1996.

Schell, Stanley. *Werner's Readings and Recitations No 31: Hallowe'en Festivities.* New York: Edgar S. Werner & Company, 1903.

Scheller, Gustav. *Operation Exodus.* Tonbridge, Kent: Sovereign World, 2001.

Schlauch, Margaret. *Romance in Iceland.* New York: Russell & Russell, 1973.

Schnell, Donald. *The Initiation.* Makawai, Maui, HI: Inner Ocean, 2002.

Schwarz, Herbert T. *Windigo: and Other Tales of the Ojibways.* Toronto: Mclelland and Steward Limited, 1969.

Schwartz, Howard. *Invisible Kingdoms: Jewish Tales of Angels, Spirits, and Demons.* New York: HarperCollins Publishers, 2002.

Schwartz, Howard. *Leaves from the Garden of Eden: One Hundred Classic Jewish Tales.* Oxford: Oxford University Press, 2009.

"Search Is Made for Armada Gold: Tuscany Galleon Was Sunk in 1588." *The Atlanta Constitution*, November 7, 1909.

Sellier, Charles. *Miracles and Other Wonders.* New York, NY: Dell Publishing, 1994.

Seraphima, Schemanun. *Saint Seraphim: His Life, Teachings, Miracles and Glorification.* Etna, CA: Center for Traditionalist Orthodox Studies, 2008.

Serdans, Beka. *I'm Moving Two: A Poetic Journey with Dystonia.* n.p.: Xlibris Corp, 2000.

Shames, Karilee Halo, compiler. *Amazing Mentors: The Real Hot Mama's Path to Power.* Scottsdale, AZ: Inkwell Productions, 2013.

Shema. *The Science of Sacred Scripture Volume I: The Blue Prints for Life.* n.p.: BluePrint Publishing, 2008.

Shipp, Richard Cottam, editor. *Champions of Light: True Experiences from the Lives of Latter-Day Champions.* Orem, UH: Randal Book, 1983.

Shiyuan, Chen. *Wandering Spirits: Chen Shiyuan's Encyclopedia of Dreams.* Translated by Richard E. Strassberg. Berkeley: University of California Press, 2008.

Sikes, Wirt. *British Goblins: Welsh Folklore, Fairy Mythology, Legends and Traditions.* London: Sampson Low, Marston, Searle, & Rivington, 1880.

Silver, Arnold. *Bernard Shaw: The Darker Side.* Stanford, CA: Stanford University Press, 1982.

Simons, Anna. *Networks of Dissolution: Somalia Undone.* Boulder, CO: Westview Press, 1995.

Singh, Hakam. *Life Stories of Great Sikh Saints.* Amritsar, India: B. Chattar Singh Jiwan Singh, 2006.

Singleton, Esther. *A Guide to the Opera: Description & Interpretation of the Words & Music of the Most Celebrated Operas.* New York: Dodd, Mead & Company, 1899.

Sloan, David L. *Ghosts of Key West.* Key West, FL: Phantom Press, 1998.

Smedley, Jenny. *Soul Mates: Magical and Mysterious Ways to Find True Love.* London: Piatkus, 2013.

Smith, Julia Crafts. *The Reason Why: or, Spiritual Experiences of Mrs. Julia Crafts Smith, Physician, Assisted by her Spirit Guides.* Boston: Published by the Author, 1881.

Sno, Herman N. "Déjà vu and Jamais vu." In *Memory Disorders in Psychiatric Practice,* edited by German E. Berrios and John R. Hodges, 338–47. Cambridge, UK: Cambridge University Press, 2000.

Sno, Herman N., and Don H. Linszen. "The Deja Vu Experience: Remembrance of Things Past?" *American Journal of Psychiatry* 147/12 (1991): 1587–95.

Snow, Loudell F. "Popular Medicine in a Black Neighborhood." In *Ethnic Medicine in the Southwest,* edited by Edward H. Spicer, 19–98. Tucson, AZ: University of Arizona Press, 1977.

Soltown, Willow Ann. *Quilting the World Over.* Radnor, PA: Chilton Book Co., 1991.

Spangler, Ann. *Dreams and Miracles: How God Speaks Through Your Dreams.* Carmel, NY: Guideposts, 2000.

Stanley, Henry Morton. *Stanley in Africa. The Paladin of the Nineteenth Century: A Succinct and Correct History of the Travels and Explorations of Henry M. Stanley.* Chicago, IL: Donahue, Henneberry & Co., 1880.

Stanton, John E. *Images of Aboriginal Australia.* n.p. The University of Western Australia, 1988.

St. Clair, Chip. *The Butterfly Garden: A Memoir.* Deerfield Beach, FL: Health Communications, 2007.

Steinmetz, Paul B. *Pipe, Bible, and Peyote: Among the Oglala Lakota.* Knoxville, TN: The University of Tennessee Press, 1990.

Stevens, William Oliver. *The Mystery of Dreams.* London: Allen & Unwin, 1950.

Stevenson, Gertrude Scott, trans. *The Letters of Madame: The Correspondence of Elizabeth-Charlotte of Bavaria, Princess Palatine, Duchess of Orleans, called "Madame" at the Court of King Louis XIV Volume II: 1709–1722.* London: Arrowsmith, 1925.

Stibal, Vianna. *Go Up and Work with God.* Roberts, ID: Rolling Thunder, 2000.

Stoia, Jeffrey. "Patient Portent: A Strong Sense of Faith." *A New Vision for Integrated Breast Care,* n.p.: n.p, 2001.

Stokes, Whitley, ed. *Lives of Saints from the Book of Lismore.* Oxford: At the Clarendon Press, 1890.

Stovel, Nora Foster. "Tatiana's Letter, A Literary Legacy: From Pushkin's Eugene Onegin to D. M. Thomas's White Hotel." *International Fiction Review* 25/1 (1998).

Sundkler, Bengt. *The Christian Ministry in Africa.* Bloomsbury Street, London: SCM Press Ltd., 1962.

Sure, Heng; Ch'au, Heng. *Silence Echoes: Journals & Letters on a Bowing Pilgrimage.* Volume Two. Burlingame, CA: Buddhist Text Translation Society, 2007.

Sutherland, Cherie. *Transformed by the Light: Life after Near-Death Experiences.* Sydney: Bantam Books, 1992.

Sweet, Louise Elizabeth. *Tell Toqaan: A Syrian Village.* Ann Arbor: University of Michigan, 1960.

Swindall, Jenny. *Freedom from Depression: Emotional Healing Through Spiritual Health and Wellness.* Lake Mary, FL: Charisma House, 2013.

Taft, Mary. *Memoirs of the Life of Mrs. Mary Taft; Formerly Miss Barritt. Written By Herself. With a Portrait. Part II.* London: Printed for, and Sold by the Author, 1827.

Tally, Frances. "American Folk Customs of Courtship and Marriage: The Bedroom." *Forms Upon the Frontier: Folklife and Folk Arts in the United States* 16/9, edited by Austin and Alta Fife and Henry Glassie, 138–159. Logan, UT: Utah State University Press, 1969.

Taylor, John. *Baptists on the American Frontier: A History of Ten Baptist Churches of Which the Author Has Been Alternatively a Member.* Macon, GA: Mercer University Press, 1995.

Taylor, Nellie T. "A Message From The World Of Spirits." In *Faith Like the Ancients Vol. 2,* Compiled by N.B. Lundwall, 27–28. Manti, UT: Mountain Valley Publishers, 1968.

Tawney, C. H., trans. *The Katha Sarit Sagara or Ocean of the Streams of Story Volume II.* Printed by J. W. Thomas, 1884.

"Telepathic Mysteries." *Buchanan's Journal of Man* 2/2 (1888): 33–43.

Thanegi, Ma. *Nor Iron Bars a Cage.* San Francisco, CA: ThingsAsianPress, 2013.

The Agawam Advertiser (Thursday, June 17, 1976).

"The Strange Story of Liz, Atlanta and a 'Vision.'" *Spastics News* (Bristol) April, 1981.

The World and Its Peoples: Germany. New York: Greystone Press, 1964.

Thomas, Daniel, and Lucy Thomas. *Kentucky Superstitions.* Princeton, NJ: University Press, 1920.

Thomas, Elizabeth Marshall. *Warrior Herdsmen: The Story of Dodoth Tribesman of Northern Uganda, By the Author of the Harmless People.* New York: Vintage Books, 1972.

Thomson, John. *The Land and the People of China: A Short Account of the Geography, History, Religion, Social Life, Arts, Industries, and Government of China and Its People.* London: Society for Promoting Christian Knowledge, 1876.

Thorpe, J. R. "Déjà Rêvé Is Déjà Vu, But For Dreams." Bustle, Oct 26, 2020.

Thurber, Robert, ed. *Believe in Miracles: Stories by People Searching for Truth.* n.a. RainBird Publishing, 1997.

Tibbits, Charles John. *Folklore and Legends: Scotland.* W. W. Gibbings, 1899.

Tiwari, Maya. *The Path of Practice: A Woman's Book of Healing with Food, Breath, and Sound.* New York: Ballantine Books, 2000.

Today's Groom Magazine. The Groom to Be's Handbook: The Ultimate Guide to a Fabulous Ring, a Memorable Proposal, and the Perfect Wedding. New York: NY: Skyhorse Publishing Inc., 2015.

Toelken, Barre. "The Moccasin Telegraph and Other Improbabilities: A Personal Essay." In *Out of the Ordinary: Folklore and the Supernatural,* edited by Barbara Walker, 46–58. Logan, UT: Utah State University Press, 1995.

Toporowitch, Bracha Perel. *At Your Command: The Remarkable Story of Reb Yechiel Mechel Rabinowicz, Talmid Chacham, Inventor, Activist, Philanthropist, and Always Faithful Jew.* Southfield, MI: Targum Press, 2003.

Tortolano, William. *Samuel Coleridge-Taylor: Anglo-Black Composer, 1875–1912.* Metuchen, NJ: Scarecrow Press, 1977.

Tosun, Necdet. *Bahauddin Naqshband (A Central Asian Sufi).* Translated by Jane Louise Kandur. Istanbul, Turkey: Insan Publications, 2008.

Trafzer, Clifford. *Earth Song, Sky Spirit: Short Stories of the Contemporary Native American Experience.* New York: Doubleday, 1993.

Trungpa, Chogyam. *The Collected Works of Chogyam Trungpa, Volume Five.* Edited by Carolyn Rose Gimian. Boston, MA: Shambala, 2004.

Ure, Jean. *Rumanian Folk Tales.* Lexington Avenue, NY: Franklin Watts, Inc., 1961.

Ury, Marion. *Tales of Times Now Past: Sixty-Two Stories from a Medieval Japanese Collection.* University of California Press for the Center for Japanese and Korean Studies University of California, 1979.

Uthaymeen, Eminent Sheikh Muhammad Bin Salih al-. *Explanation of Riyadus-Saliheen Volume 5.* Translated by Abu Naasir Ibrahim Abdur-Rauf and Abu Abdil-Barr Muhammad Yaqueen. n.p.: Darussalam, 2021.

Vajin, Antonina A. "Saint Herman Guardian Angel of The Russian Church Abroad." *The Orthodox World* 6/4 & 5 (1970): 237–38.

Vande Kieft, Kathleen. *Innersource: Channeling Your Unlimited Self.* New York: Ballantine Books, 1988.

Van Gorder, A. Christian. *Violence in God's Name: Christian and Muslim Relations in Nigeria.* Houston, TX: African Diaspora Press, 2012.

Van Natta, Bruce. *A Miraculous Life: True Stories of Supernatural Encounters with God.* Lake Mary, FL: Charisma House, 2013.

Varga, Josue. *A Call from Heaven: Personal Accounts of Deathbed Visits, Angelic Visions, and Crossings to the Other Side.* Wayne, NJ: New Page Books, 2017.

Vijavargiya, Dayakrishna. *Swami Ramanand: The Pioneer of Ram Bhakti (English rendering of the Hindi Novel Payaspayee).* Translated by Devarshi Kalanath Shastri. Shri Mhat, Panchganga, Varanasi, India: Jagadguru Ramanadacharya Smarak Seva Nyas, 2009.

Villa, Susie Hoogasian, and Mary Kilbourne Motassian. *Armenian Village Life Before 1914.* Detroit: Wayne State University Press, 1982.

Vine, Deloria. *Singing for a Spirit: A Portrait of the Dakota Sioux.* Santa Fe, NM: Clear Light Publications, 2000.

Vissell, Joyce, and Barry Vissell. *Meant to Be: Miraculous True Stories to Inspire a Lifetime of Love.* Berkeley, CA: Conari Press, 2000.

Walker, Warren S., and Ahmet E. Uysal. *Tales Alive in Turkey.* Lubbock, TX: Texas University Press, 1990.

Wareham, A. L. "Soul Science." *The Two Worlds.* June 3, 1921.

Waugh, F. W. "Canadian Folk-Lore from Ontario." *The Journal of American Folklore* 31/119 (1918): 4–82.

Webster, Jason. *Sacred Sierra: A Year on a Spanish Mountain.* London: Chatto & Windus, 2009.

Welsch, Roger. *A Treasury of Nebraska Pioneer Folklore.* Lincoln: University of Nebraska Press, 1984.

Westwood, Jennifer. "The Seasonal Round: The Folklore of Divination in Britain." In *The World Atlas of Divination: The Systems-Where They Originate and How They Work,* edited by John Matthews, 88–93. London: BCA, 1992.

Whelan, Richard. *Macbeth.* Second Edition. Ocala, FL: Llumina Press, 2013.

Wickramaratne, Colton. *My Adventure in Faith: How One Man Dared to Trust God for the Impossible.* Springfield, MO: Onward Books, 1957.

Wilde, William. *Ancient Legends, Mystic Charms, and Superstitions of Ireland.* Boston: Ticknor and Co., 1887.

Williams, Arthur Tudno. *Memories.* Florida: Florida State University, 1907.

Williston, Teresa Price. *Japanese Fairy Tales.* Chicago: Rand, McNally & Co., 1904.

Wilstach, Paul. *Richard Mansfield: The Man and the Actor.* New York: Charles Scribner's Sons, 1908.

Wintemberg, William, and Katherine Wintemberg. "Folk-lore from Grey County, Ontario." *Folklore* 31/119 (1918): 83–124.

Wooding, Dan. *Twenty-Six Lead Soldiers: A Top London Journalist and His Worldwide Search For the Truth.* Westchester, IL: Crossway Books, 1967.

Wolf, Judy. *Spiritual Life Rafts: Women's Stories of Profound Loss, Courage and Healing.* UT: Shim Institute, 2008.

Young, John. *Memoirs of John R. Young Utah Pioneer 1847 Written by Himself.* Salt Lake City, UT: Deseret News, 1920.

Yun, Hsing. *Opening the Mind's Eye: Clarity and Spaciousness in Buddhist Practice.* Translated by Amy Lam. New York: Lantern Books, 2005.

Zampounis, Christos K. *Watch Your Manners in Greece.* Translated by Christiana Lambrou. Athens, Greece: Fereniki Publications, 2003.

Zeff, Ted (Dayalu). *Amma: Inspiring Experiences with the Divine Mother.* San Ramon, CA: Mata Amritanandamayi Center, 2016.

Zimmerman, Odo John, trans. *Saint Gregory the Great Dialogues.* Washington, DC: The Catholic University of America Press, 1959.

Zipporah, Bennett. *Return, Daughter of Zion!* CA: Shekinah, 2001.

Index